Contents

Acknowledgments	xiii
Introduction	xv

Part One	**SQL Server and Extensible Markup Language (XML)**	**1**

Chapter 1	**SQL Server 2000**	**3**
	Introduction	3
	The Installation Process	5
	Step 1: Launching the Program	6
	Step 2: Invoking the Installation	6
	Step 3: Computer Name	7
	Step 4: Installation Selection	8
	Step 5: User Information	9
	Step 6: Installation Definition	9
	Step 7. Instance Name	10
	Step 8: Setup Type	12
	Step 9: Select Components	12
	Step 10: Services Account	13
	Step 11: Authentication Mode	14
	Step 12: Collation Settings	14
	Installing Additional Components	15
	Starting the Microsoft SQL Server Service Manager	15
	Starting the SQL Server Enterprise Manager	17
	Windows Management Instrumentation (WMI)	19

Chapter 2   Introduction to Extensible Markup Language (XML)   21

Background   21
    Hypertext Markup Language (HTML)   22
    XML   22
    XML Parsers   24
    XML Elements   24
    XPath Language   26
    XSL Transformations   33
    XML Namespaces   38
    XML Schema   41
    XML, HTTP, and SQL Server   45
Summary   46

Chapter 3   SQL Server and XML on the Web   47

XML and IIS   47
    The ISAPI Extension   48
    Launching the Management Tool   48
    Adding a Virtual Directory   49
    SQL and URLs   54
    The FOR XML Clause   55
    The Top-Level Element   57
    Template File Query   61
    Executing Stored Procedures   65
    Parameters   68
Summary   69

Chapter 4   The FOR XML Modes   71

The Raw Mode   71
Auto Mode   73
Explicit Mode   75
Limitations of FOR XML   78
Summary   78

Chapter 5   Annotated Schemas   79

Schema-Building   79
    Adding the Top Level   80
    Defining Data Types   80
    Tree Structures   82
Configuration   83
The Query Language   85
Locating Data in a Schema   85
Summary   86

Professional Developer's Guide

Scripting XML and WMI for Microsoft® SQL Server™ 2000

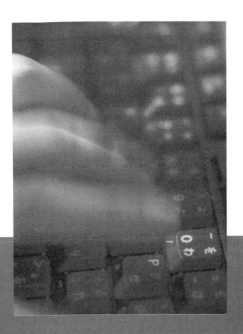

Tobias Martinsson

Wiley Computer Publishing

John Wiley & Sons, Inc.

NEW YORK · CHICHESTER · WEINHEIM · BRISBANE · SINGAPORE · TORONTO

Publisher: Robert Ipsen
Editor: Margaret Eldridge
Managing Editor: Micheline Frederick
Production Assistant: Kerstin Nasdeo
Associate New Media Editor: Brian Snapp
Text Design & Composition: D&G Limited, LLC

Library of Congress Cataloging-in-Publication Data:

ISBN: 0-471-39951-5

Printed in the United States of America.

10 9 8 7 6 5 4 3 2 1

Professional Developer's Guide Series

Other titles in the series:

Advanced Palm Programming by Steve Mann and Ray Rischpater, ISBN 0-471-39087-9

WAP Servlets by John L. Cook, III, ISBN 0-471-39307-X

Java 2 Micro Edition, by Eric Giguere. ISBN 0-471-39065-8

Chapter 6   Writing, Modifying, and Deleting XML Data   87

The OpenXML Function   87
XML System Stored Procedures   88
Element-Centric Mapping   88
Attribute-Centric Mapping   90
Edge-Table Mapping   91
Inserting Data   92
Modifying Data   94
Deleting Data   95
Summary   96

Chapter 7   Updategrams   97

Introduction   97
Inserting and Deleting Records   98
Updating Records   99
Updategram XML   100
More Information   101
Summary   101

Chapter 8   Applying XML from SQL Server   103

IIS Virtual Directory Management   103
    VDirControl   103
    SQLVDirs Collection Object   104
    SQLVDir Object   104
    VirtualNames Collection   106
    VirtualName Object   107
Microsoft Data Access Components (MDACs)   108
    The Command Object   108
    The Stream Object   109
    Microsoft XML Parser   112
    Direct Queries   113
    Posting Requests   113
    XML-to-HTML-to-ASP   114
    Parameterized XML Queries   115
    XPath and the Mapping Schema   116
Summary   117

**Part Two   SQL Server and Windows Management
Instrumentation (WMI)**   119

Chapter 9   Windows Management Instrumentation (WMI)   121

Introduction   121
The Management Architecture   123
    Windows Management Service   123
    The CIM Repository and CIM Object Manager   125
    About CIM   127

The Security Model 130
WMI and Microsoft SQL Server 132
    The Provider 133
    MSSQL Classes 134
    Creating New Objects 141
Summary 145

Chapter 10   The WMI Scripting API   147

Introduction 147
The SWbemLocator Object 148
    Overview: The SWBemLocator Object 150
The SWbemServices Object 151
    Get Instance or Class 152
    Enumerating Instances 153
    Executing Queries 154
    Overview: The SWbemServices Object 154
SWbemObject 161
    Overview: The SWbemObjectSet 161
The SWbemObject Object 162
    Overview: The SWbemObject Object 164
The SWbemSink Object 170
    Overview: The SWbemSink Object 171
The SWbemMethod and SWbemProperty Objects 173
    Overview: The SWbemMethodSet Collection, SWbemMethod
    Object SWbemPropertySet Collection, and SWbemProperty Objects 174
The SWbemPrivilegeSet Object 175
    Overview: The SwbemPrivilegeSet Collection Object 175
The SWbemObjectPath Object 177
    Overview: The SWbemLastError Object 178
The SWbemNamedValueSet Object 178
    Overview: The SWbemNamedValueSet Collection Object 179
The SWbemNamedValue Object 180
The SWbemEventSource Object 180
    Overview: The SWbemEventSource Object 180
Method Return Values 181
    Languages and Output Parameters 182
Scripting Languages and Variants 183
Common WMI Enumerated Constants 184
Summary 190

Chapter 11   WMI Query Language   191

Introduction 191
    Data Queries 192
    Event Queries 196

Schema Queries   199
Query Optimization   199
Programming with Events   200
Summary   201

Chapter 12   Common Management Tasks   203

Creating a New Database   203
Creating a New Table   205
Adding a New Column   206
Creating a New Login   207
Associating a Login with an SQL Server Role   207
Getting Information about a Login   208
Starting and Stopping SQL Server   209
Dumping Properties of a Table   209
Dumping All Instances of a Class   210
Creating a Stored Procedure   211
Assigning Permissions to a Stored Procedure   213
Enumerating Parameters of the Stored Procedure   214
Modifying Database Settings   214
Bulk-Copying a Table   215
WMI Context Objects   216
Error Checking   217
Registering for NT Log Events   218
Summary   219

Part Three   Schema Reference   221

Common Material   222

Appendix A   Aggregations   225

Appendix B   Dependent Objects   231

Appendix C   Permissions   251

Appendix D   Scoped Objects   261

Appendix E   Containment   267

Appendix F   Static Settings   271

Appendix G   Dynamic Settings   293

Appendix H   Extensions   305

Appendix I   Statistics   309

Appendix J   **Logical Elements**   **313**

Appendix K   **Users and Accounts**   **319**

Appendix L   **Service and Process Classes**   **329**

Appendix M   **Storage**   **353**

Appendix N   **Database Management System (DBMS) Objects**   **359**

Appendix O   **Top-Level Classes, Parameters, and More**   **397**

Appendix P   **What Is on the CD-ROM?**   **401**

                Index   **403**

Acknowledgments

I would like to thank a bunch of people for their help and support during the writing of this book. Michael Maston, program manager for WMI SDK and Provider, provided many good answers and great feedback as a technical reviewer for WMI. David Wohlferd and Raxit Kagalwara, developers on the WMI team, passed along some early technological insights that were very helpful. At Waggener Edstrom, Eric Foster went out of his way to make sure that I received all of the material and answers that I needed regarding Microsoft SQL Server 2000. He kind of got the ball rolling in the right direction. Finally, Jan Dubois at ActiveState was kind enough to compile a couple of files to help me sort out some issues that I had with Perl.

From the technical material to the writing process, it has been great working with Margaret Eldridge at John Wiley & Sons, Inc. I know that there are many people at Wiley who have had a hand in this book. I know that you have worked hard to put the printed material together. I never got to see you, but thanks a lot!

On a personal note, Rena's pep talks and support have of course been important. The pep talks, the many pots of coffee, the good music, and the many good ideas made life a lot easier!

Introduction

Welcome to a book that was written for the Windows developer. This book presents two features of Microsoft SQL Server that have received much attention since the introduction of SQL Server 2000.

The first topic is *Extensible Markup Language* (XML) support in the database server. Database records are typically returned in flat, relational row sets. Today, however, it is possible to also return object-oriented, hierarchical XML document fragments from SQL Server. This technology is incorporated by both the *Internet Information Services* (IIS) and *Microsoft Data Access Components* (MDACs). Additionally, SQL Server's Transact SQL makes it possible to insert, update, and delete database records using XML document fragments. My goal with this book is to help you bring this technology into your professional development environment.

The second topic is SQL Server administration (using Windows Management Instrumentation [WMI]). WMI is the management infrastructure of choice for all Windows platforms. WMI provides a consistent interface for both local and remote administration tasks, making it extremely easy to use. As an SQL Server administrator, I think that you will find WMI intuitive to work with both locally and in distributed systems. Moreover, the WMI skills that you learn can be used to leverage systems management where WMI is supported.

How This Book Is Organized

This book is divided into three parts. The first two parts are about XML and WMI. Every part has its chapters organized to begin at the basic or fundamental level and to move on through the advanced level. The XML and WMI parts each end with a code-intensive chapter.

The third part of the book is reference material. This section is a logically structured set of collections of the SQL Server classes that are exposed through WMI. This section is a compact source for a quick lookup of classes.

Chapter 1 introduces SQL Server 2000 and walks through the installation of the SQL Server itself. This chapter also covers the installation of the WMI SQL Server Administration Provider.

Chapter 2 is a whistle-stop tour of XML. The sole focus of the chapter is the background and basics of XML and a broad view of programming basics for XML-related technologies. This chapter gets you started if you are jumping into this book without previous XML experience.

Chapter 3 deals with XML support in SQL Server. Targeting Web developers, the chapter starts with configuring IIS and SQL Server to work together and then continues with the basic forms of streaming XML from SQL Server over HTTP.

Chapter 4 defines the syntax by which SQL Server builds XML document fragments. I explain in detail the three modes that can be used for retrieving XML data.

Chapter 5 discusses annotated schemas and XPath expressions for locating SQL Server data. The chapter covers the creation of schemas and how to use them with SQL Server.

Chapter 6, as opposed to previous chapters, is not about retrieving XML data. Here, XML is used for mapping XML elements to columns of relational database tables, enabling XML content to be inserted, modified, and deleted in databases.

Chapter 7 deals with updategrams. Updategrams are XML-based documents for updating, inserting, and deleting data in relational database tables.

Chapter 8 contains examples and small discussions. The XML features are scripted in Active Server Pages and Windows Script Host by using the MDACs. Additionally, I demonstrate the object model for programmatically creating virtual directories that are mapped to SQL Server databases.

How This Book Is Organized

This book is divided into three parts. The first two parts are about XML and WMI. Every part has its chapters organized to begin at the basic or fundamental level and to move on through the advanced level. The XML and WMI parts each end with a code-intensive chapter.

The third part of the book is reference material. This section is a logically structured set of collections of the SQL Server classes that are exposed through WMI. This section is a compact source for a quick lookup of classes.

Chapter 1 introduces SQL Server 2000 and walks through the installation of the SQL Server itself. This chapter also covers the installation of the WMI SQL Server Administration Provider.

Chapter 2 is a whistle-stop tour of XML. The sole focus of the chapter is the background and basics of XML and a broad view of programming basics for XML-related technologies. This chapter gets you started if you are jumping into this book without previous XML experience.

Chapter 3 deals with XML support in SQL Server. Targeting Web developers, the chapter starts with configuring IIS and SQL Server to work together and then continues with the basic forms of streaming XML from SQL Server over HTTP.

Chapter 4 defines the syntax by which SQL Server builds XML document fragments. I explain in detail the three modes that can be used for retrieving XML data.

Chapter 5 discusses annotated schemas and XPath expressions for locating SQL Server data. The chapter covers the creation of schemas and how to use them with SQL Server.

Chapter 6, as opposed to previous chapters, is not about retrieving XML data. Here, XML is used for mapping XML elements to columns of relational database tables, enabling XML content to be inserted, modified, and deleted in databases.

Chapter 7 deals with updategrams. Updategrams are XML-based documents for updating, inserting, and deleting data in relational database tables.

Chapter 8 contains examples and small discussions. The XML features are scripted in Active Server Pages and Windows Script Host by using the MDACs. Additionally, I demonstrate the object model for programmatically creating virtual directories that are mapped to SQL Server databases.

Introduction

Welcome to a book that was written for the Windows developer. This book presents two features of Microsoft SQL Server that have received much attention since the introduction of SQL Server 2000.

The first topic is *Extensible Markup Language* (XML) support in the database server. Database records are typically returned in flat, relational row sets. Today, however, it is possible to also return object-oriented, hierarchical XML document fragments from SQL Server. This technology is incorporated by both the *Internet Information Services* (IIS) and *Microsoft Data Access Components* (MDACs). Additionally, SQL Server's Transact SQL makes it possible to insert, update, and delete database records using XML document fragments. My goal with this book is to help you bring this technology into your professional development environment.

The second topic is SQL Server administration (using Windows Management Instrumentation [WMI]). WMI is the management infrastructure of choice for all Windows platforms. WMI provides a consistent interface for both local and remote administration tasks, making it extremely easy to use. As an SQL Server administrator, I think that you will find WMI intuitive to work with both locally and in distributed systems. Moreover, the WMI skills that you learn can be used to leverage systems management where WMI is supported.

Chapter 9 introduces *Windows Management Instrumentation* (WMI). I explain what WMI is, how it works, and the fundamentals about the Microsoft SQL Server implementation for WMI.

Chapter 10 introduces scripting WMI. The object model of the WMI scripting *Application Programming Interface* (API) is covered, and each object gets its own discussion. Some language peculiarities are also covered.

Chapter 11 is about *WMI Query Language* (WQL). I demonstrate different types of queries and describe programming with events.

Chapter 12 contains examples and small discussions. Different types of SQL Server WMI classes are demonstrated in a breadth that provides the essential knowledge to handle all SQL Server classes.

Who Should Read This Book?

A Windows developer who wants to learn the XML and WMI features of SQL Server should read this book. I do not assume that you understand XML or WMI; rather, I will tell you that a basic knowledge of SQL Server and relational databases is helpful. Furthermore, the WMI class reference will in places require a bit more than just a basic knowledge of SQL Server before it can be fully utilized. It is fortunately merciful on details.

Tools You Will Need

Microsoft SQL Server 7.0 or 2000 must be installed before you can run the examples in the book. Also, you must have obtained and installed the XML technology for SQL Server and the WMI provider for SQL Server 7.0. The XML technology and WMI Provider is included in SQL Server 2000.

To use the Web samples in this book, please ensure that an Active Server Pages-enabled Web server is installed. Similarly, the *Windows Script Host* (WSH) examples require WSH (the latest version can be found on Microsoft's Web site at www.microsoft.com).

Finally, if you are not using Windows 2000 or Windows Millennium Edition (which ship with WMI as a core component), you will need to install WMI by downloading it from Microsoft's Web site.

What Is on the CD-ROM?

The CD-ROM contains the scripts presented in the book. There are also scripts to demonstrate useful concepts with SQL Server's XML and WMI capabilities. A separate HTML-file with links will take you to online resources on SQL Server and WMI.

Summary

From here, we will take the plunge into SQL Server 2000 with scripting XML and WMI.

PART ONE

SQL Server and Extensible Markup Language (XML)

CHAPTER 1

SQL Server 2000

Introduced in 1988, Microsoft *Structured Query Language* (SQL) Server is the complete database solution. Much of the popularity that it has gained is thanks to the ease-of use and extensible frameworks that it provides. The database management system finds itself at home with both back-end users and developers. The back-end user enjoys SQL Server's graphical administration tools, such as the Enterprise Manager and Query Analyzer, which make life easier. But developers can take it a step farther. The management frameworks provided make it easy to build state-of-the-art applications for SQL Server or applications that are even based on the SQL Server database engine. In this book, we will cover some basics of SQL Server prior to takeoff. After the basics, this chapter will deal with the support for XML technology and the Windows Management Instrumentation provider for SQL Server.

Introduction

SQL Server is marketed as scalable, available, and reliable. Whether you want an in-house database with a limited number of users or a distributed Internet database for *electronic-commerce* (e-commerce), SQL Server 2000 is a great product. This program comes in three editions, and unless you have already picked your server, you can use the following pointers to peg the edition that fits your needs:

SQL Server 2000 Enterprise Edition is designed for all organizations, ranging from small to global. With a massive hardware capacity of up to 32 processors and

64 *gigabytes* (GB) of *Random Access Memory* (RAM) (using Microsoft Windows 2000 DataCenter), the Enterprise Edition is an extremely scalable server. This application is built for the toughest terrain. Multi-processor systems can utilize parallel scans, resulting in faster access to data, and networked servers can share the workload through distributed, partitioned views. The Analysis Services, formerly known as *Online Analytical Processing* (OLAP), see a new light of day. This edition supports the largest cubes and dimensions—10 million-plus members. You can link cubes between different servers and expose them through the *Hypertext Transport Protocol* (HTTP) and deliver them through firewalls by using the HTTP listener that is built into this edition. Security improvements in Analysis Services now work on a cell and dimension level. Furthermore, the application uses clustering and decision trees as algorithms for the integrated data mining services. Other features include indexed views for better performance, log shipping, and a failover clustering that independently reinstalls or rebuilds a node within a cluster without other nodes being impacted. The compatible operating systems for SQL Server Enterprise Edition are Windows NT Server Enterprise Edition and Windows NT Advanced Server.

SQL Server 2000 Standard Edition is designed for small- and medium-sized businesses. The hardware provides a powerful system of four processors on a symmetric multi-processor system. This edition also has the capacity of 2GB of RAM by using Microsoft Windows 2000 DataCenter. Like the Enterprise Edition, the Standard Edition integrates new features to support Internet standards such as XML, Extensible Stylesheet Language Transformations (XSLT), and XPath, and it also provides *Uniform Resource Locator* (URL) and HTTP access to the SQL Server. The operating systems that are compatible with the SQL Server Standard Edition are Windows NT Server, Windows NT Server Enterprise Edition, Windows 2000 Server, and Windows 2000 Advanced Server.

SQL Server 2000 Personal Edition is designed for workstations that have an average of five concurrent users hitting the database. This edition contains the features of the Standard Edition with single or dual processors. The operating systems that are compatible with SQL Server Personal Edition are Windows 95/98, Windows NT Workstation, Windows NT Server, Windows NT Server Enterprise Edition, Windows 2000 Professional, Windows 2000 Server, and Windows 2000 Advanced Server.

Refer to Table 1.1 for a description of the operating systems for SQL Server.

In addition to the editions of SQL Server that we mentioned, there is the Microsoft Developer Edition, *Microsoft Desktop Engine* (MSDE), the Windows CE Edition, and the Enterprise Evaluation Edition.

SQL Server 2000 Developer Edition is the Enterprise Edition designed for the software application development process. Its license limits its use to development and to test systems that are not part of a deployed production system.

Table 1.1 Operating Systems for SQL Server

Operating System	Personal	Standard	Enterprise
Windows 95	✔		
Windows 98	✔		
Windows NT Workstation	✔		
Windows NT Server	✔	✔	✔
Windows NT Server Enterprise Edition	✔	✔	✔
Windows 2000 Professional	✔		
Windows 2000 Server	✔	✔	
Windows 2000 Advanced Server	✔	✔	✔

SQL Server 2000 Desktop Engine (MSDE) is a lightweight version of SQL Server 2000 and includes the relational database engine. Some limitations apply, however. The database size and user workload in this edition are trimmed to work best in small organizations (for example, in organizations that are looking for an offline data store or maybe a software application that is built upon the SQL Server relational database engine).

SQL Server 2000 Windows CE Edition is a Windows CE version that is fully compatible with the other editions of SQL Server 2000. You can easily keep it up to date with a central database. The CE Edition gives the programmer the sane interface as the other editions.

SQL Server 2000 Enterprise Evaluation Edition is a time-limited Enterprise Edition. Its license agreement will not permit it to be used in a production environment; however, for 120 days, you can test the full features of SQL Server 2000.

The Installation Process

The Microsoft SQL Server 2000 installation process is painless. SQL Server can be put on the local computer, on a remote computer, or on part of a cluster of servers. Additionally, it can coexist on the same machine as current installations of SQL Server 6.5 or 7.0. Therefore, prior to installation, you must know where to install SQL Server. Fortunately, this location is kind of easy to determine. If you do not know whether you are on a network or on part of a virtual cluster, you probably want to install the application on the local machine. Similarly, if you know nothing about the network or virtual cluster, install the program on the local machine. Also, if it is your first experimental experience with SQL Server, install the application on the local machine. This application is easy to install and uninstall, but please become comfortable with the server before taking a leap and installing the application on a remote computer or virtual cluster. Troubleshooting the local computer is a lot easier. The scenario that we will walk through is setting up the SQL Server 2000 Standard Edition on the local computer that is running the installation CD-ROM.

Step 1: Launching the Program

Insert the SQL Server 2000 CD. The main menu with a series of options pops up. In case that fails to happen, however, open Windows Explorer and then locate the file `autorun.exe` on the SQL Server 2000 CD-ROM. Double-click the `autorun.exe` icon, and wait for the menu to be presented. When you are done, move to Step 2.

Step 2: Invoking the Installation

Now, you must install the server components. Windows 95 users might have a little extra work ahead of them, however. Actually, SQL Server does most of the work, but you need to click Install SQL Server 2000 Prerequisites before installing the software. Windows NT/2000 already has the prerequisites filled and can perform the following tasks (see Figure 1.1):

- Click Install SQL Server 2000 Components.
- Click Database Server—Standard Edition.
- Click Next in the Welcome dialog.

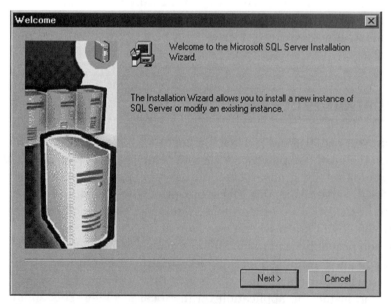

Figure 1.1   Click past the Welcome dialog.

Although we use the Standard Edition, an installation scenario is similar for most editions on the local systems. Earlier in this chapter, we discussed the previous editions.

Step 3: Computer Name

The name of the computer is also the target of the installation (see Figure 1.2). The target of the installation can be a local, remote, or virtual server. The installer, by default, selects a standalone machine[md]so from there, we can safely proceed to the next step:

- Choose Local Computer.

In case the installer did not select a standalone machine, read the following sections for an explanation of why.

Remote Installation

A remote computer involves a different process. If you install SQL Server on a remote computer, you click the Browse button and locate the computer. Or, you enter the name of the remote computer. The only requirement is that both computers must run Microsoft Windows NT or Microsoft Windows 2000 on an Intel-compatible processor. Additionally, you must have administrative privileges on the remote computer.

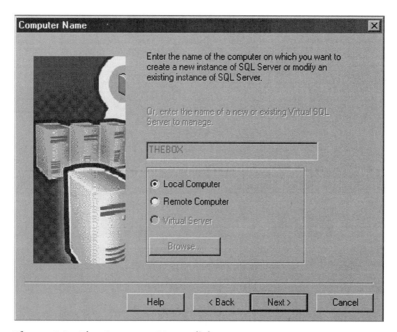

Figure 1.2 The Computer Name dialog.

Virtual Server

When a cluster is detected, a virtual server is selected by default. For that option, please read the Help information that is offered on the main menu of the installation so that you will be aware of the caveats.

Step 4: Installation Selection

The Installation Selection dialog is where the details about your installation begin (see Figure 1.3). Essentially, the type of instance to install is selected here:

- Choose Create a new instance of SQL Server.

Advanced Options

In contrast to a plain installation, try exploring the Advanced Options when you have time. You can configure unattended installations without dialogs, or you can do something totally different like repair a damaged registry. Furthermore, you can maintain a virtual server for failover clustering.

Creating an Unattended Installation

Create an unattended installation after you have installed SQL Server 2000 once. Choose Record Unattended .ISS File, and then walk through the dialogs

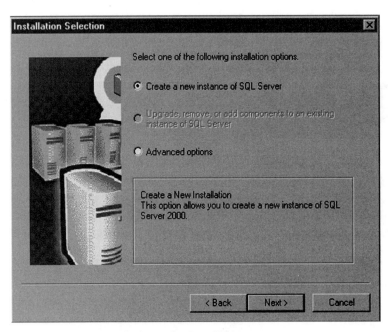

Figure 1.3 The Installation Selection dialog.

up to the start of the installation. Make sure that the choices you make are what you want for your installation. Also, as you close the last dialog, the unattended installation file that contains your installation options is saved. You will find that at the location set in the `windir` variable of the Environment Variables for the system, this variable is available through the System Properties Advanced tab in the control panel. You can later run the .ISS file by using the tool `Setup-sql.exe` located in the system directory of your SQL Server edition directory on the CD-ROM. Included on the CD-ROM are also batch files (.bat) and sample .ISS files to show you how you can run an unattended installation.

Step 5: User Information

The User Information dialog requires you to enter your name and organization (see Figure 1.4). After providing the information, click your way to the next dialog and read and accept the Software License Agreement.

Step 6: Installation Definition

The Installation Definition dialog has three options (see Figure 1.5). Client Tools Only is for when you only want access to the server. In other words, there is no administration or installation. Server and Client Tools are installed for work on the client side and server side (such as access and administrative operations):

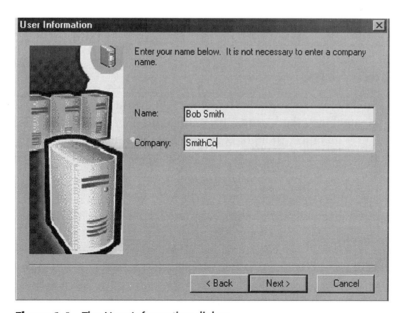

Figure 1.4 The User Information dialog.

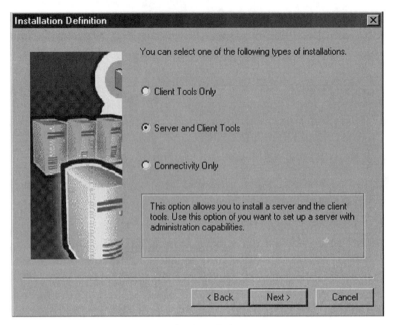

Figure 1.5   The Installation Definition dialog.

- Choose Server and Client Tools.Connectivity Only installs the *Microsoft Data Access Components* (MDAC). MDAC includes the *ActiveX Data Objects* (ADO). You can use ADO with a scripting language to access SQL Server and many other databases. Also installed are *Object Linking and Embedding Database* (OLE DB), which is the layer to which ADO gives easy access, *Open Database Connectivity* (ODBC), and DB-Library.

Step 7: Instance Name

The instance name is important when you run several instances of SQL Server 2000 on one machine (see Figure 1.6). A standalone machine with this installation as the first instance, though, is already set. The Instance Name dialog has the Default checkbox activated so that the network name of the current computer is used:

- Keep Default active and click Next.

Multiple Instances

If Default is not active, there is more work to do (but just a little). This situation probably means that an installation of SQL Server 6.5, 7.0, or 2000 is present on the machine. What you do depends on what is installed.

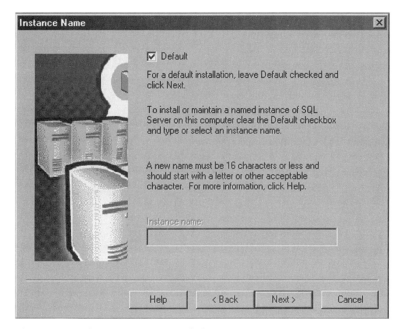

Figure 1.6 The Instance Name dialog.

You Have SQL Server 7.0 Installed

With SQL Server 7.0 installed, you will not be able to install a default instance of SQL Server 2000. You can, however, upgrade the 7.0 system to a default instance of 2000. Or, you can create a named instance of 2000.

You Have SQL Server 6.5 Installed

With 6.5, you can install a default instance of SQL Server 2000. The caveat, however, is that a default instance of 2000 cannot be running at the same time as 6.5. Therefore, the solution is to use the vswitch utility to switch between the servers, upgrade 6.5 it to 2000, or install one or more named instances of 2000.

You Have SQL Server 2000 Already Installed

SQL Server 2000 supports up to 16 instances. Also, to create a named instance in the installation, enter a new name of a maximum of 16 characters, beginning with an ampersand, underscore, or a letter. The named instance will trail the network name of the named instance separated by a backslash. The name of an instance can also be entered in order to maintain an existing instance.

Back Up Your Data

Be cautious if you share the target machine with SQL Server 6.5 or 7.0. You must back up your data before you perform any task.

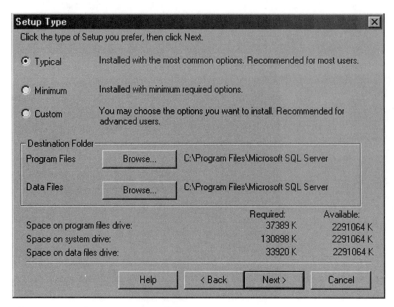

Figure 1.7   The Setup Type dialog.

Step 8: Setup Type

There are three types of setup (see Figure 1.7). The minimal installation consumes as little disk space as possible. A typical installation suits the majority of clients. The custom installation, however, is probably the developer's favorite:

- Choose Custom. (We are all curious, anyway.)

A custom installation enables you to select the components to install. The custom option also enables you to define settings such as character sets and network libraries.

Step 9: Select Components

Pick and choose among the components (see Figure 1.8). There are six major components that you can install, and each component contains subcomponents. For scripting, you can choose everything but development tools and code samples—scripting languages are not supported. When you are done, proceed to the next step.

- *Server Components.* The server components are the backbone of SQL Server. Among other things, the components contain the relational database engine.

- *Management Tools.* This set of graphical administration tools aids in the SQL Server experience.

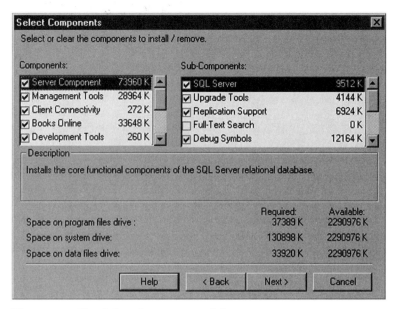

Figure 1.8   The Select Components dialog.

- *Client Connectivity.* Client connectivity refers to the miscellaneous functionality needed to connect a client application to the server.

- *Books Online.* Books online are a deep source of information for SQL Server. Topics include architecture, security, how to's, and so forth.

- *Development Tools.* Development tools are headers and libraries that are of use to the C programmer.

- *Code Samples.* Code samples are miscellaneous samples of SQL Server application programming tasks.

Step 10: Services Account

Microsoft SQL Server and the Microsoft SQL Server Agent are Windows services. A user account is required to run the two services. You can use either separate accounts for the two or have the two share one account. The default is to use the same account for both services and to auto-start the service when Windows is starting (see Figure 1.9):

- Choose Domain User Account.

The installer gives you the option of using a local system account or a domain user account. The local system account has no network capabilities because of restricted access, but it also requires no password. Therefore, it could be the ideal choice for an SQL Server that is not distributed between servers. A

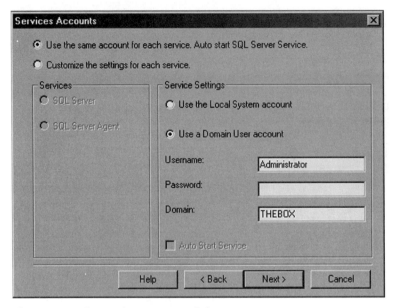

Figure 1.9   The Services Account dialog.

domain user account, on the other hand, has network permissions. The domain user account is what most people will recommend.

Step 11: Authentication Mode

You have two types of authentication from which to choose (see Figure 1.10). You can either deploy Windows Authentication Mode or Mixed Mode, and both perform Windows authentication and SQL Server authentication:

■ Choose the Windows Authentication Mode.

Windows Authentication Mode uses information stored by Windows NT or Windows 2000 to confirm the account and password, and Mixed Mode uses the Windows Authentication Mode and SQL Server authentication. The SQL Server authentication, however, is included to work with Windows 95 and Windows 98 and is compatible with older versions of SQL Server and the applications that might have been used with those applications.

Step 12: Collation Settings

In general, do not touch the collation settings unless you are tailoring them to be compatible with a current instance of SQL Server or with the locale settings

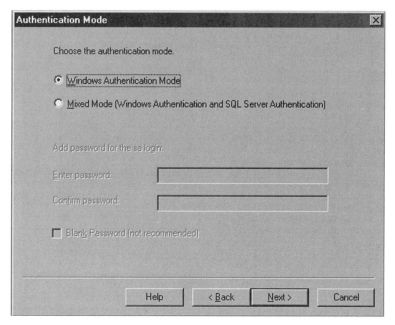

Figure 1.10   The Authentication Mode dialog.

of another Windows computer. Proceed to the next step, and then start the installation (see Figure 1.11).

The installation will copy the necessary files and set up the Microsoft SQL Server 2000 on your local computer.

Installing Additional Components

When the installation is complete, you can install additional services such as Analysis Services (formerly known as OLAP) and English Query, which provide a natural language extension for querying the SQL Server.

Starting the Microsoft SQL Server Service Manager

The Microsoft SQL Server Service Manager controls SQL Server services. This tool is lightweight and intuitive and is used to start, stop, and pause services. Figure 1.12 shows the Service Manager interface.

The Server list box displays the servers that are available on the system. The Services list box contains the services that are available. Below this display,

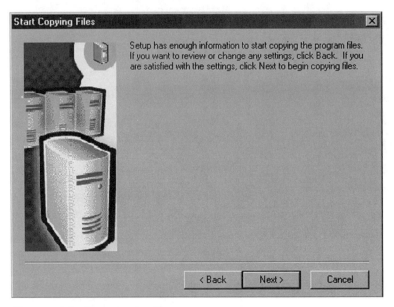

Figure 1.11   Start copying files.

buttons for starting, stopping, and pausing these services are available. A shaded button means that the option is unavailable. For example, a server that is already stopped will have a shaded Stop button, because you cannot change a stopped service's state to stopped. You can also find a textual description of the service status at the bottom of the window.

On a final note, you can choose whether a service should be started with the system by activating/deactivating the checkbox that says, "Auto start service

Figure 1.12   The Service Manager.

when OS starts." To make sure that your SQL Server installation works, you should perform the following actions:

1. Click the Stop button to make the SQL server unavailable.

2. Click the Start button to make the SQL server available again.

Starting the SQL Server Enterprise Manager

The *Enterprise Manager* (EM), seen in Figure 1.13, is *the* tool for administrating SQL Server at the console. This tool is a *Microsoft Management Console* (MMC) snap-in that comes with wizards for most thinkable SQL Server tasks.

In Figure 1.13, you have the Tree pane. This pane is a hierarchical list of all of the database objects in the selected SQL server. If you click a database, for example, the hierarchy is further expanded—and the view includes all database objects that you selected. Through this user interface, you can interact with tables, stored procedures, user-defined functions, and more. You can create, modify, delete, and examine anything that is visible. EM, however, is not meant to the scripted, so it requires your interaction and full attention.

Next, Figure 1.14 is the Properties window of the Northwind database. You can launch that window by right-clicking Northwind and then choosing Properties. Customized property windows like that are available for tables, stored

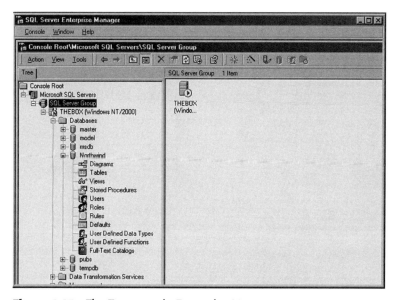

Figure 1.13   The Tree pane in Enterprise Manager.

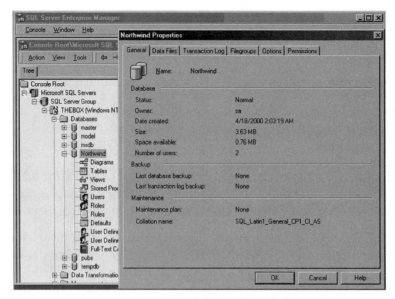

Figure 1.14 Properties window of the Northwind database.

procedures, and so forth. This interface is intuitive for managing and testing new settings.

Finally, Figure 1.15 lists the available wizards. This window can be launched from Wizards . . . under the Tool options in the top menu. The same options

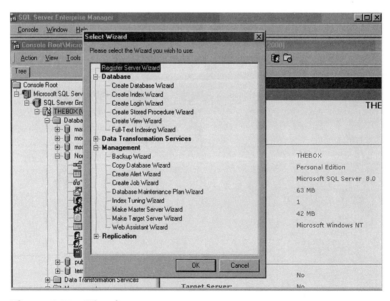

Figure 1.15 Wizards.

exist on a per-object basis. For example, if you have the Databases option selected, you can right-click it and choose New Database. The same goes for all other objects.

Windows Management Instrumentation (WMI)

Microsoft *Windows Management Instrumentation* (WMI) is the result of an industry-wide initiative. WMI provides an infrastructure based on the initiative of unifying the systems management of enterprise computing environments. While you can use WMI to manage SQL Server, WMI is in no way limited to that one family of components of Windows.

Now is a good time for a small discussion of EM and WMI. The purposes of the two are similar and not so similar. Comparing WMI to EM will not do WMI justice, but you are probably wondering why you would use WMI if EM is *the* tool for administrating SQL Server at the console. The key word here is *console*. First, EM was meant to be directed at the console. This technology requires your presence, interaction, and input. WMI, on the other hand, is used programmatically. Locally, you can write WMI scripts to deal with repetitive and tedious tasks. Remotely, your scripts or applications can directly access the management features of SQL Server 2000 through WMI. You might like to write an application that you will use for remote management of an SQL server. Now, keep in mind that this concept is shallow. As we delve deeper into WMI, we will find that it is a lot more dynamic and extensible than described here.

In WMI, software known as WMI Providers is often used to perform operations on a managed environment through WMI. Numerous environments have their own WMI Provider; for example, SQL Server, Active Directory, the Registry, and Microsoft Office 2000. Before you can program SQL Server through WMI, the WMI Provider for SQL Server administration must be installed. This component does not install with the other components of SQL Server, but it is included on the SQL Server 2000 CD-ROM. Run `SETUP.exe` in `\x86\other\wmi` on your SQL Server 2000 CD-ROM. The Microsoft Installer package will install on Intel-based systems that are running Windows 98, Windows ME, Windows NT SP 4.0+, or Windows 2000 on SQL Server 7.0 SP 2+ and SQL Server 2000.

Please note that in order for the WMI Provider for SQL Server to work, WMI must be installed on the system. Windows ME (Millennium Edition) and Windows 2000 ship with WMI as a core component, but any other system will have to double check to see that this component is installed. WMI can be downloaded from Microsoft's Web site. The run-time components install on all supported systems, but the WMI *Software Development Kit* (SDK) can only install on Windows NT 4 and later.

Introduction to Extensible Markup Language (XML)

*E*xtensible Markup Language (XML) is a technology that every Web developer should know. This chapter will introduce XML and give an overview of some of the more common technologies that are associated with XML. The main objective for this chapter is to prepare for what is to come in the next chapter.

Background

We will start with a brief history session that takes us back to 1969. That year, *Generalized Markup Language* (GML) was created at IBM. In 1986, GML became *Standard Generalized Markup Language* (SGML).

SGML is about structure and content. Entities are used to structure documents, and from the entities, a document can be broken down into bits and pieces by a parser that processes the information. Much of this tradition from SGML lives on today. Some traditions have been lost, however.

SGML parsers can extract content from and present SGML documents. It just takes a lot of code and a lot of patience to develop something along those lines. Fortunately, SGML is a generalized markup language. A generalized language is used as the basis for creating specific markup languages, and that is what led to modern-day markup languages.

Hypertext Markup Language (HTML)

In 1991, an application of SGML called *Hypertext Markup Language* (HTML) was introduced. People saw HTML as an easy-to-learn markup language that had a fixed number of HTML elements.

HTML assisted the developer with presenting documents on the Internet. The language got the job done for more than a million Web pages on the World Wide Web. Web developers soon discovered a problem with HTML, however: HTML elements had been designed for controlling the appearance of Web pages.

Why is that a problem, you might ask? You could set background colors, font styles, paragraphs, and more. And while that was fine for presentation, Web pages and services that had become more sophisticated needed a more meaningful, structured representation of data than what HTML supported.

As a result of the limitations of HTML, the *World Wide Web Consortium* (W3C) began developing an SGML subset for meaningful, structured data representation. The work later became XML.

XML

In 1998, XML became a W3C recommendation. The final recommendation came in 1999. A couple of the design goals with XML were that XML documents had to be easy to create and to programmatically process. The technology also had to be fast on the Internet and useful both in Internet applications and in other applications. In a sense, XML gathered the attributes that had made HTML popular and counteracted the attributes that had made SGML less popular.

A Cross-Platform Technology

XML documents are text based. Therefore, an XML document can be transported between and understood by interconnected machines. Many applications make use of that functionality; for example, the *Simple Object Access Protocol* (SOAP) enables a machine to invoke code on another machine by passing the instructions (properties to set, methods to call, and so on) across HTTP—embedded in an XML document. The responding machine then returns an XML document with elements containing the return value(s) of the instructions. SOAP, like XML, works just fine regardless of platform and programming language (as long as both machines support it). XML is a cross-platform technology that has universal industry support.

Extensibility

XML is extensible and enables you to define the elements of your document without restriction. With an unlimited number of elements, XML gives you the freedom to create subsets, extensions, and whatever else from XML. For example, a popular language for transforming XML documents into other XML documents is built on XML itself. These XSL transformations provide their own set of XML elements and a specification that describes how to interpret them. XML parsers implement *Extensible Stylesheet Language Transformations* (XSLT) into their application, which makes it possible to easily turn an XML document into HTML on the fly by way of XSLT.

Mainstream Characteristics

XML surrounds itself with lots of technologies. The *Common Information Model* (CIM), for example, provides a strategy that is similar to SOAP for invoking CIM operations over HTTP by using XML. Microsoft's .NET platform relies extensively on the use of XML. And Microsoft SQL Server, of course, can turn relational data into hierarchical XML documents that are sent across HTTP. Numerous other technologies are directly related to XML, and XML—although enabling the storage of information anywhere on the Internet—can be thought of as useful in a wider scope than the Internet.

A Complement to HTML

XML complements HTML, rather than replaces it. Think about XML as separating the content and structure of information from how the information is presented. XML is the solution for more sophisticated documents than for HTML documents. Commonly, you hear something along the lines of, "Since XML is only understood by a few browsers, it's not useful on the Web." The truth is that XML might not be useful in Web browsers, but it is useful on the Web.

Universal Application

XML can be used everywhere. For example, take an organization that decides to centralize its storage to an SQL server. Department A inserts data as it knows it into SQL Server databases. Then, an application in Department B retrieves the same SQL Server data in XML. A style sheet is applied in order to transform the relevant information into, say, a page to be printed in a physical product catalog. Incidentally, Department C uses the same SQL Server product data but uses another style sheet in order to publish the electronic catalog on its Internet Web site. Furthermore, Department D retrieves the product data joined with some customer information and uses different style sheets to transform it into an invoice (and so on). Wherever these SQL servers are located—or if data is joined with other XML-enabled database servers—XML bridges the gap between the sender and the recipient. The sender and the recipient work with a platform-independent, standardized format when using XML. This system enables them to work with data in the manner that they understand it or in the way that they see it as their paradigm. In addition, neither software nor firewalls get in the way of the data exchange, so Web applications for browsers and business-to-business messaging both certainly benefit from XML.

XML Parsers

XML parsers process XML documents. Applications that want to consume XML documents implement the parsers. Two significantly different methods for parsing XML documents are available: stream-based parsing and tree-based parsing.

Stream-based parsers read a single XML document as a stream of data. These parsers allocate a buffer in memory for the stream and then fire events as XML elements are crossed. A subroutine, for example, can be written to handle the `<time>` element. The subroutine could do something like present the data in a friendly format or maybe process the content into or from a 24-hour format. Stream-based parsers offer fairly good control over XML documents in your application. Maybe the top reason for using stream-based parsers is that they are fast and go easy on memory usage. The most popular stream-based parser is SAX, or Simple API for XML. API stands for Application Programming Interface.

Tree-based parsers, on the other hand, model the document as a tree that consists of a root, nodes, and subnodes. This technique is the current most common method for parsing XML, but it has a drawback. The tree is stored in memory. For this reason, a large document can be greedy for memory. The larger the document, the more memory allocated. Also, on the Web, an increasing number of concurrent users makes the situation worse. The most popular tree-based parsing model is the *Document Object Model* (DOM).

XML Elements

XML documents are made up of XML elements. The XML element is a descriptively named container of information. This container is comprised of a start and end tag, and between the tags is the content, or value, of the XML element. The following document declares the XML element `<Book>` and the content Common Information Model:

```
<?xml version="1.0"?>
<Book>Common Information Model</Book>
```

XML elements can contain subelements. Each element must be contained by a single element known as the root-level, document-level, or top-level element. With this concept in mind, we will revise the previous example:

```
<?xml version="1.0"?>
<Book>
    <Title>Common Information Model</Title>
    <ISBN>0471353426</ISBN>
</Book>
```

We have done well so far. But as our documents become more complex, our elements must nest properly. The rules for nesting are simple: An element must not end outside the content in which it was started. So, we know that a clean XML document is self-descriptive and properly nested. What else should we know? Well, XML documents should have a design that is consequential. What we have seen so far is okay on a meet-XML basis, but it is not extensible. If we wanted to add more books to the document, we would lose our top-level element. The parser croaks when that happens. Let's fix this problem by adding the top-level element <Books> to make it legal and extensible:

```
<?xml version="1.0"?>
<Books>
    <Book>
        <Title>Common Information Model</Title>
        <ISBN>0471353426</ISBN>
        <Publisher>John Wiley &amp; Sons Inc.</Publisher>
    </Book>
    <Book>
        <Title>Object-Oriented Project Management with UML</Title>
        <ISBN>0471253030</ISBN>
        <Publisher>John Wiley &amp; Sons Inc.</Publisher>
    </Book>
</Books>
```

Now, because < and > are characters that have special meaning to XML, you must encode them in your document. The same encoding applies to the ampersand, which is why John Wiley & Sons appears as John Wiley & Sons. The encoding is listed in Table 2.1.

Table 2.1 Special Character Encoding

Character	Encoding
<	&lt;
>	&gt;
&	&amp;
"	&quot;
'	&apos;

Everything in our examples so far has been element-based. XML elements can contain attributes, though. The use of attributes enables us here to also omit the end tag and to just put a forward slash before the closing of our tag:

```
<?xml version="1.0"?>
<Books>
    <Book Title="Common Information Model"
            ISBN="0471353426"
            Publisher="John Wiley &amp; Sons Inc."/>
    <Book Title="Object-Oriented Project Management with UML"
            ISBN="0471253030"
            Publisher="John Wiley &amp; Sons Inc."/>
</Books>
```

Attributes describe objects. For example, title, *International Standard Book Number* (ISBN), and publisher describe a book. You should concentrate on attributes that are important to your document. A final work on this topic, which you might have thought of already, is the ISBN number as the sole identification number. If you were to create a more elaborate list of publications, the ISBN would be a good attribute on which to base the document. The ISBN number is a 10-digit identification number that is used to identify books, pamphlets, educational kits, microforms, CD-ROMs, and Braille publications. This identification makes the document extensible to a whole host of various media (not thought of when first starting to list just books). For our examples, it is more illustrative to demonstrate elements, attributes, closing tags, and so forth when using the structure that we chose.

XPath Language

XPath essentially does two things. First, it stores an XML document in memory, modeled as a hierarchical, tree-based structure of nodes. These nodes are element, attribute, text, comment, namespace, root, or processing instruction nodes. Secondly, XPath provides the language for navigating, manipulating, and identifying and filtering the nodes of the tree. This task is performed through expressions that return objects that either are node sets, Boolean, number, or string objects.

Location Paths

A location path is analogous to a file system or URL. Paths are either absolute or relative, pointing to a node set within the tree. The difference between absolute and relative location paths is that the former begins at the top-level root element. The root element is matched by a forward slash (/).

Start at the root node, and match the `<Books>`-element:

```
/Books
```

The relative path begins from the node in the current position in the tree. Every expression, such as a location path, should result in a node set. If not, an error occurs. So, if your current position in the tree is /Books, the following relative location path returns all book/author elements:

```
Book/Author
```

What we know so far is that expressions that specify an absolute path begin with a forward slash, indicating that the location path starts at the root document. A relative path starts at the context node, or the current position.

Location Steps

The location step is part of a location path. A location step has an axis that describes the tree relationship between the selected nodes and the context node. For examples, the axis tells whether the selected nodes and the context relation are related as a parent-child or as a child-parent.

Building XPath expressions, an abbreviation of the axis' name tells the language how to move along the axis. This process is simple: A forward slash moves to the right along the location step axis, returning children of the context node. A double forward slash moves to the left, or reverses, along the axis, thus returning the parents. Here is an expression to return all <Book> elements that are children of <Books>:

```
/Books/Book
```

Find all author elements:

```
/Books/Book/Author
```

Both of these expressions start at the root node and use the forward slash. They also build absolute paths. If you wanted to get all <Book> elements relative to your current position, however, your code would look like the following:

```
Book
```

The forward slash is one of many abbreviations. For example, you can use the @ ("at" sign) character to build expressions that return attributes. Return the title attribute of each <Book> as follows:

```
/Books/Book/@Title
```

XPath Expressions

XPath expressions are created by using special characters and operators. The listing in Table 2.2 will aid you with XPath expressions.

Table 2.2 XPath Expressions

Operators	Meaning
/	Child Operator
//	Recursive Descent
.	Current Context
*	Wildcard
@*name*	Selects the attribute name
@	Selects all attributes
:	Namespace-separator
[*index*]	Subscript Operator
+	Addition Operand
-	Subtraction Operand
div	Floating-point division
*	Multiplication
mod	Modulus

You could use the subscript operator to match a node within a set. The index starts at one, and to get the title of the second `<Book>` node, use the following:

```
/Books/Book[2]/@Title
```

To match all `<Author>` elements in the first position of an element-based document, use the following:

```
/Books/Book/Author[1]
```

XPath includes powerful navigation and addressing capabilities. This functionality is furthered by specifying a core function library that can be used in any XML parser that fully supports XPath.

Core Functions

XPath has a core function library. Its functions deal with Node set-, string-, Boolean-, and number-related expressions (see Table 2.3). Tables 2.4, 2.5, and 2.6 are tables with XPath core functions.

Node Tests

Node tests are used to read the node type and the expanded name that are selected by the location step. Typical node tests are `text()`, `comment()`, and `processing-instruction()`. Each returns `True` for nodes of the type cor-

Table 2.3 Node-Set Functions

Function	Description
number last( )	Context-size of expression evaluation context.
number position( )	Index of the node within the parent.
number count(node-set)	Number of nodes in node-set.
node-set id(object)	Returns a node-set selected by the id in object.
string local-name(node-set?)	Returns the local part of the expanded name. It is possible to get an empty string.
string namespace-uri(node-set?)	Returns the namespace URI of the expanded name.
string name(node-set?)	Returns a qualified name representing the expanded name.

Table 2.4 String Functions

Function	Description
string concat(string, string*)	Returns a concatenated string of all strings.
boolean contains(string, string)	Returns True if first string contains second string.
string normalize-space(string)	Returns the string with white space removed.
string string(object)	Returns object converted to string.
boolean starts-with(string, string)	Returns True if the first string starts with the text in the second string.
string substring-before(string, string)	Returns a substring of all characters in the first string before the occurrence of the text in the second string.
string substring-after(string, string)	Returns a substring of all characters in the first string after the occurrence of the text in the second string.
string substring(string, number, length?)	Returns a substring of the first string, starting at the index of number and limiting it to optionally the index in length.
number string-length(string)	Returns the number of characters in string.
string translate(string, string, string)	Returns the first string with the characters in the second string translated into the character at the corresponding position in the third string.

Table 2.5   Boolean Functions

Function	Description
boolean boolean(object)	Returns true if object is a non-empty node-set, a non-zero length string, not negative or positive zero, not NaN.
boolean true( )	Return True
boolean false( )	Returns False
boolean lang(string)	Returns True if the **xml:lang** attribute of the context node is the same as a sublanguage of the language specified by the argument string.

Table 2.6   Numeric Functions

Function	Description
number number(object?)	Converts object to a number.
number sum(node-set)	Converts each node in the set to a number and returns the sum adding their values.
number floor(number)	Returns the largest number that is not greater than number and an integer value.
number ceiling(number)	Returns the smallest number that is not less than number and an integer value.
number round(number)	Returns the number that is closest to number and an integer value.

responding to their name. For example, `text()` returns `True` for a text node. To test for nodes along the axes, you can use the name of the axis separated by double colons and a node test of some type (see Table 2.7 for information about XPath axes).

The abbreviations that we have used are equivalent to the more verbose syntax. You can use either one in your applications. Personally, I prefer the abbreviation, because less typing is required.

The expression `child::text()` selects the text in bold:

```
<?xml version="1.0"?>
 <Books>
   <Book>
    <Title>Common Information Model</Title>
    <ISBN>0471353426</ISBN>
    <Publisher>John Wiley &amp; Sons Inc.</Publisher>
   </Book>
```

Table 2.7   XPath Axes

Axis	Description
child	Children of the context node
descendant	Descendants of the context node
parent	Parent of the context node
ancestor	Ancestors of the context node
following-sibling	Following siblings of the context node
preceding-sibling	Preceding siblings of the context node
following	Next context node
preceding	Preceding context node
attribute	Attributes of the context node
namespace	Namespace nodes of context node
self	The context node
descendant-or-self	The context node and its descendants
ancestor-or-self	The context node and its ancestors

```
<Book>
 <Title>
 Object-Oriented Project Management with UML
     </Title>
 <ISBN>0471253030</ISBN>
 <Publisher>John Wiley &amp; Sons Inc.</Publisher>
 </Book>
</Books>
```

Also, `child::node()` returns `True` for any node, so if you replace the previous expression with that expression, all except for the `<?xml version="1.0"?>` declaration will be selected.

Executing XPath

Here is a snippet of how you use XPath from Microsoft XML Parser 3.0 or greater:

```
Set xmlDoc = CreateObject("MSXML2.DOMDocument")
 xmlDoc.setProperty "SelectionLanguage", "XPath"
' Load XML source document or report error
If Not xmlDoc.load("file.xml") Then
    WScript.Echo xmlDoc.parseError.reason
    WScript.Quit
```

```
End If
Set nodes = xmlDoc.selectNodes("Books/Book/ISBN")
For Each node in nodes
    WScript.Echo node.xml
Next
```

Predicates

Predicates are filter node sets. Find the `<Book>` node where the ISBN element is equal to 047135346:

```
/Books/Book[ISBN='0471353426']
```

Match each `<Book>` that was written or co-authored by Murray R. Cantor:

```
/Books/Book[Author='Murray R. Cantor']
```

Then, match all authors of the book titled *Common Information Model.*

```
/Books/Book[@Title='Common Information Model']/Author
```

These operations result in a new node set. There are a number of operators and characters for operations that can be used in XPath (see Table 2.8).

There are a couple more operators listed in Table 2.9.

Table 2.8 Operators and Characters for Use with XPath

Predicates	Meaning
=	Equality
!=	Not equal
<	Less than
<=	Less than or equal
>	Greater than
>=	Greater than or equal

Table 2.9 More Operators

Operator	Meaning
and( )	Logical And
or( )	Logical Or
not( )	Negation
( )	Grouping
[*pattern*]	Filter-pattern
		Union

The union operation performs a union of several expressions and creates a new node set. The following operation creates a node set of all title and publisher elements:

```
Title | Publisher
```

XPath puts up a great language for navigating XML documents. The specification states a pattern-matching portion, a set of manipulation functions, and a variety of predicates and more. Next, we will look at a technology that implements XPath: XSLT.

XSL Transformations

XSL Transformations generates a new text-based document from an XML source document. This language is a template-driven language (templates are small blocks of transformations). The templates are applied to XML elements or to attributes that are matched by an XPath expression.

In XSLT, templates are grouped into a style sheet. By associating, or applying, the style sheet to an XML document, you generate your new tree structure. For example, it is possible to convert an XML tree into an HTML tree. We will look at some common uses for XSLT and processing instructions.

What Does XSLT Look Like?

XSLT is XML-based. XSLT is an XML document, so to differentiate it from other XML documents, we will start with a small declaration:

```
<?xml version='1.0'?>
<xsl:stylesheet xmlns:xsl="http://www.w3.org/1999/XSL/Transform"
 version="1.0">
...
</xsl:stylesheet>
```

Here, we declare the XML document a style sheet. XSLT has its own namespace and its own XML elements, so we import the namespace in order to use the processing instructions for transformation. Some common instructions in XSLT are iteration, conditional processing, sorting, and accessing of an XML source tree.

For-Each Processing

For-each processing is the capability to iterate over all nodes that match an XPath expression. We will write a simple style sheet for generating an HTML tree with the <Title>-elements in the <Books> tree. A short summary of what happens is as follows:

- `<xsl:stylesheet>` declares the document a style sheet and uses the XSL namespace.

- `<xsl:template match="/">` matches the root element of our XML source document, and its content encapsulates the code for handling the resulting node set.

- `<xsl:for-each select="Books/Book">` iterates over each XML element returned by the XPath expression.

- `<xsl:value-of select="Title"/>` gets the value of every title element that is a child of the `<Book>` element; we mix some HTML in with this element to make it familiar-looking.

Here is the full style sheet:

```xml
<?xml version="1.0"?>
<xsl:stylesheet
 xmlns:xsl="http://www.w3.org/1999/XSL/Transform" version="1.0">
 <xsl:output method="html"/>
    <xsl:template match="/">
        <html>
            <xsl:for-each select="Books/Book">
                <b><xsl:value-of select="Title"/></b><br/>
            </xsl:for-each>
        </html>
    </xsl:template>
</xsl:stylesheet>
```

When XSLT converts XML into HTML, the XML rules that we discussed previously apply to HTML. Nesting and the structure of HTML elements within a style sheet must be correct in order for the tree to be generated.

Conditional Processing and Sorting

Our standard document will be conditionally processed and sorted this time. The new structure for the book element is as follows:

```xml
<?xml version="1.0"?>
<Books>
    <Book Title="Common Information Model">
        <ISBN>0471353426</ISBN>
        <Author Firstname="John"
                Middle="W"
                Lastname="Sweitzer"/>
        <Author Firstname="Winston"
                Lastname="Bumpus"/>
        <Author Firstname="Raymond"
                Middle="C"
                Lastname="Williams"/>
        <Author Firstname="Patrick"
                Lastname="Thompson"/>
```

```
            <Author Firstname="Andrea"
                    Middle="R"
                    Lastname="Westerinen"/>
            <Publisher>John Wiley &amp; Sons Inc.</Publisher>
        </Book>
        <Book Title="Object-Oriented Project Management with UML">
            <ISBN>0471253030</ISBN>
            <Author Firstname="Murray"
                    Middle="R"
                    Lastname="Cantor"/>
            <Publisher>John Wiley &amp; Sons Inc.</Publisher>
        </Book>
    </Books>
```

There are several author elements, and we will use this situation for our excuse to sort them by last name. In addition, we will concatenate the names into a single string. This task could be done in a single operation, but quite a number of authors include their middle initial in their title. We will have to check to make sure that we are including a middle initial in the format "Firstname I. Lastname," or we can just enter it as "Firstname Lastname." First comes the code, and then comes the talk:

```
<?xml version="1.0"?>
<xsl:stylesheet xmlns:xsl="http://www.w3.org/1999/XSL/Transform"
version="1.0">
 <xsl:output method="html" version="4.0"/>
 <xsl:template match="/">
   <html>
     <table border="1" cellpadding="5" align="center">
       <xsl:for-each select="Books/Book">
         <tr>
           <td bgcolor="#666666">
               <font face="arial" size="+1" color="#ff0000">
               <b><xsl:value-of select="@Title"/></b>
               </font>
           </td>
         </tr>
         <xsl:for-each select="Author">
           <xsl:sort select="@Lastname"/>
           <tr>
             <td bgcolor="#ffffff">
               <font face="verdana" size="-1">
               <b>
                <xsl:choose>
                  <xsl:when test="@Middle">
                  <xsl:value-of select="concat(@Lastname, ' ',
                                               @Middle, '. ',
                                               @Firstname)"
                  />
                  </xsl:when>
                  <xsl:otherwise>
```

```
                        <xsl:value-of select="concat(@Lastname, ' ',
                                                      @Firstname)"
                        />
                        </xsl:otherwise>
                      </xsl:choose>
                    </b>
                    </font>
                  </td>
                </tr>
              </xsl:for-each>
            </xsl:for-each>
          </table>
        </html>
      </xsl:template>
    </xsl:stylesheet>
```

The output is shown in Figure 2.1. These elements are what is new:

- `<xsl:output method="html" version="4.0"/>` sets the output to HTML, conforming to HTML version 4.0.

- `<xsl:sort select="@Lastname">` sorts the node set alphabetically by last-name.

- `<xsl:choose>` starts a block where `<xsl:when test="@Middle">` executes its block of code when a middle attribute is present in the author element. `<xsl:otherwise>` contains the code to run if no middle attribute is present.

- The `concat(string, string, string*)` function concatenates all author attributes into a single string.

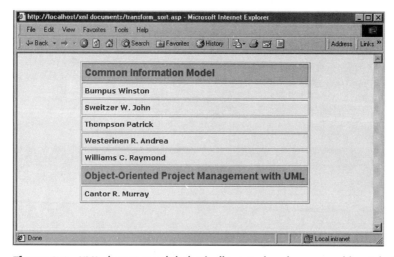

Figure 2.1 XML document alphabetically sorted and processed by stylesheet.

Applying Templates

XSL style sheets have transformed XML documents in a single blow so far. This method is not generally the way that it is done, however. You can define blocks of code, or templates, for each pattern to match, and you call them like subroutines. We will use this method later as we transform XML from SQL Server into HTML.

The Actual Transformation

The burning question is, "Where does the transformation take place?" Well, you will have to write the code that handles the loading, transformation, and date display to find out.

Basically, the code must instantiate two free-threaded DOMDocument objects. These free-threaded objects are optimized for server-side usage. Microsoft's initial XML parser strategy existed in the client-side processing of XML data, thus putting the workload on the client.

The Microsoft XML Parser, however, turned out to be heavily used on the server side, and performance was somewhat of an issue. Microsoft began improving its server-side performance (and soon). Free-threaded objects were released, addressing this problem.

The XSLTemplate object is a major improvement. This object compiles a style sheet and enables you to store it in the ASP Application or Session object in order to be reused. By doing so, the costly process of recompiling the object is avoided.

XSLProcessor is the object that handles the transformation. This object was spawned from the XSLTemplate object's `createProcessor()` method. This object contains the compiled style sheet, which it applies to the XML source document that you pass to it. With all of these concepts in mind, let's get on with the code:

```
<%@ Language=VBScript %>
<%
    Dim xmlDoc, xslDoc, xslTmp, xslProc
    Set xmlDoc = CreateObject("MSXML2.FreeThreadedDOMDocument")
    Set xslDoc = CreateObject("MSXML2.FreeThreadedDOMDocument")
    Set xslTmp = CreateObject("MSXML2.XSLTemplate")
    xmlDoc.async = 0
    xmlDoc.async = 0
    ' Load XML source document or report error
    If Not xmlDoc.load(Server.MapPath("Books-ElementBased.xml")) Then
        Response.Write xmlDoc.parseError.reason
        Response.End
    End If
```

```
' Load XSLT stylesheet or report error
If Not xslDoc.load(Server.MapPath("Books-ElementBased.xsl")) Then
    Response.Write xslDoc.parseError.reason
    Response.End
End If
' IXSLTemplate that contains the compiled stylesheet
xslTmp.stylesheet = xslDoc
' IXSLProcessor that transforms the compiled stylesheet
Set xslProc = xslTmp.createProcessor()

' XML-tree to transform
xslProc.input = xmlDoc
' Transform it
xslProc.transform()
' Send to ASP "standard output"
Response.Write(xslProc.output)
%>
```

If the load() method for either XML or XSL fails, a textual description of the error is outputted—and the script is aborted. Please check with your Microsoft XML Parser for the latest progIDs of all of the objects that are instantiated.

NOTE

Sometimes it is tricky to get a style sheet to do what you want it to do. To make matters worse, there is effective caching. Before you tear your script and style sheets into pieces, empty the browser's cache and refresh the page.

What Else?

XSLT is quite extensive. This application has conditionals, for-each processing, and so forth in common with programming languages. Table 2.10 lists some more common instructions but is nowhere near listing every feature.

XSLT is implemented in Microsoft's XML Parser. This application provides the XSLT functionality that is found in the examples that we are using, and there is enough material about XSLT to justify a book on that topic alone. Luckily, those books have been written, and there is a wealth of resources on the Internet.

XML Namespaces

XML elements can be protected within namespaces. This technique is a way of saying, "These elements and attributes belong to this XML application." Technically, these elements are called qualifying elements and attribute names.

A qualified name (Qname) has two parts: a namespace Uniform Resource Identifier (URI) and a local part. The namespace URI is the name of the namespace.

Table 2.10 XSLT Instructions

Element	Description
`<xsl:apply-imports />`	Invokes an overridden template rule.
`<xsl:apply-templates, select=expression mode=Qname />`	Begins processing the source document by finding the templates that match the selected nodes or nodes in the select-expression.
`<xsl:attribute, name="attributename" namespace="URI-reference"/>`	Attaches an attribute element to an output element. For example: `<a> <xsl:attribute name="href"> <xsl:value-of select="@url"/> </xsl:attribute> </a>`.
`<xsl:call-template, name=Qname />`	Calls a named template specified in the name attribute.
`<xsl:comment>`	Inserts a comment in the generated document.
`<xsl:element name="element-name" namespace"URL-reference" use-attribute sets=Qname />`	Creates a new element.
`<xsl:if  test = boolean expression> </xsl:if>`	Conditional statement that processes the block of code in the element's content if the statement evaluates to `True`.
`<xsl:import href="URI-reference"/>`	Imports another XSLT style sheet.
`<xsl:param, name=Qname select=expression/>`	Declares a named parameter for use within a style sheet and optionally a default value.
`<msxsl:script, language="language" implements-prefix="namespace">`	Declared at the top level of the style sheet, where it defines global variables and functions or subroutines. The namespace is used when an instruction accesses a variable or calls a subroutine that was declared within `</msxsl:script>`.

This element points to the namespace where the local part, or name of the element or attribute, is accessed. So the local part is simply the name of the XML element.

The proper use of namespaces ensures integrity. This integrity is especially useful when your XML data is grabbed from different machines. If, for example, two XML elements share the same name in the final document, they can be uniquely identified by their namespaces. Finally, namespaces can map back to XML schemas that define the rules for XML elements.

Declaring a Namespace

Declaring a namespace is done either explicitly or implicitly. Implicit declarations result in an unnamed, default namespace to which elements without a namespace URI belong:

```
<?xml version="1.0"?>
<Books xmlns="http://mycomputer.com/">
    <Book>
        <Title>Common Information Model</Title>
        <ISBN>0471353426</ISBN>
        <Publisher>John Wiley &amp; Sons Inc.</Publisher>
    </Book>
</Books>
```

The <Book> element and its children belong to the default namespace. The best way to illustrate the difference between default and explicit is through code. So, if you want to explicitly create a namespace called lib (short for library), you would write the code as follows:

```
<?xml version="1.0"?>
<Books xmlns:lib="http://mycomputer/">
    <lib:Book>
        <lib:Title>Common Information Model</lib:Title>
        <lib:ISBN>0471353426</lib:ISBN>
        <lib:Publisher>John Wiley &amp; Sons Inc.</lib:Publisher>
    </lib:Book>
    <lib:Book>
        <lib:Title>
        Object-Oriented Project Management with UML
        </lib:Title>
        <lib:ISBN>0471253030</lib:ISBN>
        <lib:Publisher>John Wiley &amp; Sons Inc.</lib:Publisher>
    </lib:Book>
</Books>
```

What Is xmlns=?

The namespace that we used points to a URL. This technique is not the only option, however. The namespace can point to a URI, URL, or *Uniform Resource Name* (URN). We could have been more specific with our URL and pointed it to a schema, as follows:

```
<Books xmlns="http://mycomputer.com/Schemas/BookSchema.xml">
```

The schema would then provide the declarations of the XML elements. Let's look at the schema.

XML Schema

The schema is the declarations of the elements and attributes that can appear in an XML document. Several things are defined in the schema. You can model hierarchies of parent and child elements, the sequence and number of children, and similar relationships. In addition, data types, data constraints, and default values are defined in the schema.

XML schemas are said to have an open content model. The open model enables you to declare elements as particular data types or lengths and also enables you to apply default values to them without a hassle. Also, typed elements accept data only of their own type, so they provide validation of the content. Also, you can specify a maximum and minimum length of the element. Lengths are on a character basis for strings and numeric data and on a byte basis for hexadecimal and binary data. Additionally, in the open model you can add further information to the schema for elements and attributes without rewriting the schema.

Microsoft provides its own dialect of XML schema called XML Data Reduced. The file extension for XML Data Reduced schemas is .xdr, and while schemas can be external files, inline schemas are possible. Whichever you use does not matter to the parser, but how you reference a schema from your XML document varies. Inline schemas, when referenced, must be prefixed with a pound sign (#). In addition, the XML schema must have gone through the parser before an element defined in the schema goes through it. The schema is an XML document itself, and the first thing that you declare is for the document to be a schema:

```
<Schema
    name  = "name"
    xmlns = "namespace"  >
. . .
```

Adding Elements and Attributes

The schema contains the elements and attributes of the XML document. You declare them with *<ElementType>*, *<AttributeType>*, *<element>*, and *<attribute>*.

<ElementType> creates a new element type. To add an XML element to the structure of an XML document that is associated with the schema, you would type the following code:

```
<ElementType
content = "{empty | textOnly | eltOnly | mixed}"
dt:type = "datatype"
```

```
model   = "{open | closed}"
name    = "idref"
order   = "{one | seq | many}"  >
```

Give the element a sense of identity with *name*. Set the *content* attribute if you need your content to be empty, text only, or elements only. The use of both named elements and text, known as mixed content, is the default.

Optionally specify a *datatype* and *model*. In a closed model, elements and mixed content that are not defined in the content model cannot be used. The *order* can be defined as a sequence in which the elements must occur: *one*, *seq*, or *many*. The *one* value permits only one element in the sequence. *seq* requires the elements to be ordered in a specified sequence, and *many* does not care how they are ordered.

The *<AttributeType>* lets you create a new attribute type. This element, too, is an essential declaration:

```
<AttributeType
        default   = "default value to assign"
        dt:type   = "data type"
        dt:values = "enumerated values"
        name      = "idref"
        required  = "{yes | no}"  >
```

Note that an *<AttributeType>* declared within an *<ElementType>* falls under the *<ElementType>*'s scope. The default attribute assigns a default value to the attribute type, and like the name attribute, this value is necessary for it to work properly. The *dt:type* attribute defines the data type for the attribute. The data type varies with the implementation of XML components that you are using. When the enumeration type is defined for *dt:type*, the *dt:values* attribute must list the possible values. The required attribute indicates whether the attribute is required for the element.

Example: Adding an Element

Using the following XML document,

```
<?xml version="1.0"?>
<Books xmlns:lib="x-schema:SimpleSchema.xml">
    <lib:Book>Common Information Model</lib:Book>
    <lib:Book>Object-Oriented Project Management with UML</lib:Book>
</Books>
```

the schema would look like the following:

```
<Schema name="Books" xmlns="urn:schemas-microsoft-com:xml-data">
    <ElementType name="Book"/>
</Schema>
```

Because the schema has defined <Book> as the only element of your XML document, changing

```
<lib:Book>
Common Information Model
</lib:Book>
```

into

```
<lib:ComputerBook>
Common Information Model
</lib:ComputerBook>
```

would result in the parser complaining that the element `lib:ComputerBook` is used but is not declared in the schema.

Example: Adding an Attribute

We will change our previous example to using attributes. We declare the `<AttributeType>` within the scope of the `<ElementType>` and then include it by using the attribute declaration:

```
<?xml version="1.0"?>
<Books xmlns:lib="x-schema:SimpleSchema3.xml">
    <lib:Book Title="Common Information Model"/>
    <lib:Book Title="Object-Oriented Project Management with UML"/>
</Books>
```

We will use the attribute element with this document. Create an `<Attribute-Type>` element, then place the attribute within an `<ElementType>` declaration:

```
<attribute
    default  = "default value"
    type     = "attribute type"
    [required = "{ yes | no }"] >
```

The default attribute assigns a default value to the attribute type, which is referred to by the name of an `<AttributeType>` through the type attribute. The required attribute indicates whether the attribute should be required for the element. Of course, if you have a book in the library, a title is available—so let's use that as a basic rule.

```
<Schema name="Books" xmlns="urn:schemas-microsoft-com:xml-data">
    <ElementType name="Book">
        <AttributeType name="Title"/>
        <attribute type="Title" required="yes"/>
    </ElementType>
</Schema>
```

Nesting Elements and Attributes

Think scope when you nest elements. The attribute element places a typed attribute within the scope of an `<ElementType>`. Similarly, if you want to place a typed element within another element, there is an element for that. To use `<element>`, we have to declare it within an `<ElementType>`:

```
<element
    type = "element type"
    [minOccurs = "{0 | 1}"]
    [maxOccurs = "{0 | *}"] >
```

The type attribute is the name of an `<ElementType>`; the namespace can be included, too. Both *minOccurs* and *maxOccurs* can be set in order to indicate how many times the element can appear within another element. An integer value can be used as a constraint in *maxOccurs*, and the asterisk (*) specifies an unlimited number of occurrences. If the `<ElementType>` content is mixed, the default *maxOccurs* is *. Otherwise, it is 1. Let's work out a version of the initial document:

```
<?xml version="1.0"?>
<lib:Books xmlns:lib="x-schema:SimpleSchema3.xml">
    <lib:Book Title="Common Information Model">
        <lib:ISBN>0471353426</lib:ISBN>
        <lib:Author>Winston Bumpus</lib:Author>
        <lib:Author>John W. Sweitzer</lib:Author>
        <lib:Author>Patrick Thompson</lib:Author>
        <lib:Author>Andrea R. Westerinen</lib:Author>
        <lib:Author>Raymond C. Williams</lib:Author>
        <lib:Publisher>John Wiley &amp; Sons Inc.</lib:Publisher>
    </lib:Book>
    <lib:Book Title="Object-Oriented Project Management with UML">
        <lib:ISBN>0471253030</lib:ISBN>
        <lib:Author>Murray R. Cantor</lib:Author>
        <lib:Publisher>John Wiley &amp; Sons Inc.</lib:Publisher>
    </lib:Book>
</lib:Books>
```

The corresponding schema is as follows:

```
<Schema name="Books" xmlns="urn:schemas-microsoft-com:xml-data"
                      xmlns:dt="urn:schemas-microsoft-com:datatypes">
    <ElementType name="ISBN" dt:type="int"/>
    <ElementType name="Author" dt:type="string"/>
    <ElementType name="Publisher" dt:type="string"/>
    <ElementType name="Book">
        <AttributeType name="Title" dt:type="string"/>
        <attribute type="Title" required="yes"/>
        <element type="ISBN"/>
        <element type="Author"/>
        <element type="Publisher"/>
    </ElementType>
    <ElementType name="Books">
        <element type="Book"/>
    </ElementType>
</Schema>
```

Caching Schemas

Since the introduction of version 3.0 of MSXML Parser, schemas can be cached. You can use this functionality to cache them in objects such as the ASP Application object, where they are frequently accessed (possibly by several concurrent users).

```
Set xmlDoc = CreateObject("MSXML2.DOMDocument")
Set xmlSchemaCol = CreateObject("MSXML2.XMLSchemaCache")

    xmlSchemaCol.add("urn:simpleschema", "simpleschema3.xml")

    xmlDoc.schemas=xmlSchemaCol

    xmlDoc.async = False
    xmlDoc.validateOnParse = False
    xmlDoc.load("books-simpleschema3.xml")

    xmlDoc.validate()
```

The `xmlSchemaCol` object is a collection of schemas, and the `add()` method places another schema into the collection. This physical schema is the file `simpleschema3.xml`, and it is associated with the `urn:simpleschema` namespace. You can place several schemas into the schema collection by calling `add()` several times. The schemas property of the `xmlDoc` object is then used to tell the parser from which schema collection it should find the namespace.

XML, HTTP, and SQL Server

On the Internet, Web applications can certainly benefit from pulling XML from SQL Server. There are some considerations that need attention, however.

A script pulling XML data from SQL Server consumes memory and processing power during the transfer. If you store the XML document in memory, even more memory is gone. Moreover, a Web application normally presents HTML. You must, then, transform XML into HTML. This transformation applies an additional layer to the logic needed for the transformation. Now, multiply the resources that are consumed with the average number of concurrent clients to see the demands that are being placed on the server. The moral of the story is that unless the Web service has tight code and the hardware to match the applied XML, a hardware upgrade becomes necessary. You can easily turn this scenario into something positive. Instead of delivering all of the data dynamically, think about how you define up-to-date data. Maybe the Web application at certain times of the day can pull XML documents from SQL Server, apply the necessary styles, and save a static HTML document that displays the results? That process saves enormous amounts of processing and memory usage. Also, it is also a solution that does not have too many kinks and complicated implementations. Only a small percentage of all data might have to be served from SQL Server in real time.

XML is a standard, cross-platform format, so you can use SQL Server and XML for specialized applications. Imagine an XML document based on records from diverse data sources all over the world. You get some records from an SQL Server here, from an Oracle server there, and from an Informix server elsewhere. These records could be collected into a single XML document.

Knowing XML provides you with a wealth of knowledge. When you learn to script it, you can come up with innovative solutions. But figuring out where to use XML is a problem when you are new and just starting. Fortunately, there are some good sources of inspiration. Try to find various implementations of XML. They do not have to be related to SQL Server. Look at what, how, and possibly why an application uses XML when you find one. Then, think about a similar implementation at an SQL Server paradigm, and see what ideas come to mind. XML is in use in many creative areas. Windows Media Player 7.0 is one technology that uses SQL Server's XML support to stream details such as author information over the Internet. Another one is the MSDN Subscription index (http://msdn.microsoft.com/subscriptions/index/). This Web application queries SQL Server 2000 for XML data. On the server side it uses XSLT, ADO, and ASP to sort, filter, and transform the XML. The client is then presented the HTML.

Learning to use XML involves learning to think in XML. If you have not yet used XML, it will most likely take some implementation experience before you shout "Eureka!" over XML. You might know that SQL Server comes with XML features, but you might have no clue what to do with them. Well, the question, "Where can I use XML?" is similar to the question, "What's the meaning of life?" You will either get no answer or tons of answers. Then, some answers will make sense, and others will not. The best advise that I can give is to take a hobby project that is lying around your desk and see if you can do something positive to it with XML. Let it develop over time, and start doing things with the XML document (such as parsing it and transforming the content). Sometimes activities like that, which might seem pointless, will put new ideas in the back of your mind. That way, even if you do not find a use for XML today, a future problem that comes up might be perfect for XML.

Summary

In this chapter, the basics of XML have been covered. Technologies like markup-languages and XML-related languages, how they are used, and so forth were discussed. The next chapter will continue where this one left off: SQL Server and XML for Internet-applications.

CHAPTER 3

SQL Server and XML on the Web

T he *Extensible Markup Language* (XML) features in SQL Server 2000 mark a milestone in the product's history. Instead of working with flat row sets, you can turn your relational data into hierarchical, tree-shaped XML document fragments that are easily transported between machines and through firewalls. On the Web, the *Internet Information Services* (IIS) incorporates XML features into its Web server. Specially configured virtual directories can be mapped to Microsoft SQL Server databases, thanks to an Internet Server API (ISAPI) extension. The extension sends XML-yielding queries to the data access layer, which returns XML documents or document fragments over the *Hypertext Transport Protocol* (HTTP). In this chapter, we will examine how to configure virtual directories for data access, how to execute queries against them, and how to transform XML into *Hypertext Markup Language* (HTML).

XML and IIS

XML support for *Internet Information Server* (IIS) is configured rather quickly. An easy-to-use *Microsoft Management Console* (MMC) snap-in, the IIS Virtual Directory Management tool provides a user interface for creating and configuring virtual directories for the ISAPI extension. We will take a tour of the tool, where you will specify parameters such as location paths, authentication, underlying data source, and the allowed types of queries for XML. When this section is completed, you will have a virtual directory mapped to the Northwind database.

The ISAPI Extension

The ISAPI extension enables XML support in the Web server. With the Virtual Directory Management tool, you mark the virtual directories that are to be handled by the extension. Each virtual directory is configured for how it is accessed itself but also for how the SQL Server is accessed in terms of the authentication mode and the database source to query. The ISAPI makes calls to the *Object Linking and Embedding Database* (OLE DB) data access layer (more precisely, the OLE DB provider for SQL Server). The provider understands XML-queries, so it runs your query against the SQL Server database to which the virtual directory maps. Microsoft SQL Server then returns the results through the OLE DB layer to the Web application. See Figure 3.1 for a diagram of this process.

Launching the Management Tool

Open the Microsoft SQL Server program group and launch the IIS Management tool. This tool is an MMC snap-in, so you might already be familiar with its layout. In the left windowpane, there is a tree that contains the hierarchy of com-

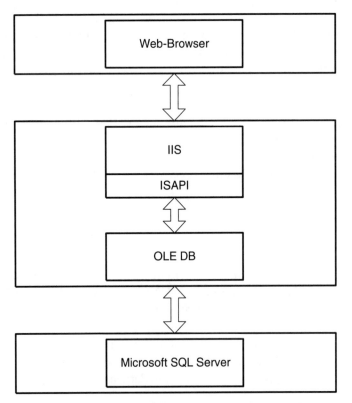

Figure 3.1 Connecting to SQL Server through a virtual root.

puters, Web sites, and virtual directories. You can expand further on these items in the right pane. By right-clicking an item, you can view its properties and perform operations such as deleting or renaming the item. In addition, by right-clicking the empty space in the window, you can create new items of the same type (see Figure 3.2).

NOTE

Microsoft recommends that if you are using Windows 2000 Professional systems, you should install `adminpak.msi` before using the IIS Virtual Directory Management tool for SQL Server. `adminpak.msi` is available on the System32 directory of Windows 2000 Server. This situation makes it complicated if you do not have Windows 2000 Server, however. So, for what it is worth, during the beta cycles of the Microsoft SQL Server 2000, I ran the XML technology just fine on a Windows 2000 Professional development station without `adminpak.msi`. The big disclaimer and key word here is *beta*.

Adding a Virtual Directory

Here, a virtual directory will be created and configured by using the IIS Virtual Directory Management tool. Begin by expanding the host computer, or click the plus sign (+) to the left of the computer icon. Next, pick the Web site that you want to open for access to XML. If you are unsure what to do here, choose the default Web site.

To create the virtual directory, navigate the top menu through Action and New, and then click Virtual Directory (see Figure 3.3). Or, you can right-click in the

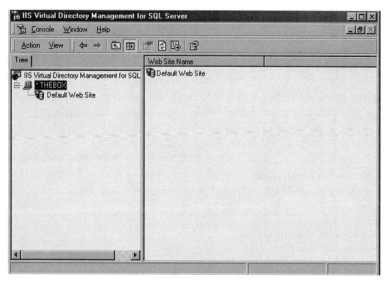

Figure 3.2 The Virtual Directory Management tool.

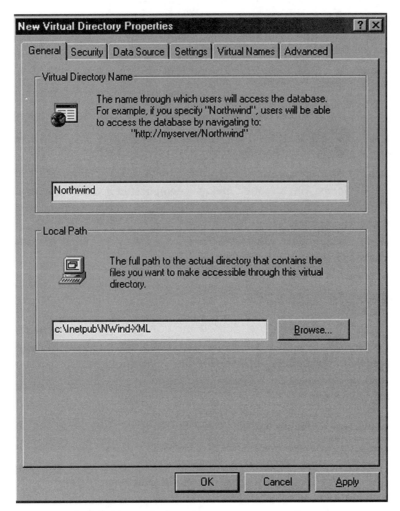

Figure 3.3 The IIS Virtual Directory Management tool.

right window pane and choose New and Virtual Directory. Enter Northwind in the Virtual Directory Name dialog. This name will be the name that you use to access it through the Web browser.

In order to specify the physical location, choose Browse. Expand the directory for your Web server—probably `<device>:\Inetpub\`, where `<device>` is C. Then, create a New Folder named `Nwind-XML`. Click OK.

Configuring the Security

The security under the Security tab sets up how SQL Server is accessed from the virtual directory. There are three options for authentication. A standard login (a Windows or SQL Server account) is listed first. The more special cases of Windows Integrated authentication and basic authentication follow. Of course, the setting that you choose has to correspond with how your SQL Server installation is set up.

First, should you choose a Windows or SQL Server account? Either account is combined with standard IIS anonymous access, which means that users are not prompted for a username and password when they are accessing the public areas of your Web site. Instead, the Web server assigns the user account IUSR_computername to the user. So, if your SQL Server authentication selects a Windows account, it will attempt to log on to the SQL server by using that Windows account. The virtual directory tool automatically selects the default Internet account (typically IUSR_Name). The user and password for the Windows account can be reconfigured in this management tool. If, on the other hand, you define an SQL Server account to use when logging onto SQL Server, it again uses the standard IIS authentication and then sends your defined SQL Server user and password information to SQL Server when requesting a connection (see Figure 3.4).

Secondly, Integrated Windows authentication uses the information that is stored on the client computer. An exchange is made between the browser and the Web server, so your Windows NT account is used to run the Web site and is also used to access the SQL server. No passwords are sent over the network with this method of authentication. The limitation is that for this process to work, you need to be using Microsoft Internet Explorer. Ideally, this type of authentication is used over an intranet, where you know the client computers.

Finally, Basic Authentication is an HTTP authentication method that is about as old as the Web browser. When you visit a site that has basic authentication, you are first denied access and are then prompted for a username and password. When you enter your Windows username and password, the information is sent for verification. If both the username and password were valid, you are granted access. If not, you get to try again. This method is not very secure because it does not encrypt your password, and when seen, it is mainly in combination with *Secure Socket Layers* (SSL).

For development purposes, the most bulletproof setting is integrated authentication. This setting is clearly the least hassle to configure, so pick that option.

The Data Source

In the Data Source tag, you decide the database to which the virtual directory will map. Keep it on the local server, as defined by default, unless you want to specify another database that is known to you. The Database drop-down menu

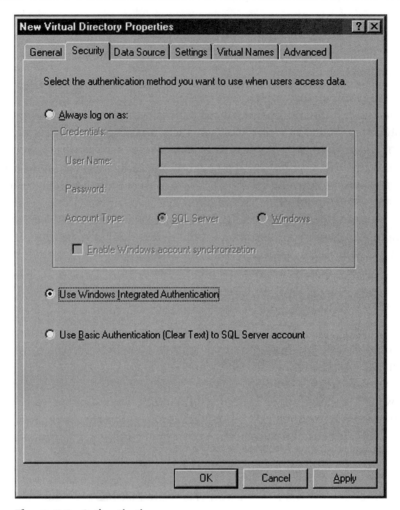

Figure 3.4 Authentication.

is the key theme for this tab. Select the Northwind database, which results in the virtual directory being mapped to Northwind.

Typically, if you are not seeing any databases on the list or are being denied access, check the security settings once more.

Access Types

The Access Types tab is where you configure the access types of the database that is supported by the virtual directory. The three types are: *Uniform Resource Locator* (URL), Template Files, and XPath.

Allow URL Access results in the URL being parsed for the query. In other words, if you embed a valid query in the URL, it is fired off against the database, which hopefully returns an XML document. For the first sample in the book, it is enough for you to check Allow URL Queries and uncheck other active options (see Figure 3.5).

Allow Template Queries enables template files to be executed. Template files are XML documents in which you mark up the parts that are essential to your query. They contain the text of your SQL statement and can contain additional information as well. Template files are more sophisticated than URL access. In addition, they are much more manageable and secure than URL access.

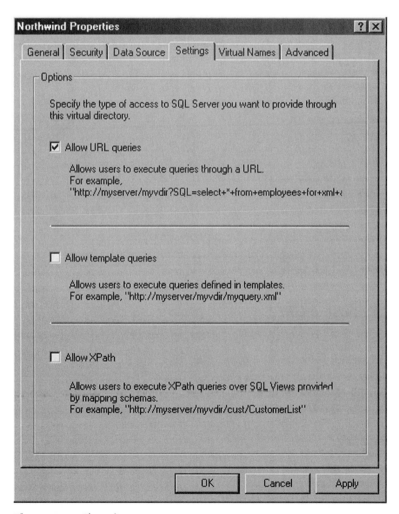

Figure 3.5 Choosing access types.

Finally, Allow XPath Queries enables XPath queries to be run against an XML data-reduced schema. The XPath queries can well be embedded in a URL but can also be marked up in a template file. You will use this option with one of the other two options.

Now That We Are Done . . .

Start an XML-enabled browser, such as Microsoft Internet Explorer. Enter the URL `http://IISServer/Northwind?sql=SELECT+TOP+1+ContacName+FROM+Customers`. Provided that you followed the previous steps, `Maria Anders` should be printed on the screen. In other words, the Northwind virtual directory has been successfully set up, and we can proceed.

If you see nothing or get an error, however, recheck the settings for the virtual directory. Please open the management tool again and make sure that Allow URL Queries is checked under the Settings tab.

SQL and URLs

Within our virtual directory, we can execute queries that are embedded in the URL. In other words, the browser passes the data on to the ISAPI extension. Then, the extension parses the URL for the query, makes sense of it, and fires it off at the data access layer. There are two ways to pass data from the browser to the ISAPI.

Traditionally, data that is sent from a browser to the server is contained either in the `querystring` portion of the URL or in the body of the HTTP request. In this case, the focus is on the `querystring`.

Should You Use a URL?

Should you use URLs for your queries? In my opinion, the answer is both yes and no. Template files are much more secure than URLs, so I think that URLs should never be used in a production environment. They are, however, a good way of getting to know SQL Server and XML. Start with URLs, but avoid them in professional development (or once you know how to use template files).

The querystring

The `querystring` is part of the URL. This variable is an environment variable of the Web server's that is set by the client. With the `querystring` being part of the URL, some limitations apply to embedding XML queries in this variable.

First of all, a URL has a maximum-length of about 2,000 characters, and the `querystring` must abide by that limitation. Some characters must also be encoded when they are part of the query string. These characters are those that have special meaning to the structure of URLs. For them to be interpreted as pure character data, you will have to encode them for the `querystring`. Last, the `querystring` is appended after the actual location is defined in the URL. This action makes it readable by the client (which might be a bad idea). The `querystring` is separated from the URL by a question mark (?). See Table 3.1 for more information about URL encoding.

```
http://yoursite.com?querystring
```

The `querystring` is a collection of name-value pairs, or variables. The name and value of each pair are separated by an equals sign (=), just like when you assign values to variables. Each pair is separated from the other pair by an ampersand (&). For example,

```
http://yoursite.com?name=value&name2=value2
```

Whatever you do, do not make a database *really* public. A client can easily modify the query, write personal queries, and view everything in the database. At the very least, this situation can turn into a destructive scenario with someone who gets a kick out of requesting 10MB of XML documents through your Web server 100 times per minute. Having said that, think about the programmer (most likely you) who has to sit and write, test, and fire off queries through URL-embedded queries. All of the character encoding and typos are a pain.

The FOR XML Clause

Microsoft SQL Server 2000 extends the `SELECT` statement with a `FOR  XML` clause. `FOR  XML` tells the database that you want the results returned as an XML document instead of as a row set. The syntax of a typical query that uses `FOR  XML` is as follows:

```
SELECT <statement>
FOR XML   (
Raw |
```

Table 3.1 URL Encoding

Character	Encoded
/	%2F
?	%3F
#	%23
%	%25
&	%26

```
Auto [,ELEMENTS] |
Explicit
)
[,XMLDATA][,BINARY Base64]
```

The most essential piece of information in the query is the *mode* argument. FOR XML uses one of three modes to generate an XML document fragment (see Table 3.2). By changing the *mode* of your query, you change the fundamental structure of the XML that is generated by SQL Server.

In addition to the mode argument, the ISAPI extension can be passed user-defined variables. How you handle those variables will also affect the output of the XML that is returned from the database. URL queries and template queries support these variables, but in their own fashion. The parameters that you can embed in the querystring are listed in Table 3.3.

Table 3.2 The FOR XML Mode Argument

Mode	Meaning
RAW	Each row is returned as a single XML element whose attributes are named and set in accordance with each returned non-null, queried column's name and value.
AUTO	Each row is returned as an XML element that is identified by a table name whose attributes are named and set in accordance with each queried column's name and value. The result is a simple, nested XML tree with the leftmost table in the query as the top element in the hierarchy of the tree.
EXPLICIT	An XML tree—the returned tree is formatted and shaped by writing the query in a special way.

Table 3.3 The HTTP Embedded URL Query Parameters

Parameter	Meaning
Root	The top-level element, or root element, of the produced XML document. This parameter is a required parameter for a valid XML document if the result contains more than one record, but with one record, that record in particular would be the root element for the valid XML document.
ContentType	The definition for the type of content of the data that is retrieved from the database. For example, binary data such as an image might use image/jpeg, provided that it is a jpeg image. The default content type, however, does not need to be specified (text/XML).
XSL	The path to a style sheet that is to be applied to the XML document that is returned from the query. Note that if the style sheet transforms the XML into HTML, the content type must be text/HTML.

The Top-Level Element

An XML document that is returned from Microsoft SQL Server is assigned a top-level XML element by using the Root parameter. XML documents that contain only a single element, such as the result of a singleton select, have themselves as the top level, so it will work without the Root parameter being defined. An XML document that was created from multiple database records, on the other hand, will break without a top-level element.

An Attribute-Based Example

By default, XML documents are returned as attribute based. A query that limits the number of records to only one record by using the TOP keyword

```
http://IISServer/Northwind?sql=SELECT+TOP+1+*+FROM+Customers+FOR+XML+AUTO
```

yields the following XML:

```
<Customers CustomerID="ALFKI"
  CompanyName="Alfreds Futterkiste"
  ContactName="Maria Anders"
  ContactTitle="Sales Representative"
  Address="Obere Str. 57"
  City="Berlin"
  PostalCode="12209"
  Country="Germany"
  Phone="030-0074321"
  Fax="030-0076545"
/>
```

<Customers> is the top-level element. Furthermore, as defined by AUTO, the leftmost table name in the query becomes the top element. We only used the Customers table, so that is what we get. Attributes are then named and set after the queried column's name and value. XML documents do not have to be attribute-based, though.

An Element-Based Example

XML documents can be element based. We used an attribute-based mode earlier, and shifting into element-based mode is as simple as including the Elements argument of the FOR XML clause. This action changes the form of the XML document. The top-level element is, by nature, still the Customers element—because only that single record is returned from the query. Consider the following query with the Elements argument:

```
http://IISServer/Northwind?sql=SELECT+TOP+1+*+FROM+Customers+FOR+XML+AUT
O+,ELEMENTS
```

Now, consider the output in element-based form:

```
<Customers>
 <CustomerID>ALFKI</CustomerID>
 <CompanyName>Alfreds Futterkiste</CompanyName>
 <ContactName>Maria Anders</ContactName>
 <ContactTitle>Sales Representative</ContactTitle>
 <Address>Obere Str. 57</Address>
 <City>Berlin</City>
 <PostalCode>12209</PostalCode>
 <Country>Germany</Country>
 <Phone>030-0074321</Phone>
 <Fax>030-0076545</Fax>
</Customers>
```

When Good Queries Go Bad

So, how do you break either one of these queries? Request multiple records. For example, execute a `SELECT TOP 10...FOR XML AUTO` query, and the XML parser will greet you with an error.

The integrity of the top-level element is lost unless you stick with single records. Multiple records from the Customers table would result in multiple `<Customers>` elements. So, we will have to explicitly name and assign a unique top-level element for queries that have multiple records. Compare these queries:

- Bad query:

  ```
  http://IISServer/Northwind?sql=SELECT+TOP+10+*+FROM+Customers+FOR+
  XML+AUTO+,ELEMENTS
  ```

- Good query:

  ```
  http://IISServer/Northwind?sql=SELECT+TOP+10+*+FROM+Customers+FOR+
  XML+AUTO+,ELEMENTS&Root=myRoot
  ```

The bad query skips the top-level element, which will not work. We want 10 customer elements, so we need a top-level element that contains that number. The good query solves this problem by defining a Root parameter. If you execute the good query, you will get the following structure contained by the `<myRoot>` element:

```
<myRoot>
 <Customers>
  <CustomerID>ALFKI</CustomerID>
  ...
 </Customers>
</myRoot>
```

Content Types

We are almost ready to abandon singleton queries. Let's just talk about the `ContentType` argument first.

The content type describes the content that is coming with the HTTP response. For example, a FOR XML query that returns images from the database can use ContentType to tell the browser that it should render the data into an image. Furthermore, if you want to transform your XML into HTML, you must specify the content type.

The default content type is text/XML. This type is the header with the document returned from a FOR XML query. An HTML document, on the other hand, must be text/HTML. Otherwise, the browser will not render it as HTML. Likewise, a text/HTML document cannot be interpreted as XML. If, for example, you attempt to transform the returned XML into HTML by using XSL transformations without indicating the content type, it will not matter. The browser will never interpret it as HTML unless the content type tells it to render it as HTML.

Moreover, to come to terms with binary data that is stored in the database (such as images), the FOR XML query must tell the browser what type of image to display. To illustrate this situation, I prefer working with the SQL Server Pubs database. This database has .gif files easy at hand, and we know that .gif files display in most browsers without hassle.

Presenting Images from the Database

Use the Virtual Directory Management tool to prepare a virtual root for the Pubs database. Then, experiment with displaying an image.

Streaming Binary Data

When retrieving single columns, we can omit FOR XML by design. Enter the following location:

```
http://IISServer/Pubs?sql=SELECT+logo+FROM+pub_info+WHERE+pub_id+=+'0736'
&ContentType=image/gif
```

Streaming Binary Data in HTML

The good old HTML IMG-element can be used to execute a URL query and to present the image in the browser:

```
<img src="http://IISServer/Pubs?sql=SELECT+logo+FROM+pub_info+WHERE+
pub_id+=+'0736'"/>
```

You need to make sure that the full URL is in one single line. Any white space, such as newline, will break the query.

Database Objects

The XPath language and the dbobject virtual name type is used to access binary data. Because Microsoft SQL Server in some instances returns an XPath reference to a binary object, people think that the dbobject type can be used to resolve the reference if passed the address by your application. You can set up a `dbobject` in the management tool under Virtual Names. Just create a new `dbobject` named, say, `myObject`, and when you get an XPath location path to binary data returned instead of actual binary data, pass it to `myObject`.

```
http://IISServer/Northwind/myObject/XPath
```

or

```
http://IISServer/Northwind/myObject/Employees[@EmployeeID='1']/@Photo
```

Applying XSL Transformation

XSL Transformations are cool, mainly because they are a real easy and powerful technology to apply to XML documents. Include the XSL parameter, pointing to a valid style sheet, in your URL, and pass the query. The style sheet for this example looks like the following:

```
<?xml version="1.0"?>
<xsl:stylesheet
 xmlns:xsl="http://www.w3.org/1999/XSL/Transform"
 version="1.0">
<xsl:template match="/">
  <html>
    <body bgcolor="#ffffff">
      <table align="center"
        border="1"
        cellpadding="3"
        cellspacing="0">
        <tr>
        <td bgcolor="#aaaaaa"><b>pub_id</b></td>
        <td bgcolor="#aaaaaa"><b>pr_info</b></td>
        </tr>
        <xsl:apply-templates/>
      </table>
    </body>
  </html>
</xsl:template>
<xsl:template match="pub_info">
  <tr>
   <td bgcolor="#eeeeee">
   <xsl:value-of select="@pub_id"/>
   </td>
   <td bgcolor='#eeeeee'>
   <xsl:value-of select="substring(@pr_info,1,60)"/> ...
   </td>
  </tr>
</xsl:template>
</xsl:stylesheet>
```

Place the style sheet within the Pubs virtual directory. Then, type the following URL (see Figure 3.6):

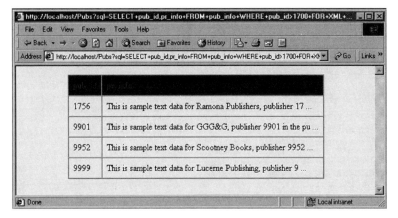

Figure 3.6   XSL Transformations on XML from SQL Server.

```
http://IISServer/Pubs?sql=SELECT+pub_id,pr_info+FROM+pub_info+WHERE+pub_
id>1700+FOR+XML+AUTO&Root=root&xsl=Pubs.xsl&ContentType=text/HTML.
```

All three parameters that have been discussed thus far are applied to the URL. Without the text/HTML content type—a simple, frustrating detail sometimes— we would not get the expected result. The data would just not be interpreted as HTML. Additionally, without a root element, we would not have a valid XML document. Also, without an XSL Transformation style sheet, XML could not easily be turned into HTML. To make sure that no details are left out, the function `substring()` of the transformation language, XPath, that is supported in XSL limits the number of characters shown from the returned value for the `pr_info` column to only 60 characters in length. It does not, however, modify this restriction at the level of the XML document, because it is modified only at the transformation time from XML to HTML.

Template File Query

A template file is a structured XML document that is marked up with elements that define things such as the `FOR XML` statement. It is absolutely more manageable and secure than HTTP URL access directly to the SQL Server database.

XML in a Template File

Built on XML itself, a template file contains optional elements that can be used to create a file that executed a query. The XML file can be accessed directly through its URL, but no information about the actual database is made public to the client (because it is all contained within the template). A sample template file is as follows:

```
<document
 xmlns:sql="urn:schemas-microsoft-com:xml-sql"
 sql:xsl="Filename.xsl">
    <sql:header>
      <sql:param name="ParameterName">
          ParameterValue
      </sql:param>
    </sql:header>
    <sql:query>
          SELECT Statement
    </sql:query>
    <sql:XPath-query mapping-schema="SchemaFilename.xml">
        XPath Expression
    </sql:XPath-query>
</document>
```

Using Template Files

In order to utilize templates, template support must be activated. Open the tool for configuring the SQL Server XML support for IIS. Locate the Northwind virtual root, right-click it, select Properties, and follow the next few steps:

1. Click the Settings tab.
2. Check Allow Template Queries.
3. Click the Virtual Names tab.
4. Click New.
5. Enter `myTemplate` as the Virtual Name.
6. Select Template as Type.
7. For Path, click to browse.
8. Expand Inetpub.
9. Expand Nwind-XML.
10. Click New Folder.
11. Create Templates.
12. Click Save.
13. Click OK.

Now, you can create a template file that contains a query, save it within the virtual space for template files, and execute it through its URL. For each template file, the `sql` namespace needs to be declared. That namespace defines the `sql:element`(s), which are completely optional elements. The following query can be executed by placing the file `Customers.xml` within the template-enabled virtual directory and then entering the following URL:

```
http://IISServer/Northwind/myTemplate/Customers.xml
```

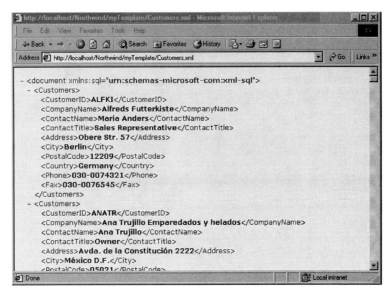

Figure 3.7 Output of FOR XML AUTO, ELEMENTS query.

The following is the output of Customers.XML (see Figure 3.7):

```
<document xmlns:sql="urn:schemas-microsoft-com:xml-sql">
  <sql:query>
    SELECT *
    FROM Customers
    FOR XML AUTO, ELEMENTS
  </sql:query>
</document>
```

Like URL-embedded queries, you can include an XSL attribute for an associated XSL Transformation style sheet. For example, let's redo the previous example:

```
<document xmlns:sql="urn:schemas-microsoft-com:xml-sql" sql:xsl="nwind-
transform.xsl">
  <sql:query>
    SELECT CustomerID,
           CompanyName,
           ContactName,
           ContactTitle
    FROM Customers
    FOR XML AUTO, ELEMENTS
  </sql:query>
</document>
```

To transform the document into HTML, specify the ContentType in the URL as

```
http://IISServer/Northwind/myTemplate/nwind-transform.xml?
ContentType=text/HTML
```

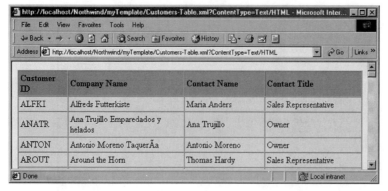

Figure 3.8 Transformed FOR XML query.

and place this style sheet in the same directory (see Figure 3.8):

```
<?xml version="1.0"?>
<xsl:stylesheet
 xmlns:xsl="http://www.w3.org/1999/XSL/Transform"
 version="1.0">
  <xsl:template match="/">
    <html>
      <body bgcolor="#ffffff">
        <table align="center"
        border="1" cellpadding="3" cellspacing="0">
        <tr>
        <td bgcolor="#aaaaaa"><b>Customer ID</b></td>
        <td bgcolor="#aaaaaa"><b>Company Name</b></td>
        <td bgcolor="#aaaaaa"><b>Contact Name</b></td>
        <td bgcolor="#aaaaaa"><b>Contact Title</b></td>
        </tr>
           <xsl:apply-templates/>
        </table>
      </body>
    </html>
  </xsl:template>
  <xsl:template match="Customers">
        <tr>
        <td bgcolor="#eeeeee">
        <xsl:value-of select="CustomerID"/>
        </td>
        <td bgcolor="#eeeeee">
        <xsl:value-of select="CompanyName"/>
        </td>
        <td bgcolor="#eeeeee">
        <xsl:value-of select="ContactName"/>
        </td>
        <td bgcolor="#eeeeee">
        <xsl:value-of select="ContactTitle"/>
        </td>
```

```
        </tr>
    </xsl:template>
</xsl:stylesheet>
```

Template files can also be embedded directly within the URL, not unlike an SQL statement, and can be executed through that medium. The parameter in such a `querystring` is the template parameter instead of the sql parameter. Because it is a query string, the same encoding rules apply to the URL—which leads us to a new topic: encoding within template files.

Encoding Rules

Because the template file is an XML file, the symbols greater-than and less-than, for example, must be encoded to their proper representation—or else they signify markup tags within the document. The query

```
http://IISServer/Pubs?sql=SELECT+pub_id,pr_info+FROM+pub_info+WHERE+
pub_id>1700+FOR+XML+AUTO&Root=document&xsl=Pubs-transform.xsl&
ContentType=text/HTML
```

is used to show how to transform an XML document into HTML. Provided that a template virtual root is set up for the Pubs database, this query could have to be refined within a template file.

```
<document xmlns:sql="urn:schemas-microsoft-com:xml-sql"
 sql:xsl="Pubs-transform.xsl">
  <sql:query>
    SELECT pub_ud,
           pr_info
    FROM pub_info WHERE pub_id &gt; 1700
    FOR XML AUTO
  </sql:query>
</document>
```

Executing Stored Procedures

A common database object, the stored procedure can be executed by way of a URL. You can either embed it within the URL or contain it within a template file.

In order to execute a stored procedure through a URL-embedded query, let's first use the base of an existing stored procedure in the Northwind database and make it into an XML-returning procedure. We are using the "Ten Most Expensive Products," and when we are done with the code, it will look like the following:

```
CREATE PROCEDURE xml_TenProducts AS
SET ROWCOUNT 10
    SELECT Products.ProductName
        AS TenMostExpensiveProducts,
```

```
                    Products.UnitPrice
        FROM Products
        ORDER BY Products.UnitPrice DESC
        FOR XML AUTO
    GO
```

To execute this code, enter the following URL:

```
http://IISServer/Northwind?sql=EXECUTE+xml_TenProducts&Root=document
```

Within the stored procedure, you can set the top-level element of the XML document by selecting it before and after the actual query result is returned. We will perform this action in the next query, which also expects an input parameter. The code base is the Northwind `CustOrdersOrders` procedure, and the XML version that we end up with looks like the following:

```
CREATE PROCEDURE xml_CustOrdersOrders
    @CustomerID nchar(5)
AS
    SELECT '<document>'
    SELECT OrderID,
      OrderDate,
      RequiredDate,
      ShippedDate
    FROM Orders
    WHERE CustomerID = @CustomerID
    ORDER BY OrderID
    FOR XML AUTO
    SELECT '</document>'
GO
```

The expected input parameter can be included in one of two ways:

- `http://IISServer/Northwind?sql=EXECUTE+`
  `xml_CustOrdersOrders+@CustomerID=QUEEN`

- `http://IISServer/Northwind?sql=EXECUTE+`
  `xml_CustOrdersOrders+QUEEN`

If the stored procedure expected several parameters,

```
CREATE PROCEDURE xml_CustOrdersOrders2
    @CustomerID nchar(5) ,
    @OrderID int
AS
    SELECT '<document>'
    SELECT OrderID,
            OrderDate,
            RequiredDate,
            ShippedDate
    FROM Orders
```

```
       WHERE CustomerID = @CustomerID AND OrderID = @OrderID
       FOR XML AUTO
       SELECT '</document>'
GO
```

separate multiple parameters with a comma.

- A standard call to execute a stored procedure:

```
http://IISServer/Northwind?sql=EXECUTE+xml_
CustOrdersOrders2+@CustomerID=QUEEN+,+@OrderID=10372
```

- If you are familiar with ODBC,

```
http://IISServer/Northwind?sql={CALL+xml_
CustOrdersOrders2}+@CustomerID=QUEEN+,+@OrderID=10372
```

When working with template files, the syntax for calling a stored procedure over the URL is only different with the template file's XML elements. Let's remove `SELECT '<document>'` and `SELECT '</document>'` from the stored procedure. We perform this task because the template file declares the root element. For the reader, who visualizes the examples, the stored procedure will look like the following:

```
CREATE PROCEDURE xml_CustOrdersOrders4
    @CustomerID nchar(5),
    @OrderID int
AS
    SELECT OrderID,
           OrderDate,
           RequiredDate,
           ShippedDate
    FROM Orders
    WHERE CustomerID = @CustomerID AND OrderID = @OrderID
    FOR XML AUTO
GO
```

The XML template file keeps the input parameter information in its header, and if we predefine the parameters, it will be a straightforward document that is run by `http://IISServer/Northwind/myTemplate/nwind-sp.xml`.

```
<document xmlns:sql="urn:schemas-microsoft-com:xml-sql">
 <sql:header>
  <sql:param name="CustomerID">QUEEN</sql:param>
  <sql:param name="OrderID">10728</sql:param>
 </sql:header>
 <sql:query>
    EXECUTE CustOrdersOrdersXML @CustomerID, @OrderID
 </sql:query>
</document>
```

Override the default parameter values by passing your own parameters to the document. The query

```
http://IISServer/Northwind/myTemplate/nwind-sp.xml?
CustomerID=OCEAN&OrderID=10898
```

uses the same template, but it fetches the information for the CustomerID and OrderID as the values that they are assigned in the `querystring`.

Parameters

Queries support parameterized calls. As already seen, a template file can declare parameters and their default values for stored procedures. Now, we will instead look at how queries can accept parameters.

In Template Files

To begin, our template file in the following format has two parameters and a predefined SQL statement within its query element:

```
<document xmlns:sql="urn:schemas-microsoft-com:xml-sql">
<sql:header>
    <sql:param name="CustomerID">OCEAN</sql:param>
    <sql:param name="OrderDate">10/27/1997</sql:param>
</sql:header>
<sql:query>
    SELECT CustomerID,
           OrderID,
           ShippedDate,
           Freight
    FROM Orders
    WHERE CustomerID = @CustomerID AND OrderDate &gt; @OrderDate
    FOR XML AUTO
</sql:query>
</document>
```

The query will list all orders that were made later than 10/27/1997 and that involved the customer identified as OCEAN. The template file can be called without parameters, because you only enter its URL into the browser. It can also be called with parameters, however. For example, `http://IISServer/Northwind/myTemplate/nwind-parameter.xml?OrderDate=3/26/1998` would return only one matching record, while the default parameter would return three records. Here is a template fragment shown on the accompanying CD-ROM from `nwind-parameter-style.xsl`:

```
...
  <xsl:template match="OrderInfo">
     <tr>
     <td bgcolor="#eeeeee">
     <xsl:value-of select="@CustomerID"/>
     </td>
     <td bgcolor="#eeeeee">
     <xsl:value-of select="@OrderID"/>
     </td>
     <td bgcolor="#eeeeee">
     <xsl:value-of select="substring(@ShippedDate, 1, 10)"/>
     </td>
     <td bgcolor="#eeeeee">
     $<xsl:value-of select="format-number(@Freight, '####')"/>
     </td>
     </tr>
  </xsl:template>
...
```

In URLs

Likewise, an embedded URL query that utilizes parameters indicates a parameter by using the question mark character (?). The parameter later is assigned its value within the `querystring`, where its column name is used. Multiple parameters are separated by the ampersand (&):

```
http://IISServer/Northwind?sql=SELECT+CustomerID,OrderID,ShippedDate,
Freight+FROM+Orders+WHERE+CustomerID+=+?+FOR+XML+AUTO&CustomerID=
OCEAN&Root=document
```

The query creates an XML document from matching the OCEAN customer identification string with the records in the Orders table. The parameters in the URL are passed to the template file.

Summary

This chapter has discussed how the IIS ISAPI extension works for SQL Server, as well as the basic FOR XML query, and the XML data it returns. The various approaches for a Web application to pull XML data from SQL Server, plus how to transform it into HTML, were demonstrated. The next chapter is going to take a deeper look at the FOR XML query capabilities and how to write more complex queries.

The FOR XML Modes

Microsoft SQL Server 2000 can build *Extensible Markup Language* (XML) documents in three different modes. Modes are used to control the structure of your document, ranging from a flat document to a nested tree. Each one of the modes varies in degree of complexity. So, starting at the most basic level, we will work our way up through the most advanced mode.

The Raw Mode

The Raw mode is the easiest mode to understand. Each row from the underlying data store is returned as a single XML element. The attributes of that element are set in accordance with each queried column's returned name and value—provided that the value is non-null.

The XML document will contain the top-level element, followed by the elements that are spawned from the query. For a simple query, when the Northwind database's Categories-table is queried for its data that is returned in Raw mode by the following,

```
http://IISServer/Northwind?sql=SELECT+*+FROM+Categories+FOR+XML+RAW&Root
=document
```

the resulting XML document will resemble the underlying database table.

```
<document>
 <row CategoryName="Beverages"
     Description="Soft drinks, coffees, teas, beers, and ales" />
```

```
...
</document>
```

Furthermore, a query can perform joins on multiple tables, yet each queried column in every table is placed as an attribute within the generic row created by the Raw mode. Please note that the Elements argument is not available with Raw mode, so attributes are the only way to get the result. In this example, we alias—which means using the AS keyword to alias, or rename—columns and tables in order to alter the naming convention for the XML attributes. Consider the following query:

```
SELECT   Orders.OrderID          AS [ID],
         Orders.OrderDate        AS [Date],
         Orders.ShipName         AS [To],
         Orders.ShipAddress      AS [Address],
         Orders.ShipCity         AS [City],
         Orders.ShipPostalCode   AS [PostalCode],
         Orders.ShipCountry      AS [Country],
         Orders.Freight          AS [ShippingCost],
         Details.ProductID,
         Details.UnitPrice,
         Details.Quantity,
         Details.Discount,
         Product.UnitsInStock,
         Product.Discontinued,
         Product.ProductName
FROM Orders
    INNER JOIN
      [Order Details] AS Details ON Orders.OrderID = Details.OrderID
    INNER JOIN
      Products AS Product ON Details.ProductID = Product.ProductID
WHERE (Orders.OrderDate > '1/1/1998' AND Details.Quantity > 75)
ORDER BY Orders.ShipName
FOR XML RAW
```

Here is the output:

```
<document>
  <row ID="10854" Date="1998-01-27T00:00:00" To="Ernst Handel"
   Address="Kirchgasse 6" City="Graz" PostalCode="8010"
   Country="Austria" ShippingCost="100.22" ProductID="10"
   UnitPrice="31" Quantity="100" Discount="0.15000001"
   UnitsInStock="31" Discontinued="0" ProductName="Ikura"
  />
  <row ID="10895" Date="1998-02-18T00:00:00" To="Ernst Handel"
   Address="Kirchgasse 6" City="Graz" PostalCode="8010"
   Country="Austria" ShippingCost="162.75" ProductID="24"
   UnitPrice="4.5" Quantity="110" Discount="0" UnitsInStock="20"
   Discontinued="1" ProductName="Guaraná Fantástica"
  />
  ...
</document>
```

In spite of the several queried columns belonging to several tables, the XML document contains a number of generic XML elements: the row elements, or nodes, that do not contain any nodes within themselves. The Raw mode cannot create a nested tree. Additionally, no distinction about the table from which the attributes of the generic XML element were retrieved is produced.

When retrieving data in Raw mode, you can return data in Binary Base64 encoded format by adding the `BINARY BASE64` clause to the `FOR XML RAW` full SQL statement. This statement is not set by default, so a reference is returned to any binary data. The reference can be resolved by the `dbobject` virtual name. A schema describing the XML document can also be requested for the XML document. The query

```
http://IISServer/Northwind?sql=SELECT+*+FROM+Categories+WHERE+1=2+FOR+XM
L+RAW,BINARY+BASE64,XMLDATA
```

returns an XML data schema for the Categories table in the Northwind database.

```
<Schema name="Schema"
 xmlns="urn:schemas-microsoft-com:xml-data"
 xmlns:dt="urn:schemas-microsoft-com:datatypes">
 <ElementType name="row" content="empty" model="closed">
  <AttributeType name="CategoryID" dt:type="i4" />
  <AttributeType name="CategoryName" dt:type="string" />
  <AttributeType name="Description" dt:type="string" />
  <AttributeType name="Picture" dt:type="bin.base64" />
  <attribute type="CategoryID" />
  <attribute type="CategoryName" />
  <attribute type="Description" />
  <attribute type="Picture" />
 </ElementType>
</Schema>
```

Next, we will look at Auto mode. This mode is capable of producing a nested tree and can create either an attribute-based or element-based XML document.

Auto Mode

Auto mode builds a simple XML tree. Here, each row is returned as an XML element that is identified by a table name whose attributes are named and are set in accordance with each queried column's name and value. The resulting tree keeps the leftmost table of the SQL query as the top element in the tree hierarchy. Sibling relationships are not supported in Auto mode. Attribute-based documents are returned by default. You could, however, specify the Elements argument of the `FOR XML` clause, and the resulting XML tree will become element-based.

As we previously mentioned, the table to the left in the SQL statement is the element that falls directly under the top-level root element. The name of the returned XML elements will reflect the names of the queried tables unless they are aliased. Let's revisit this query:

```
SELECT   Orders.OrderID          AS [ID],
         Orders.OrderDate        AS [Date],
         Orders.ShipName         AS [To],
         Orders.ShipAddress      AS [Address],
         Orders.ShipCity         AS [City],
         Orders.ShipPostalCode   AS [PostalCode],
         Orders.ShipCountry      AS [Country],
         Orders.Freight          AS [ShippingCost],
         Details.ProductID,
         Details.UnitPrice,
         Details.Quantity,
         Details.Discount,
         Product.UnitsInStock,
         Product.Discontinued,
         Product.ProductName
FROM Orders
    INNER JOIN
      [Order Details] AS Details ON Orders.OrderID = Details.OrderID
    INNER JOIN
      Products AS Product ON Details.ProductID = Product.ProductID
WHERE (Orders.OrderDate > '1/1/1998' AND Details.Quantity > 75)
ORDER BY Orders.ShipName
FOR XML AUTO
```

In contrast to Raw, when in Auto mode, the output is hierarchical:

```
<document>
 <Orders ID="10854" Date="1998-01-27T00:00:00"
  To="Ernst Handel"
  Address="Kirchgasse 6" City="Graz" PostalCode="8010"
  Country="Austria" ShippingCost="100.22">
  <Details ProductID="10" UnitPrice="31" Quantity="100"
   Discount="0.15000001">
   <Product UnitsInStock="31" Discontinued="0"
    ProductName="Ikura" />
  </Details>
 </Orders>
 <Orders ID="10895" Date="1998-02-18T00:00:00"
  To="Ernst Handel"
  Address="Kirchgasse 6" City="Graz" PostalCode="8010"
  Country="Austria" ShippingCost="162.75">
  <Details ProductID="24" UnitPrice="4.5" Quantity="110"
   Discount="0">
   <Product UnitsInStock="20" Discontinued="1"
    ProductName="Guaraná
    Fantástica" />
  </Details>
```

```
    <Details ProductID="40" UnitPrice="18.4" Quantity="91"
     Discount="0">
     <Product UnitsInStock="123" Discontinued="0"
      ProductName="Boston
      Crab Meat" />
    </Details>
    <Details ProductID="60" UnitPrice="34" Quantity="100"
      Discount="0">
     <Product UnitsInStock="19" Discontinued="0"
      ProductName="Camembert Pierrot" />
    </Details>
   </Orders>
   ...
  </document>
```

Like Raw mode, the Auto mode can return an XML data schema by defining XMLDATA and posting the FOR XML clause. Unlike Raw mode, the Auto mode (by default) turns on Binary Base64 encoding.

Explicit Mode

The third mode is the most dynamic and also the most complex. With its special syntax, Explicit mode enables the programmer to shape the hierarchy of the well-formed, returned XML tree.

When building an XML tree in Explicit mode, you must first create a universal table. The table is then used to represent the nodes and values of the XML tree. Each column that is defined in the universal table should be equivalent to a queried column, with the exception of two columns: Tag and Parent. These columns dictate the relationship between the nodes of the XML tree, and these two columns are used when the XML tree is finally built. For structure, the Tag column contains the number for the current element or a number representing the current element, while the Parent column contains the number for its parent element. 0 or null represents the first level that falls under the top level of the XML document. Both the arbitrary nesting of elements and sibling relationships are possible while in Explicit mode.

An XML element that is created from a universal table can only be created if the query specifies 1) the name of the XML element, 2) the Tag representation, and 3) either an Attribute name or a Directive, because they are necessary in order to build the XML tree.

Syntactically, building a basic XML element is easy. The basic form for creating the representation within the universal table is as follows:

```
GenericIdentifier!TagRepresentation!AttributeName!Directive
```

Bit by bit, the Element name will define the name of the node, and the Tag representation will be the unique identifier for the element. The Attribute name will be the name of the attribute that belongs to the element or subelement if the Directive indicates an element, and the Directive can be used to specify how the data is returned within the XML tree or how its text is mapped to XML. You can decide which columns map to attributes and which columns map to elements. Before proceeding, let's look at an example query that uses the Northwind database.

```
SELECT  1 AS Tag, NULL AS Parent,
    Orders.OrderID        AS [Order!1!ID],
    Orders.OrderDate      AS [Order!1!Date],
    Orders.ShipName       AS [Order!1!ShipTo!Element],
    Orders.ShipAddress    AS [Order!1!ShipAddress!Element],
    Orders.ShipCity       AS [Order!1!ShipCity!Element],
    Orders.ShipPostalCode AS [Order!1!ShipPostalCode!Element],
    Orders.ShipCountry    AS [Order!1!ShipCountry!Element]
    FROM Orders
    WHERE Orders.OrderDate > '5/1/1998'
    FOR XML EXPLICIT
```

Provided that the document is the name of the top-level element, the following code is part of the output:

```
<?xml version="1.0" encoding="utf-8" ?>
 <document>
  <Order ID="11067" Date="1998-05-04T00:00:00">
   <ShipTo>Drachenblut Delikatessen</ShipTo>
   <ShipAddress>Walserweg 21</ShipAddress>
   <ShipCity>Aachen</ShipCity>
   <ShipPostalCode>52066</ShipPostalCode>
   <ShipCountry>Germany</ShipCountry>
  </Order>
  ...
 </document>
```

In essence, the first two columns of the Orders table become attribute-based. Next, the directive called Element is set for each column, and as a result, they are inserted as elements under the Orders element—rather than becoming attributes. It is not unreasonable to want an XML document structured like the following:

```
<?xml version="1.0" encoding="utf-8" ?>
 <document>
  <Order ID="11067" Date="1998-05-04T00:00:00">
   <Customer CustomerID="DRACD"
    RequiredDate="1998-05-18T00:00:00">
    <ShipTo>Drachenblut Delikatessen</ShipTo>
    <ShipAddress>Walserweg 21</ShipAddress>
    <ShipCity>Aachen</ShipCity>
    <ShipPostalCode>52066</ShipPostalCode>
    <ShipCountry>Germany</ShipCountry>
```

```
    </customer>
   </Order>
   ...
  </document>
```

These fields are all available within the Orders table, so what it takes is to fabricate a customer element as a child element and put the subnodes of customer information within the customer element, right? The answer is yes. Unfortunately, the initial release of SQL Server 2000 does not support fabricating XML elements. The standard syntax for creating parents and children within the universal table must be used. See Table 4.1 for more information.

```
SELECT TOP 10 1 AS Tag, NULL AS Parent,
        Orders.OrderID   AS [Order!1!ID],
        Orders.OrderDate AS [Order!1!Date],
        NULL AS [Customer!2!CustomerID],
        NULL AS [Customer!2!RequiredDate],
        NULL AS [Customer!2!ShipName!element],
        NULL AS [Customer!2!ShipAddress!element],
        NULL AS [Customer!2!ShipCity!Element],
        NULL AS [Customer!2!ShipPostalCode!Element],
        NULL AS [Customer!2!ShipCountry!Element]
FROM Orders WHERE Orders.OrderDate > '5/1/1998'
UNION ALL
SELECT TOP 10 2 AS Tag, 1 AS Parent,
      Orders.OrderID,
      NULL,
      Orders.CustomerID,
      Orders.RequiredDate,
      Orders.ShipName,
      Orders.ShipAddress,
      Orders.ShipCity,
      Orders.ShipPostalCode,
```

Table 4.1 Explicit Mode Directives

Directive	Meaning
cdata	Wraps text-type values within a CDATA section
element	Creates a column as an XML element instead of as an attribute
hide	Hides the attribute name and value
ID	ID-type attribute
IDREF	Refers to an ID-type attribute
IDREFS	Refers to an ID-type attribute with multiple values separated by white space
xml	No entity encoding
xmltext	Wraps text-type values within a single tag

```
        Orders.ShipCountry
FROM Orders WHERE Orders.OrderDate > '5/1/1998'
ORDER BY [Order!1!ID],[Customer!2!ShipName!element]
FOR XML EXPLICIT
```

At first glance, `ID`, `IDREF`, and `IDREFS` can seem odd. They enable many-to-many relationships. The ID attribute of an XML element signifies a unique identifier. If the same ID appears twice or more in the same document, an error results. (It is up to the processor to return an error.) The `IDREF` is a reference to an ID within the document, so the relationship between the two is analogous to primary and foreign key.

Limitations of FOR XML

`FOR XML` cannot be used with the following:

- Nested select statements are accepted but are invalid if they contain `FOR XML <mode>`
- Views can be queries but cannot be created as `CREATE VIEW ... FOR XML <mode>`.
- COMPUTE expressions are incompatible with `FOR XML <mode>`.
- Rowset commands returning user-defined functions cannot return `FOR XML <mode>`.
- SELECT statements calling additional stored procedures cannot use `FOR XML <mode>`.
- INSERT statements cannot call a stored procedure containing `FOR XML <mode>`.

Summary

This chapter has dealt with the FOR XML syntax. The most basic syntax of FOR XML were covered, but also complex queries that create hierarchical results joined from multiple tables. The next chapter is about annotated schemas and what they are.

CHAPTER 5

Annotated Schemas

icrosoft SQL Server includes its own annotations to the XML Data Reduced schema. Annotations are actual extensions. These extensions are especially designed for working with XML views and trying XPath expressions against SQL Server databases. Annotations involve user-defined information about databases, instances, relations (tables or views), and columns. Furthermore, you can define the relationships that are required to express hierarchical relationships of your relational data in XML.

Schema-Building

So, what we need to do is declare a schema and import our annotations. This procedure should be fairly simple at the start:

```
<Schema
 name="mySchema"
 xmlns="urn.schemas-microsoft-com:xml-data"
 xmlns:sql="urn:schemas-microsoft-com:xml-sql">
...
</Schema>
```

We import two namespaces. The first namespace, xmlns, declares the document a schema. Afterwards, the Microsoft Annotation, xmlns, follows. Here, we continue building our schema with some new annotations:

```
<ElementType name="Order" sql:relation="Orders" >
    <AttributeType name="OrderID" />
```

```
        <AttributeType name="OrderDate" />
        <attribute type="OrderID" sql:field="OrderID" />
        <attribute type="OrderDate" sql:field="OrderDate" />
    </ElementType>
```

We used two annotations: `sql:relation` and `sql:field`. `sql:relation` defines the relational database table, and `sql:field` defines the columns of the relational table that are mapped by the schema. Both are optional, but we use them so that we will be familiar with annotations.

Adding the Top Level

What if you do not want an element that is mapped to a database? Because the root element does not map to a valid database column, you must declare it as a constant:

```
    <ElementType name="Order" sql:relation="Orders" >
        <AttributeType name="OrderID" />
        <AttributeType name="OrderDate" />
        <attribute type="OrderID" sql:field="OrderID"/>
        <attribute type="OrderDate" sql:field="OrderDate" />
    </ElementType>
    <ElementType name="document" sql:is-constant="1">
        <element type="Order"/>
    </ElementType>
```

The `sql:is` constant attribute says that the element is not mapped to the database. Consequently, it creates the document element, and Order is placed as a child of the document.

Defining Data Types

The XDR schema lets you get specific with data types. Structuring elements and attributes, data types directly affect `<ElementType>` and `<Attribute-Type>`. All data types are defined within the `dt:datatype` namespace. Because SQL Server is platform specific and has its own data types, XML as a multi-platform standard will be naturally different. The schema is as follows (see Table 5.1):

```
    <?xml version="1.0" ?>
    <Schema xmlns="urn:schemas-microsoft-com:xml-data"
            xmlns:dt="urn:schemas-microsoft-com:datatypes"
            xmlns:sql="urn:schemas-microsoft-com:xml-sql"
    >
    <ElementType name="Order" sql:relation="Orders" >
        <AttributeType name="OrderID"   dt:type="i4"/>
        <AttributeType name="OrderDate" dt:type="dateTime"/>
```

Table 5.1 SQL Server to XML Data Type Mapping

SQL Server Data Type	XML Data Type
binary	bin.base64
bit	Boolean
char	char
datetime	dateTime
decimal	r8
float	r8
image	bin.base64
int	int
money	r8
nchar	string
ntext	string
nvarchar	string
numeric	r8
real	r4
smalldatetime	dateTime
smallint	i2
smallmoney	fixed.14.4
text	string
timestamp	ui8
tinyint	ui1
varbinary	bin.base64
varchar	bin.base64
uniqueidentifier	uuid

```
      <attribute type="OrderID" sql:field="OrderID"/>
      <attribute type="OrderDate" sql:field="OrderDate" />
  </ElementType>
  </Schema>
```

XML and SQL Server do not exactly agree on Binary Large Objects (BLOBs).
BLOB data maps only to `bin.base64` with XML data types. The `sql` namespace solves this problem by supporting SQL Server data types. Thanks to that,
a varchar does not have to be set as `dt:type="bin.base64"`, and it is better
used as `sql:datatype="varchar"`.

Tree Structures

An XML document is often tree-based. Sooner or later, we will want nested hierarchies—and that will require us to declare relationships between the nodes. A special annotation is used to declare relationships. If the objective is the following output,

```
<document>
...
 <Order attributes>
   <Details attributes>
     <Product attributes></Product>
   </Details> ... n
 </Order>
...
</document>
```

then we need each `<Order>` element organized with one or more `<Details>` elements as subnodes. Let's think for a second. The Order table and the Order Details table relate to each other through an OrderID key. To be able to verify that the query is on the right track, the OrderID from both the Order and Order Details tables is visible in the XML document. Our primary table is the Order table. The foreign table for the relation is the Order Details table. Essentially, we just need to do a join of the two (in XML syntax). Let's declare the Products-element first, because it has no children:

```
<ElementType name="Product" sql:relation="Products" >
    <AttributeType name="UnitsInStock" />
    <AttributeType name="Discontinued" />
    <AttributeType name="ProductName" />
    <attribute type="UnitsInStock" />
    <attribute type="Discontinued" />
    <attribute type="ProductName" />
</ElementType>
```

The underlying SQL Server table Products is under the covers related to the table Order Details. The XML schema thus must declare the relationship between Products and Order Details, and this procedure is done with the `sql:relationship` annotation. The next new thing is the `sql:map` field annotation. This annotation is used here to hide a field. Hiding a field causes the attribute not to be returned in the rowset when the mapping schema is referenced in an XPath query. This procedure has nothing to do with the relationship that is declared in `sql:relationship`.

```
<?xml version="1.0" ?>
<Schema xmlns="urn:schemas-microsoft-com:xml-data"
        xmlns:dt="urn:schemas-microsoft-com:datatypes"
        xmlns:sql="urn:schemas-microsoft-com:xml-sql">
```

```
<ElementType name="Details" sql:relation="[Order Details]" >
    <AttributeType name="OrderID" />
    <AttributeType name="ProductID" />
    <AttributeType name="UnitPrice" />
    <AttributeType name="Quantity" />
    <AttributeType name="Discount" />
    <attribute type="OrderID" sql:map-field="0"/>
    <attribute type="ProductID" />
    <attribute type="UnitPrice" />
    <attribute type="Quantity" />
    <attribute type="Discount" />
</ElementType>
<ElementType name="Order" sql:relation="Orders" >
    <AttributeType name="OrderID" />
    <AttributeType name="OrderDate" />
    <attribute type="OrderID" />
    <attribute type="OrderDate" />
    <element type="Details" >
      <sql:relationship
         key-relation="Orders"
         key="OrderID"
         foreign-key="OrderID"
         foreign-relation="[Order Details]" />
    </element>
</ElementType>
<ElementType name="document" sql:is-constant="1">
    <element type="Order"/>
</ElementType>
</Schema>
```

Here, `sql:relationship` is declared within the Product element. The element refers to a declared element and indicates the scope in which the element lives. Our Product element itself is within the context of the Details element. So, it is a Product's child. This element contains some interesting annotations. Let's break it down. We essentially create the hierarchy by using `sql:relationship,` and it works like an SQL join. The key relation attribute points to the primary table, and the foreign relation points to the foreign table. The primary key and the foreign key are defined in the key and foreign key attributes (see Table 5.2).

Configuration

First, store all schemas in the Northwind virtual directory. Create a new folder named Schemas, and move every schema into that location. Then, start the IIS Virtual Directory Management tool, and select Properties for Northwind. Check Allow XPath under the Settings tab, and click the Virtual Names tab. Choose New, and then enter `mySchema` for Virtual Name.

Table 5.2 XML Data Annotations

Annotation	XML Element	Type	Meaning
sql:is-mapping-schema	\<Schema\>	boolean	Indicates whether the mapping mapping schema is inline.
sql:id	\<Schema\>	string	The inline mapping schema's unique identifier.
sql:target-namespace	\<Schema\>	string	A namespace other than the default to place elements and attributes in the mapping schema.
sql:field	\<attribute\> \<element\>	string	The mapped database column.
sql:relation	\<ElementType\> \<element\> \<attribute\>	string	The mapped relation (table or view).
sql:relationship	\<element\> \<attribute\>	string	The definition of the relationship that defines the hierarchy of the XML elements.
sql:key-fields	\<ElementType\>	string	The column(s) that is the unique identifier for the row in the table. Multiple columns are separated by a space.
sql:use-cdata	\<ElementType\> \<element\>	boolean	A CDATA-section will wrap the returned value. CDATA escapes characters that are recognized for markup.
sql:is-constant	\<ElementType\>	boolean	The XML element does not map to a database.
sql:map-field	\<ElementType\> \<element\> \<attribute\>	boolean	The XML element is excluded from the result.
sql:limit-field	\<element\> \<attribute\>	string	The column to which the `sql:limit` value applies.
sql:limit-value	\<element\> \<attribute\>	string	The limiting value for the column.
sql:url-encode	\<element\> \<attribute\>	boolean	A URI reference, instead of `Base64` encoding, BLOB columns.
sql:id-prefix	\<AttributeType\>	string	The string prepends ID, IDREF, and IDREFS attributes.
sql:overflow-field	\<ElementType\>	string	Get unconsumed data from the specified column.

Now, select Schema as the type for the virtual name. Create a new directory called schema, and select the full path for the Path option. Accept the selections, and close the windows. The server is now set up for XPath queries against your annotated schemas. We will use schema-document.xml, which is available on the accompanying CD-ROM.

The Query Language

XPath is the language for querying XML views. Fire off a simple query at your annotated schema:

```
http://IISServer/Northwind/mySchema/schema-document.xml/document
```

Here is the output:

```
<document>
 <Order OrderID="10248" OrderDate="1996-07-04T00:00:00" />
 <Order OrderID="10249" OrderDate="1996-07-05T00:00:00" />
 ...
</document>
```

With XPath location paths resembling URLs, they fall naturally into actual URLs. For example, locate an XML node that carries an attribute value that you want:

```
http://IISServer/Northwind/mySchema/schema-
document.xml/document/Order[@OrderID=10252]
```

The query for OrderID 10252 produces the following output:

```
<Order OrderID="10252" OrderDate="1996-07-09T00:00:00" />
```

The underlying code behind SQL Server's XML support actually translates XPath expressions into FOR XML Explicit-mode queries. Consequently, annotated schemas and XPath expressions can, in some instances, turn out to be an easier solution than an otherwise Explicit-mode query.

Locating Data in a Schema

XPath expressions can be passed in the URL as well as in a template file. The structure for a template file containing an XPath expression is as follows:

```
<document xmlns:sql="urn:schemas-microsoft-com:xml-sql">
 <sql:xpath-query mapping-schema="mySchemaPath">
 XPath Expression
 </sql:xpath-query>
</document>
```

With template files, make sure that they are contained in a virtual root that is of the template type. In this case, it makes no sense to declare a root element inside the schema-file, as we did before, because the template file declares the top-level element.

Summary

This chapter covered the annotated XML schemas and how to query those by XPath. The next chapter leaves simple select queries in favor of inserting, updating, and deleting data with help of XML.

Writing, Modifying, and Deleting XML Data

Microsoft SQL Server 2000 is not limited to the retrieval of XML documents. The technology works both ways, so it is fully possible to take an XML document and map the contained XML elements to database columns. This functionality is provided by the rowset function called OpenXML.

The OpenXML Function

Before you write data with OpenXML, you must create an internal representation of an XML document. This representation is created by using the `sp_xml_preparedocument system` stored procedure. The stored procedure returns a handle to a tree of the various nodes in the document. The handle references the internal representation of the XML document. The handle is passed on to OpenXML, which provides rowset views of the document based on an XPath expression. When you are done, remove the XML document from memory by calling the `sp_xml_removedocument system` stored procedure. The syntax of OpenXML is as follows:

```
OpenXML (
    idoc int [in],
    rowpattern nvarchar[in],
    [flags byte[in]]
) [WITH (SchemaDeclaration | TableName)]
```

The XML document handle `idoc` and the XPath `rowpattern` are required parameters. The handle is created by `sp_xml_preparedocument`. The XPath pattern matches the elements of the XML document that are to be processed. The flags parameter is a byte value that represents the mapping that is used between the relational rowset and XML data. XML attributes are used by default. The default has a value of zero, and XML attributes have a value of one. Essentially, the default points to XML attributes. Attributes can be used with elements that have a flag value of one, however.

XML System Stored Procedures

Before exposing an XML document as a rowset, we must know the system stored procedures that are used to prepare and remove the documents.

```
sp_xml_preparedocument
    hdoc OUTPUT
    [, xmltext]
    [, xpath_namespaces]
```

The `hdoc` output parameter is the integer handle to the internal representation, and `xmltext` is the XML document upon which you want to base your rowset. The `xpath_namespaces` is the namespace declaration used in XPath expressions on OpenXML; the default value is `<root  xmlns:mp="urn: schemas-microsoft-com:xml-metaprop">`.

Once you are finished with your OpenXML operation, use `sp_xml_remove-document` to remove the internal representation and destroy the handle:

```
sp_xml_removedocument hdoc
```

Pass the handle integer to `hdoc`, and it will take care of removal and destruction. Both system stored procedures return 0 if they are successful, and they return a value greater than zero if unsuccessful. Execute permission on both defaults to the public role.

Element-Centric Mapping

At the beginning, we will extract the elements of an XML document and insert one element each into the database. It is reasonable to believe that the *International Standard Book Number* (ISBN) would be suitable as an identity column for the database table. But we will not specify any such details, because you might want to insert the same data over and over again as you play with OpenXML. Here is an element-centric use of OpenXML:

```
DECLARE @idoc int
DECLARE @doc varchar(1000)
SET @doc ='
<?xml version="1.0"?>
```

```
<Books>
    <Book>
        <Title>Common Information Model</Title>
        <ISBN>0471353426</ISBN>
        <Author>Winston Bumpus</Author>
        <Author>John W. Sweitzer</Author>
        <Author>Patrick Thompson</Author>
        <Author>Andrea R. Westerinen</Author>
        <Author>Raymond C. Williams</Author>
        <Publisher>John Wiley &amp; Sons Inc.</Publisher>
    </Book>
    <Book>
        <Title>Object-Oriented Project Management with UML</Title>
        <ISBN>0471253030</ISBN>
        <Author>Murray R. Cantor</Author>
        <Publisher>John Wiley &amp; Sons Inc.</Publisher>
    </Book>
</Books>
'
- Create the internal representation
EXEC sp_xml_preparedocument @idoc OUTPUT, @doc
- SELECT statement using OPENXML rowset provider
    SELECT * FROM
        OPENXML (@idoc, '/Books/Book',2)
            WITH (ISBN     int,
                  Title    varchar(50),
                  Publisher varchar(50))
- Remove the internal representation
EXEC sp_xml_removedocument @idoc
```

Run it with the Query Analyzer tool, and you will find that a relational table with three columns is displayed (or created, but not saved). See Figure 6.1.

The XML elements ISBN, title, and publisher populate the columns. Moreover, because there are two unique Book elements in the XML document, there are two rows in the rowset. With our knowledge of XPath, we can easily understand what is happening. The columns are mapped directly to the XML elements of the same name. If you want control over the column names, you can explicitly name them and use an XPath expression per column basis to indicate the source of data:

```
- Create the internal representation
EXEC sp_xml_preparedocument @idoc OUTPUT, @doc
- SELECT statement using OPENXML rowset provider
    SELECT * FROM
        OPENXML (@idoc, '/Books/Book', 2)
            WITH (ISBN           int        'ISBN',
                  MediaTitle     varchar(50) 'Title',
                  MediaPublisher varchar(50) 'Publisher')
- Remove the internal representation
EXEC sp_xml_removedocument @idoc
```

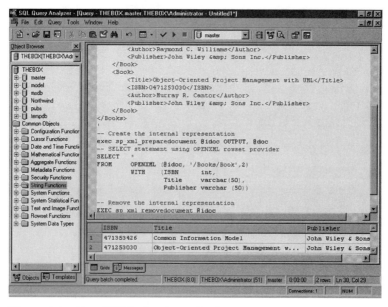

Figure 6.1 OpenXML in the Query Analyzer.

Attribute-Centric Mapping

Attribute-centric mapping does not differ much from element-centric mapping. Basically, we change the flags parameter to 1:

```
DECLARE @idoc int
DECLARE @doc varchar(1000)
SET @doc ='
<?xml version="1.0"?>
<Books>
    <Book Title="Common Information Model"
        ISBN="0471353426"
        Publisher="John Wiley &amp; Sons Inc."
    />
    <Book Title="Object-Oriented Project Management with UML"
            ISBN="0471253030"
            Publisher="John Wiley &amp; Sons Inc."
    />
</Books>
'
- Create the internal representation
EXEC sp_xml_preparedocument @idoc OUTPUT, @doc
- SELECT statement using OPENXML rowset provider
    SELECT * FROM
        OPENXML (@idoc, '/Books/Book', 1)
            WITH (ISBN      int,
                Title      varchar(50),
```

```
                        Publisher varchar(50))
- Remove the internal representation
EXEC sp_xml_removedocument @idoc
```

The query can be explicitly mapped to the attributes for the column:

```
- Create the internal representation
EXEC sp_xml_preparedocument @idoc OUTPUT, @doc
- SELECT statement using OPENXML rowset provider
   SELECT * FROM
      OPENXML (@idoc, '/Books/Book', 1)
         WITH (ISBN            int          '@ISBN',
               MediaTitle      varchar(50)  '@Title',
               MediaPublisher varchar(50)  'attribute::Publisher')
- Remove the internal representation
EXEC sp_xml_removedocument @idoc
```

Edge-Table Mapping

Edge-table mapping results in a format that is close to the XML structure. This mapping provides a detailed overview of the settings, such as how the elements relate by `id`, `nodetypes`, `data types`, `namespaceURI`, and so forth. You receive an edge table by simply omitting the `WITH` clause of OpenXML (see Figure 6.2).

```
- Create the internal representation
EXEC sp_xml_preparedocument @idoc OUTPUT, @doc
```

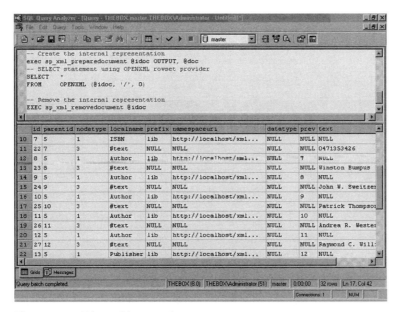

Figure 6.2 Edge-table mapping.

```
- SELECT statement using OPENXML rowset provider
SELECT * FROM OPENXML (@idoc, '/', 0)
- Remove the internal representation
EXEC sp_xml_removedocument @idoc
```

Metaproperties in an XML document provide extra information about the document. They are not visible in the document, but by using Microsoft SQL Server 2000, you can access them through the namespace urn:schemas-microsoft-com:xml-metaprop. You have already seen them in the edge-table format, and they are listed here in Table 6.1.

Get the XML document text of all Book elements and their descendants:

```
- Create the internal representation
exec sp_xml_preparedocument @idoc OUTPUT, @doc
- SELECT statement using OPENXML rowset provider
SELECT * FROM OPENXML (@idoc, '//*', 0)
        WITH (fs varchar(1000) '@mp:xmltext')
- Remove the internal representation
EXEC sp_xml_removedocument @idoc
```

Inserting Data

In this example, we will create a new table and insert some data in the XML document into the new table. By using the previous attribute-centric XML document, we will execute the following code in the Query Analyzer:

```
- Create the PublishedMedia table in Northwind
USE Northwind
CREATE TABLE PublishedMedia
```

Table 6.1 Metaproperty Attributes

Attribute	Description
@mp:id	Identifier
@mp:parentid	Identifier of parent
@mp:localname	The local name part of the node name
@mp:parentlocalname	The local name part of the current node's parent
@mp:namespaceuri	The namespace URI of the current node
@mp:parentnamespaceuri	The namespace URI of the current node's parent
@mp:prefix	The namespace prefix of the current node
@mp:parentprefix	The namespace prefix of the current node's parent
@mp:xmltext	Textual representation of the node set
@mp:prev	Previous sibling of the node

```
(
 ISBN int,
 Title varchar(50),
 Publisher varchar(50)
)
GO
DECLARE @idoc int
DECLARE @doc  varchar(1000)
SET @doc ='
    <?xml version="1.0"?>
    <Books>
    <Book Title="Common Information Model"
          ISBN="0471353426"
          Publisher="John Wiley &amp; Sons Inc."
    />
    <Book Title="Object-Oriented Project Management with UML"
              ISBN="0471253030"
              Publisher="John Wiley &amp; Sons Inc."
    />
</Books>
'
- Create the internal representation
EXEC sp_xml_preparedocument @idoc OUTPUT, @doc
- INSERT statement using OPENXML rowset provider
    INSERT INTO PublishedMedia
      SELECT * FROM
        OPENXML (@idoc, '/Books/Book', 1)
          WITH (ISBN      int        '@ISBN',
                Title     varchar(50) '@Title',
                Publisher varchar(50) '@Publisher')
- Remove the internal representation
EXEC sp_xml_removedocument @idoc
```

When we insert data into the database, a stored procedure has unmatched performance. Continuing on what we have built so far, here is a stored procedure that takes an XML document as parameter and inserts the data in the database:

```
CREATE PROCEDURE [dbo].[xml_insert] (@doc NTEXT)
AS
BEGIN
    DECLARE @idoc int
    - Create the internal representation
    EXEC sp_xml_preparedocument @idoc OUTPUT, @doc
    - INSERT statement using OPENXML rowset provider
    INSERT INTO PublishedMedia
      SELECT * FROM
        OPENXML (@idoc, '/Books/Book', 1)
          WITH (ISBN      int        '@ISBN',
                Title     varchar(50) '@Title',
                Publisher varchar(50) '@Publisher')
    - Remove the internal representation
    EXEC sp_xml_removedocument @idoc
```

```
END
GO
```

To call the stored procedure, we use the following code:

```
USE northwind
EXEC xml_insert '<?xml version="1.0"?>
                <Books>
                <Book Title="Common Information Model"
                 ISBN="0471353426"
                 Publisher="John Wiley &amp; Sons Inc."
                />
                <Book Title="Object-Oriented Project Management
                 with UML"
                 ISBN="0471253030"
                 Publisher="John Wiley &amp; Sons Inc."
                />
                </Books>'
```

Modifying Data

In the next example, we're going to use OpenXML to update existing records in a database. The update information is passed as an XML data fragment, and the OpenXML function is used for mapping it into a relational mode. First, insert a record into the PublishedMedia table by:

```
...
set @doc ='
<?xml version="1.0"?>
<Books>
    <Book Title="Update Example"
        ISBN="1234567890"
        Publisher="Publishing Media."
    />
</Books>
'

- Create the internal representation
exec sp_xml_preparedocument @idoc OUTPUT, @doc
- SELECT statement using OPENXML rowset provider
INSERT INTO PublishedMedia
    SELECT   *
    FROM     OPENXML (@idoc, '/Books/Book', 1)
     WITH    (ISBN      int        '@ISBN',
             Title      varchar(50) '@Title',
             Publisher varchar(50) '@Publisher')
...
```

After that, you freely modify it by using OpenXML and an UPDATE statement as follows:

```
/*
Only the Title of the book will be updated. ISBN is used to match
    the record you want to update in the database.
*/

use Northwind
declare @idoc int
declare @doc varchar(1000)
set @doc ='
    <Book Title="Update this Example"
        ISBN="1234567890"
        Publisher="Publishing Media."
    />
'

- Create the internal representation
exec sp_xml_preparedocument @idoc OUTPUT, @doc
- UPDATE statement using OPENXML rowset provider
UPDATE PublishedMedia
    SET Title = xmlTitle
    FROM OPENXML( @idoc, 'Book')
    WITH( xmlTitle varchar(50) '@Title', xmlISBN int '@ISBN')
    WHERE ISBN = xmlISBN

- Remove the internal representation
EXEC sp_xml_removedocument @idoc
```

Or, if you want to update multiple columns at once:

```
UPDATE PublishedMedia
    SET Title = xmlTitle, Publisher = xmlPublisher
    FROM OPENXML( @idoc, 'Book')
    WITH( xmlTitle varchar(50) '@Title',
        xmlISBN int '@ISBN',
        xmlPublisher varchar(50) '@Publisher')
    WHERE ISBN = xmlISBN
```

Deleting Data

Finally, it is time to delete some of the data inserted. The OpenXML function is again used for performing the DELETE statement on a relational table. Execute the following code in the Query Analyzer:

```
use Northwind
declare @idoc int
declare @doc varchar(1000)
set @doc ='
    <Book Title="Update this Example"
        ISBN="1234567890"
        Publisher="Publishing Media."
```

```
            />
    '

- Create the internal representation
exec sp_xml_preparedocument @idoc OUTPUT, @doc

- DELETE statement using OPENXML rowset provider
DELETE PublishedMedia
    FROM OPENXML( @idoc, 'Book')
    WITH( xmlTitle varchar(50) '@Title',
          xmlISBN int '@ISBN',
          xmlPublisher varchar(50) '@Publisher')
    WHERE ISBN = xmlISBN

- Remove the internal representation
EXEC sp_xml_removedocument @idoc
```

Summary

This chapter looked at the OpenXML Transact SQL function. It was used for inserting, updating, and deleting relational data from XML. The next chapter will take a look at purely XML-based inserts, updates, and deletes.

CHAPTER 7

Updategrams

Until now, the chapters in this book have demonstrated the retrieval of *Extensible Markup Language* (XML) data and mapping of XML data to relational database columns. This chapter looks at a technology that Microsoft has released and updated on the Web: XML-based insert, update, and delete operations.

Introduction

Microsoft supports updating SQL Server data by using XML. This functionality is not, however, part of the Microsoft SQL Server 2000 released product. The technology is called a Web release, and you can download it from Microsoft's Web site at www.microsoft.com.

Updategrams are an XML-based technology for updating SQL Server database records. A lot of things can be said about updategrams, but the core of their functionality comes down to two things:

- Your database record before the update
- Your database record after the update

An XML file is composed of elements describing the database record before and after it has been updated. The `<updg:before>` element contains the data that is needed to locate the database record to be updated, and the `<updg:after>` element contains the values with which you update the record. These operations are wrapped into a transaction by an `<updg:sync>` element, so the most basic template for an XML-based update looks like the following:

```
<document xmlns:updg="urn:schemas-microsoft-com:xml-updategram">
  <updg:sync>
    <updg:before>
      <TABLENAME [updg:id="value"]
       col="value" col="value" ... n    />
    </updg:before>
    <updg:after>
        <TABLENAME [updg:id="value"]
         [updg:at-identity="value"]
          col="value" col="value" ... n />
      </updg:after>
  </updg:sync>
</document>
```

The common prefix to the Updategrams namespace (urn:schemas-microsoft-com:xml-updategram) that you will see is updg. This prefix can be anything that you want, however, so feel free to change it. In addition, updategrams can contain more than one transaction, so you can include several <sync> elements. Updategrams can also contain several <before> and <after> elements in a single <sync> container.

Inserting and Deleting Records

Updategrams behave in an interesting, intuitive manner. For example, if you leave the <before> element and omit the <after> element, you are deleting a database record:

```
<document xmlns:updg="urn:schemas-microsoft-com:xml-updategram">
  <updg:sync>
    <updg:before>
      <TABLENAME [updg:id="value"]
       col="value" col="value" ... n    />
    </updg:before>
  </updg:sync>
</document>
```

On the other hand, omitting the <before> element and leaving the <after> element results in an inserted database record:

```
<document xmlns:updg="urn:schemas-microsoft-com:xml-updategram">
  <updg:sync>
    <updg:after>
      <TABLENAME [updg:id="value"]
       col="value" col="value" ... n    />
    </updg:after>
  </updg:sync>
</document>
```

Updating Records

Here is what an updategram might look like, using default behavior and mapping XML-element names to direct columns of the database by using attributes:

```
<document xmlns:updg="urn:schemas-microsoft-com:xml-updategram">
  <updg:sync>
    <updg:before>
      <myTable myColName="Irena" myColPhone="555-543-4343" />
    </updg:before>
    <updg:after>
      <myTable myColName="Irena" myColPhone="555-232-1765" />
    </updg:after>
  </updg:sync>
</document>
```

Here is the element-centric version:

```
<document xmlns:updg="urn:schemas-microsoft-com:xml-updategram">
  <updg:sync>
    <updg:before>
      <myTable>
        <myColName>Irena</myColName>
        <myColPhone>555-543-4343</myColPhone>
      </myTable>
    </updg:before>
    <updg:after>
      <myTable>
        <myColName>Irena</myColName>
        <myColPhone>555-232-1765</myColPhone>
      </myTable>
    </updg:after>
  </updg:sync>
</document>
```

If you do not want to use the default values, you can use an XML data-reduced schema to map the columns to their respective tables. Just include the schema in the `<sync>` element:

```
<document xmlns:updg="urn:schemas-microsoft-com:xml-updategram">
  <updg:sync mapping-schema="mySchema.xdr">
    ...
  </updg:sync>
</document>
```

Updategram XML

Tables 7.1 and 7.2 include a listing of the XML elements and attributes of an updategram.

Named parameters are declared within the `<updg:header>` elements. You give a parameter a name by using the name attribute of the `<param>` element, and then you use $name to access the parameter.

```
<document xmlns:updg="urn:schemas-microsoft-com:xml-updategram">
    ...
    <updg:header>
        <updg:param name="myName"  />
        <updg:param name="myPhone"  />
```

Table 7.1 Updategram Elements

XML Element	Meaning
`<updg:sync> </updg:sync>`	The updategram transaction
`<updg:before> </updb:before>`	The database record to match
`<updg:after> </updg:after>`	The database record to affect
`<updg:header> </updg:header>`	Updategram header information
`<updg:param/>`	A named parameter

Table 7.2 Updategram Attributes

Attribute	Applies to	Type	Meaning
updg:nullvalue	`<before>` `<after>`	string	A string-value that you use to represent database-NULL in the XML document; XML has no NULL-value.
updg:at-identity	`<table>`	string	A string that name a placeholder to receive the identity value from an insert operation; equivalent to `@@identity` in SQL Server.
updg:returnid	`<after>`	string	Returns the identity.
updg:id	`<table>`	string	An update operation can use the `updb:id` to match the record in `<before>` with the record in `<after>`; deletes and inserts can use this attribute, too.
Name	`<param>`	string	Defines the name of a parameter.

```
        </updg:header>
        ...
        <myTable myColName="$myName" myColPhone="$myPhone" />
        ...
    </document>
```

The same approach can be used to access parameters that were declared within a standard XML-based template file through the element `<sql:param-name="name" />`.

When you use `<updg:returnid>` to receive the identity value, it will be returned in the following format, where

```
        <updg:after updg:returnid="myName myPhone">
```

yields the output

```
    <returnid>
        <myName>Irena</myName>
        <myPhone>555-232-1765</myPhone>
    </returnid>
```

More Information

For more information about updategrams, keep checking the Web release of the technology. The Web release will contain the latest binary builds, sets of documentation, and samples. There are a few caveats to be aware of, however, about how updategrams relate to data types, but it does not directly affect anything. Your core installation of SQL Server requires the application to download updategrams first before you install the application. This program is available from www.microsoft.com.

Summary

This chapter has looked at the updategrams technology. Updategrams are not a part of the initial Microsoft SQL Server 2000 release, but they are available over the Internet. In the next section, we will cover some common access methods for streaming XML from SQL Server to Web applications and to Windows Script Host.

Applying XML from SQL Server

I n this chapter, we will see which parts of the *Extensible Markup Language* (XML) support in SQL Server 2000 can be scripted. First is virtual directory management, and then follows the *Microsoft Data Access Components* (MDACs).

IIS Virtual Directory Management

The Internet Information Services (IIS) virtual directory management tool for SQL Server is great. This tool provides a clean, concise *graphical user interface* (GUI) that is easy to use. Sometimes, though, this interface is just too easy, too time consuming, and "too GUI." We will look at how to create scripts for setting up virtual directories. Small scripts can set up all of the virtual directories that are needed for an XML-enabled SQL Server. If you continuously allocate disk space for new clients of a standard Web server, SQL Server, and so on, you definitely want to automate the process of creating virtual directories. You would probably create Web-based tools for the client's virtual directory management, as well. Let's move on to the object model for virtual directory management.

VDirControl

The `SQLVDir.SQLVDirControl` is *the* management object. This object opens, closes, and maintains a virtual directory management session with IIS.

To use the `Connect()` method of IIS, pass the *IIS Server Name* and *Web Site Number*, or leave the fields empty if the target is your local server. Once you

Table 8.1 The `SQLVDirControl` Object

Method	Description
Connect(IISName, WebSiteNumber)	Connects to the IIS server. Defaults to the local machine and default Web site if no parameters are passed.
Disconnect( )	Disconnects from the IIS server.

are connected, `SQLVDirControl.SQLVDirs()` returns a collection of virtual directory objects. `SQLVDirControl.Disconnect()` closes the connection as follows (see Table 8.1):

```
Set objVdm = CreateObject("SQLVDir.SQLVDirControl")
    objVdm.Connect

    Set objVdirs = objVdm.SQLVDirs
    WScript.Echo "There are " & objVdirs.Count & _
                " virtual directory objects."
    objVdm.Disconnect
```

This object is not designed for directory management, per se. Instead, it spawns new or existing object instances. You need to get this object at all times, though. This object is the only object in the object model that can return the other virtual directory objects.

SQLVDirs Collection Object

`SQLVdirs` is a management-oriented collection object. This object adds, removes, and navigates the virtual directories. The collection object cannot be instantiated by itself, however. Instead, it is returned from `SQLVDir.SQLVDirControl` after calling `SQLVDirControl.SQLVDirs()` (see Table 8.2).

You can use `SQLVDirsCol.Count()` to get the number of IIS XML virtual directories in the collection. Also, `SQLVDirsCol.Item()` returns a virtual directory by index or key name. `SQLVDirsCol.AddVirtualDirectory()` and `SQLVDirsCol.RemoveVirtualDirectory()` can be used to manage the current virtual directories.

SQLVDir Object

The directory object controls the virtual directory properties in the same manner as they are controlled through the GUI tool. The object is dropped through the Virtual Directory collection, and either `SQLVDirsCol.Item()` or `SQLVDirsCol.AddVirtualDirectory()` returns this object (see Tables 8.3 and 8.4).

Table 8.2 The SQLVDirs Collection Object

Method	Description
Next(numDirs)	Gets the next virtual directory or the number of virtual directories specified in *numDirs*
Skip(numDirs)	Skips the next virtual directory or the number of virtual directories specified in *numDirs*
Reset( )	Resets the collection by moving to the first virtual directory
Clone( )	Returns a cloned copy of this object
Count( )	Returns the number of virtual directories
Item(index|key)	Returns a virtual directory specified by integer index or key name
AddVirtualDirectory(name)	Creates and returns the virtual directory name
RemoveVirtualDirectory (name)	Removes the virtual directory name

Table 8.3 The SQLVDir Object

Property	Description
ServerName	Microsoft SQL Server instance name
Name	Virtual directory name
PhysicalPath	Physical path to the virtual directory
DatabaseName	Default database to connect
UserName	User login
SecurityMode	Authentication method to use
AllowFlags	Allowed Access types
Password	User password
DLLPath	Path to SQLISAPI.dll
AdditionalSettings	OLE DB connection string
EnablePasswordSync	Enables IIS' capability to handle password synchronization
Method	**Description**
VirtualNames( )	Returns the VirtualNames collection object

Table 8.4 Settings: AllowFlags

Value	Description
1	Allow URL Queries
8	Allow Template Queries
64	Allow XPath Queries

Table 8.5 Security: SecurityMode

Value	Description
1	SQL Server Login
2	Windows NT Login
4	Basic Authentication
8	Integrated Windows Authentication

```
Set objVdm = CreateObject("SQLVDir.SQLVDirControl")
    ' Connect to IIS
    objVdm.Connect
    ' Get a new virtual directory
    Set objVdir = objVdm.SQLVDirs.AddVirtualDirectory(strVDirName)
    ' Set its properties
    objVdir.ServerName   = " {local}"
    objVdir.DatabaseName = "Northwind"
    objVdir.PhysicalPath = "C:\\Inetpub\\Nwind-XML\\Templates"
    objVdir.SecurityMode = 8
    objVdir.AllowFlags   = 8 ' 73 Allows all modes
    ' Disconnect
    objVdm.Disconnect
```

These values can also be combined, thus enabling several settings. For example, 73 (1 + 8 + 64) enables all access types. You can use a bitwise OR operator or simple addition to combine the flags (see Table 8.5).

The different types of authentication modes for accessing SQL Server were described in an earlier chapter.

VirtualNames Collection

The VirtualNames collection contains the defined virtual names of a virtual directory. You can use it to iterate, add, and remove virtual names in the current virtual directory (see Table 8.6).

SQLVirtualNames.AddVirtualName() and SQLVirtualNamesRemove-VirtualName() manage the virtual names. This object is returned when SQLVDir calls SQLVDir.VirtualNames(). You can pass the configuration data for the virtual name with SQLVirtualNames.AddVirtualName(), or you can set their properties in the returned VirtualName object.

Table 8.6 The Virtual Names Collection Object

Method	Description
Next(numDirs)	Gets the next virtual directory or the number of virtual directories specified in *numDirs*
Skip(numDirs)	Skips the next virtual directory or the number of virtual directories specified in *numDirs*
Reset( )	Resets the collection by moving to the first virtual directory
Clone( )	Returns a cloned copy of this object
Count( )	Returns the number of virtual directories
Item(index|key)	Returns a virtual directory specified by integer index or key name
AddVirtualName(name, type, path)	Creates and returns the virtual directory *name* of *type* located at the physical *path*
RemoveVirtualName(name)	Removes the virtual name *name*

Table 8.7 Virtual Name

Property	Description
Name	Name of virtual name
Type	Type of virtual name
Path	Physical path to virtual name

Table 8.8 Types of Virtual Names

Value	Description
1	dbobject
2	schema
4	template

VirtualName Object

VirtualName controls the properties of a virtual name within a virtual directory. Here is how you can define a template (see Tables 8.7 and 8.8):

```
objVName.Name - "myTemplate"
objVName.Type = 4
objVName.Path = "C:\\Inetpub\\Nwind-XML\\myTemplates"
```

The VirtualName object's properties define the virtual name that you are setting up. Often, you can set these properties by passing parameters to `Virtual-Names.AddVirtualName(name, type, path)`.

Microsoft Data Access Components (MDACs)

The *Microsoft Data Access Components* (MDACs) implement Microsoft's Universal Data Access strategy. These data access components are available through the *Component Object Model* (COM), so the majority of programming and scripting languages can use MDACs for applications. MDACs can access data regardless of whether it is relational or non-relational, and the two main enablers for this task are *Object Linking and Embedding Database* (OLE DB) and *ActiveX Data Objects* (ADO).

OLE DB enables access to the data store. This functionality is a low-level interface that is available in C++ only. ADO, on the other hand, is a COM wrapper around OLE DB that provides an *Application Programming Interface* (API) for Automation-aware languages.

Because OLE DB supports `FOR XML` queries with the release of Microsoft SQL Server 2000, ADO can be used to retrieve XML documents. Our examples will revolve around how ADO can be used to access XML document fragments from SQL Server.

ADO supports XML retrieval through the Command object. XML applications that use SQL Server will find that ADO is intuitive and easy to handle. This interface can be used to execute XML-yielding queries against SQL Server. Then, MSXML Parser can be used to process the returned documents. With this toolkit, the scope of your applications that consume XML data ranges from simple Windows Script Host files to Web servers to complete Windows Applications.

The Command Object

The ADO Command object represents a textual command to run against the database. You can, for example, represent an ordinary query or the name of a stored procedure as its command text. The text that forms the command is run against the database when you call `Command.Execute()`, and the result is returned to you through ADO.

Certain properties of the Command object are used to indicate the type of query in the command text. This feature is an optional optimization feature of ADO, and it is set by default to use a standard SQL language. This situation is quite the contrary when you are issuing an XML query. With an XML query, you

Table 8.9   Command Dialects

GUID	Meaning
{C8B521FB-5CF3-11CE -ADE5-00AA0044773D}	OLE DB provider default behavior
{C8B522D7-5CF3-11CE -ADE5-00AA0044773D}	Interpret the command text as a T-SQL query
{5D531CB2-E6Ed-11D2 -B252-00C04F681B71}	Interpret the command text as an XML template
{EC2A4293-E898-11D2 -B1B7-00C04f680C56}	Interpret the command text as an XPath expression

are required to indicate the nature of the query, which is done through the `Command.Dialect` property (see Table 8.9).

Next, we will present the basics about the ADO Stream object and some of the various ways in which the Command object is used to execute a FOR XML query.

The Stream Object

When working with files, you are handling streams of data. There are input streams and output streams. Binary and textual streams of data can be accessed through ADO by using the Stream object. Consequently, this object can be used to represent two things in the XML world of SQL Server. You can first use a Stream object to store the XML document that is returned from SQL Server. The Stream object's native methods enable you to treat the XML document as the text-based document that it is. Secondly, the Stream object can contain a template file that is passed to the SQL Server with an XML query.

When the Stream object is initialized with the returned XML data from SQL Server, it is an output stream. You can point the Command object to use a Stream object for returned data. This object is set as a dynamic property, which is available through the Properties collection. The ones affecting the returned stream are presented in Table 8.10.

Using a Windows Script File (.wsf), format for Windows Script Host files, begin importing the type library constants and objects that you will use:

```
<?XML version="1.0"?>
<job ID="ADOXML">
  <reference object="ADODB.Stream"/>
  <reference object="ADODB.Command"/>
  <object id="objConn" progid="ADODB.Connection"/>
```

Table 8.10 ADO Command Object's Dynamic Properties for SQL Server

Dynamic Property	Description
Output Encoding	The encoding used by the Stream object that contains the XML data. UTF8 is the default, but you can specify ANSI or Unicode to change the setting.
Output Stream	The output stream is a reference to the Stream object to which you want to return the XML data.
XML Root	Name of the top-level element that you want inserted.

```
<object id="objCmd"  progid="ADODB.Command"/>
<object id="objStr"  progid="ADODB.Stream"/>
```

Because Windows Script files are XML documents, the actual script code is wrapped up inside CDATA sections.

```
<script language="VBScript">
<![CDATA[
```

Then, store the MSSQLXML dialect in a variable:

```
Dim DBGUID_XML
DBGUID_XML= "{5D531CB2-E6Ed-11D2-B252-00C04F681B71}"
```

Open a connection to the Northwind database on the SQL server:

```
objConn.Open "Provider=SQLOLEDB.1;"        &_
             "Integrated Security=SSPI;"    &_
             "Persist Security Info=False;" &_
             "Initial Catalog=Northwind"
```

If we get this far without an error, the connection was successful. The next step is to associate the Command object with the active connection. That way, when it executes its query (defined in CommandText), it goes through the Connection object:

```
' The active connection to Northwind on SQL Server
objCmd.ActiveConnection = objConn
' Here's the query
objCmd.CommandText = "<root xmlns:sql" &_
                     "='urn:schemas-microsoft-com:xml-sql'>" &_
                     "<sql:query>" &_
                     "SELECT TOP 1 * FROM Orders FOR XML AUTO" &_
                     "</sql:query>" &_
                     "</root>"
' The CommandText will be Interpreted as an XML-query
objCmd.Dialect = DBGUID_XML
' Open the outstream
objStr.Open
' Define the outstream
```

```
objCmd.Properties("Output Stream") = objStr
' Execute the query; adExecuteStream tells It to return the
' result as a stream
objCmd.Execute , , adExecuteStream
' Print It to the screen
WScript.Echo objStr.ReadText(adReadAll)
```

Finally, we close the CDATA section and the XML document:

```
    ]]>
  </script>
</job>
```

The ADO Connection object can execute queries through `Connection.Execute()`. The Command object is the only object that can be used to return an object that represents an outstream, however. You can make further optimizations to the application, as well. `Command.CommandText`, although it does not imply so, expects a Unicode string. If the XML template used is not Unicode, it has to convert the template. In addition, time and memory is consumed by reading the XML template into memory. Although the effort of reading a template file remains, you can work around the non-Unicode issue (if it is an issue). Instead of setting the `Command.CommandText` property, set the property `Command.CommandStream`. The property expects a Stream object containing the XML template. You can point the Stream object to an existing template, or you can push the string into the object by hand. For the purpose of illustration, the template text is just directly written to the Stream object:

```
<?XML version="1.0"?>
<job ID="ADOXML">
  <reference object="ADODB.Stream"/>
  <reference object="ADODB.Command"/>
  <object id="objConn" progid="ADODB.Connection"/>
  <object id="objCmd" progid="ADODB.Command"/>
  <object id="objOutStr" progid="ADODB.Stream"/>
  <object id="objInStr" progid="ADODB.Stream"/>`
  <script language="VBScript">
<![CDATA[
  objConn.Open "Provider=SQLOLEDB.1;"         &_
               "Integrated Security=SSPI;"    &_
               "Persist Security Info=False;" &_
               "Initial Catalog=Northwind"
  objCmd.ActiveConnection = objConn
  objInStr.Open
  objInStr.WriteText "<document xmlns:sql" &_
                     "='urn:schemas-microsoft-com:xml-sql'>" &_
                     "<sql:query>" &_
                     "SELECT TOP 2 * FROM Orders FOR XML AUTO" &_
                     "</sql:query>" &_
                     "</document>", adWritechar
```

```
        objInStr.Position = 0
        objOutStr.Open
        objCmd.Dialect = "{5D531CB2-E6Ed-11D2-B252-00C04F681B71}"
        objCmd.CommandStream = objInStr
        objCmd.Properties("Output Stream") = objOutStr
        objCmd.Execute , , adExecuteStream
        WScript.Echo objOutStr.ReadText()
    ]]>
    </script>
</job>
```

Technically, an instream is something to which we write. Our Stream object called `objInStr` is written to, is never saved, and then is sent to the property `CommandStream` of the Command object.

Microsoft XML Parser

In the previous section, we initialized the XML data into an ADO Stream object. It is fully possible to substitute the outstream for an instance of the DOMDocument object in Microsoft's XML Parser. Use the following code instead of creating an instance of `ADODB.Stream`:

```
<object id="objConn" progid="ADODB.Connection"/>
<object id="objCmd"  progid="ADODB.Command"/>
<object id="objInStr" progid="ADODB.Stream"/>
<object id="objDOM"  progid="MSXML2.DOMDocument"/>
```

The connection settings and such remain. The dynamic Output Stream property, however, is given a reference to our DOMDocument:

```
' Set output stream to our DOMDocument
objCmd.Properties("Output Stream") = objDOM
objCmd.Execute , , adExecuteStream
' Use XPath as the selection-language
objDOM.setProperty "SelectionLanguage", "XPath"
' Select the EmployeeID-nodes
Set objNodes = objDOM.selectNodes("/root/Orders/EmployeeID")
' Echo each node and Its typed value; types values are those assigned
' a data-type
For Each objNode In objNodes
    WScript.Echo objNode.nodeName & "=" & objNode.nodeTypedValue
Next
```

Once you have the DOMDocument, you can do pretty much anything you want to it.

Direct Queries

The query in this example executes as a simple T-SQL statement. It initializes the returned XML document into a DOMDocument object.

```vbscript
<?XML version="1.0"?>
<job ID="MSXML-FOR-XML">
  <reference object="ADODB.Command"/>
  <object id="objConn" progid="ADODB.Connection"/>
  <object id="objCmd" progid="ADODB.Command"/>
  <object id="objDOM"  progid="MSXML2.DOMDocument"/>
  <script language="VBScript">
  <![CDATA[
      Dim strQuery
      objConn.Open "Provider=SQLOLEDB.1;"          &_
                   "Integrated Security=SSPI;"     &_
                   "Persist Security Info=False;" &_
                   "Initial Catalog=Northwind"
      objCmd.ActiveConnection = objConn
      objCmd.CommandText = "SELECT TOP 1 * FROM Orders " &_
                           "FOR XML AUTO, ELEMENTS "
      objCmd.Properties("Output Stream") = objDOM
      objCmd.Properties("XML Root") = "document"
      objCmd.Execute , , adExecuteStream
      WScript.Echo objDOM.xml
  ]]>
  </script>
</job>
```

Posting Requests

Here is an example of code that applications can use to query a Web server for an XML document. This example uses the HTTP POST method through the XMLHTTP object:

```vbscript
<?XML version="1.0"?>
<job ID="MSXML-FOR-XML-POST">
  <object id="objDOM"  progid="MSXML2.DOMDocument"/>
  <object id="objHTTP"  progid="MSXML2.XMLHTTP"/>
  <script language="VBScript">
  <![CDATA[
    objDOM.loadXML "<?xml version='1.0'"  &_
                   "encoding='UTF-16'?>" &_
                   "<document xmlns:sql" &_
                   "='urn:schemas-microsoft-com:xml-sql'>" &_
                   "<sql:query>" &_
                   "SELECT TOP 1 * FROM Orders FOR XML AUTO" &_
```

```
                      "</sql:query>" &_
                      "</document>"
        objHTTP.Open "POST", "http://localhost/Northwind", False
        objHTTP.send objDOM
        WScript.Echo objHTTP.statusText
        WScript.Echo objHTTP.responseBody
        ]]>
      </script>
    </job>
```

XML-to-HTML-to-ASP

The *Active Server Pages* (ASP) Response object is an output stream. Whenever you want to output text in an ASP, you call the `Response.Write()` method. Our ADO code so far is pretty portable. Let's throw in an XSLT transformation style sheet there. And let's also persist the document tree to the ASP Response object.

```
<%@ Language=VBScript %>
<%
  Set objConn = CreateObject("ADODB.Connection")
  Set objCmd  = CreateObject("ADODB.Command")
  objConn.Open "Provider=SQLOLEDB.1;"         &_
               "Integrated Security=SSPI;"     &_
               "Persist Security Info=False;" &_
               "Initial Catalog=Northwind"
  objCmd.ActiveConnection = objConn
  objCmd.CommandText = "<root xmlns:sql" &_
                       "='urn:schemas-microsoft-com:xml-sql'>" &_
                       "<sql:query>" &_
                       "SELECT TOP 5 " &_
                       "CustomerID, " &_
                       "CompanyName, " &_
                       "ContactName, " &_
                       "ContactTitle " &_
                       "FROM Customers FOR XML AUTO, ELEMENTS " &_
                       "</sql:query>" &_
                       "</root>"
  objCmd.Dialect = "{5D531CB2-E6Ed-11D2-B252-00C04F681B71}"
  objCmd.Properties("XSL") = "http://localhost/Customers-Table.xsl"
  objCmd.Properties("Output Stream") = Response
  objCmd.Execute , , 1024
%>
```

The Response object is intrinsic and is built into ASP. So, it is not necessary to create an instance of it. The dynamic property XSL is appended to the `Command.Properties` collection. The property is set to the absolute URL of the style sheet that we will apply; it is the same style sheet used in the previous

Table 8.11 ADO Command Object's Dynamic Properties for XML Data

Dynamic Property	Description
XSL	XSLT transformation style sheet that is applied to FOR XML, template, and XPath queries; path or URL
Mapping Schema	Mapping schema applied to XPath-queries; path or URL
Base Path	The base path of a relative path to an XSL or mapping schema specified in the dynamic properties

chapter. The following dynamic properties are available in addition to Output Stream and Output Encoding (see Table 8.11).

Parameterized XML Queries

XML Queries can use Named Parameters through ADO. Here's a basic sample demonstrating how to use them:

```
Set conn = CreateObject("ADODB.Connection")
Set cmd = CreateObject("ADODB.Command")
Set str = CreateObject("ADODB.Stream")
Set xml = CreateObject("ADODB.Stream")

str.Open
str.WriteText_
    "<document xmlns:sql='urn:schemas-microsoft-com:xml-sql'>" &_
    "<sql:header>" &_
    "<sql:param name='CustomerID'>OCEAN</sql:param>" &_
    "<sql:param name='OrderDate'>10/27/1997</sql:param>" &_
    "</sql:header>" &_
    "<sql:query>" &_
    "    SELECT CustomerID, " &_
    "           OrderID, " &_
    "           ShippedDate," &_
    "           Freight " &_
    "    FROM Orders" &_
    "    WHERE CustomerID = " &
    "    @CustomerID AND OrderDate " &
    "    &gt; @OrderDate" &_
    "    FOR XML AUTO" &_
    "</sql:query>" &_
    "</document>"

str.Position = 0

conn.Open "Provider=SQLOLEDB.1;"      &_
          "Integrated Security=SSPI;"   &_
```

```
                    "Persist Security Info=False;" &_
                    "Initial Catalog=Northwind"

    cmd.ActiveConnection = conn

    xml.Open

    cmd.CommandStream = str

    cmd.Dialect = "{5D531CB2-E6Ed-11D2-B252-00C04F681B71}"

    cmd.Properties("Output Stream").Value = xml

    ' You can uncomment the next two lines for the default parameters
    ' in the template file to be applied
    Set prm = cmd.CreateParameter("@OrderDate", 129, 1, _
    20, "3/26/1998")
    cmd.Parameters.Append prm

    cmd.NamedParameters = True

    cmd.Execute , , 1024

    WScript.Echo xml.ReadText
```

XPath and the Mapping Schema

XPath queries can be issued against your custom mapping schemas by ADO.
The main difference from the approaches that we have seen so far is that you
set `Command.CommandText` to your query and to the XPath dialect. Here is a
sample that asks for the user to write a query:

```
<?XML version="1.0"?>
<job ID="ADO-XPath">
  <reference object="ADODB.Stream"/>
  <reference object="ADODB.Command"/>
  <object id="objConn" progid="ADODB.Connection"/>
  <object id="objCmd" progid="ADODB.Command"/>
  <object id="objOutStr" progid="ADODB.Stream"/>
  <script language="VBScript">
  <![CDATA[
   objConn.Open "Provider=SQLOLEDB.1;"          &_
                "Integrated Security=SSPI;"     &_
                "Persist Security Info=False;" &_
                "Initial Catalog=Northwind"
    objCmd.ActiveConnection = objConn
    objOutStr.Open
    ' Our XML-mapping schema
    objCmd.Properties("Mapping Schema") = "C:\\NestedElements.xml"
```

```
  objCmd.Properties("Output Stream") = objOutStr
  ' XPath dialect
  objCmd.Dialect = "{EC2A4293-E898-11D2-B1B7-00C04f680C56}"
  ' Try document/Order[@OrderID = '10255']
  objCmd.CommandText = InputBox("Enter XPath Query:")
  objCmd.Execute , , adExecuteStream
  ' Echo the results to standard output
  WScript.Echo objOutStr.ReadText(adReadAll)
  ]]>
  </script>
</job>
```

Summary

This examples chapter showed you the ADO and XML objects can be used for pulling SQL Server data as XML. The examples can be applied online as well as offline. Up next is Part II of the book, introducing Windows Management Instrumentation (WMI).

SQL Server and Windows Management Instrumentation (WMI)

Windows Management Instrumentation (WMI)

Microsoft *Windows Management Instrumentation* (WMI) is the simple, powerful infrastructure for systems management on the Windows platform. This application has actually been around for quite some time, but just recently Microsoft's products have begun moving into WMI. As a result, WMI is becoming the way to manage systems. This product is easy to learn, even easier to use, and gets the job done in no time. In a line of many products that support WMI, Microsoft SQL Server 2000 has leveraged its family of components from a traditional, proven object model called SQL DMO into the realm of WMI.

Introduction

WMI is the Windows implementation of *Web-Based Enterprise Management* (WBEM). Without repeating too much history here, WBEM was started as an industry-wide initiative towards unifying the systems management of enterprise computing environments. Managing large, distributed systems has always been considered an increasingly tedious and costly task. WBEM wanted to make it easier and less expensive.

WBEM is overseen by the *Distributed Management Task Force* (DMTF). Giants such as Microsoft, Novell, Intel, Silicon Graphics, Inc., and IBM are actively supporting WBEM and early realized the long-term benefits of its results. The technology quickly took spin, but before hitting the mainstream, there was a waiting period during which WBEM, although available, was waiting to be adapted to the industry. Right now, with Microsoft SQL Server 2000, enterprise applications are serious about the WBEM implementation on Windows (WMI).

WMI addresses various aspects of management on Windows. Foremost, whether you are managing a personal workstation or a distributed system, it should be easy. WMI does not care about the location of the managed computer. Rather, it just connects to the computer. Once it is connected, whether working with a particular object or a bunch of different objects, operations are consistent. Why would creating a file be different from creating an NT user account? Well, it is not different in WMI. WMI does not care if you are operating on a physical device or are operating a piece of software, so every kind of management operation is streamlined by a consistent set of methods in the WMI API. Creating, deleting, and updating objects is done by calls through the WMI API—not by the underlying object. The WMI API can map its methods for creating, deleting, and updating objects to the native methods of the underlying object. But it is nothing that the programmer will ever notice. In addition, the methods remain the same regardless of whether you manage a local or a remote system.

A core part of WMI is the query services. The query language is called *WMI Query Language* (WQL), and this language is similar to SQL. WQL can be used to enumerate the objects of any particular class; for example, all NT user accounts, SQL Server databases, or Windows services. Queries that are targeting more specific object matching based on user-defined criteria are also possible (for example, retrieving all .zip files in directory z that are no older than x days and y minutes). Furthermore, WQL can utilize event services. Even if the underlying system has no events, WMI provides standard events that consistently fire. We'll be exploring event handling in WMI a little later. Of course, when the system has built-in events, WMI enables you to register for those events, too.

WMI hides the complexity of systems management. If you know how to execute a script file, you will get started in less than a day. It takes time to fully understand WMI, but even with the most basic knowledge, you can streamline access and the sharing of managed objects in Windows. Table 9.1 lists some of the environments that can be administrated through WMI.

Windows itself has several hundred classes for the operating system, network, devices, and more that are included with WMI. Windows 2000 and *Windows Millennium Edition* (Windows ME) ship with WMI as a core component of their operating systems. WMI is available on the Internet for Windows 95, Windows 98, Windows 98 SE, and Windows NT 4.0 SP 4+. WMI is Microsoft's primary management strategy for the Windows platform.

Table 9.1 Examples of Managed Environments

WMI Provider
Active Directory
Windows NT Event Log
Microsoft Installer
Registry
WMI for WDM
SNMP
Office 2000
DNS
SNA Server

The Management Architecture

The WMI management infrastructure consists of managed environments, managed objects, and management applications.

First, managed environments are systems management environments. For example, the Windows operating system, UNIX, and Microsoft SQL Server are all management environments.

Managed objects, on the other hand, are the items in a managed environment. These include, but are not limited to, Windows services, Windows processes, and SQL Server databases, tables, and logins.

Last, the consumers of WMI services are management applications. In other words, we are referring to the code that you write in order to make the calls to WMI. This application can be directed to enumerate, update, create, and delete managed objects.

Windows Management Service

The Windows Management Service (`WinMgmt.exe`) is the core of WMI. This application is responsible for a great deal of things, including handling client requests, talking to providers, and managing the CIM Repository.

The Windows Management Service is exposed to programmers through two APIs that are built on top of it. C/C++ programmers use the COM API, which is the lowest-level access to WMI that you can obtain. And automation-aware

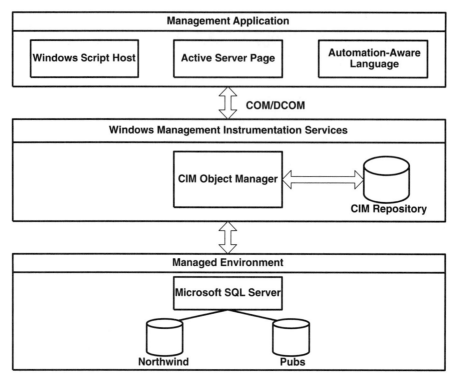

Figure 9.1 The three management layers in WMI illustrated as how a scripting language can access it through the Scripting API.

scripting languages make their calls through the Scripting API, which is a wrapper around the COM API (see Figure 9.1).

WMI is always invoked on the local or remote computer that you want to manage. So, the machine to be managed has to invoke WMI. This is an important concept to get across, so I'll try to elaborate a little more. The computer that you are managing is called a host computer. The host computer could be your local machine, or it could be a remote machine. The local machine is the one you're maybe logged in to right now. And as you make calls for management operations through the WMI Scripting API, every operation is performed by the WMI service on your local machine. Next, a remote machine is the one you're managing remotely. This means that you sit at your machine and use the WMI Scripting API to connect to a remote machine located by its computer name, DNS name, or IP address. When you make a call through the WMI Scripting API, it instructs the WMI Service on the remote computer to perform the operation. So if a remote computer hasn't got WMI installed, you can't manage it through WMI—even if you have WMI installed on your machine. As a result, the software that is providing the WMI Service with data from a management environment only has to be installed on the host computer, not on every client machine that wants to manage the host computer.

NOTE
WMI had to be scalable in network situations. The WMI team solved this problem by using *Distributed COM* (DCOM) for WMI's connections and data transfer. To obtain top performance, WMI does some custom marshaling of data.

The WMI Administration Provider for Microsoft SQL Server is the software that WMI uses to manage Microsoft SQL Server. Managed environments that provide dynamic, or frequently changing, data are generally exposed through WMI providers (see Table 9.2).

A WMI provider can be one or a combination of several of the providers that are listed in Table 9.2. For example, a provider might only support the retrieval of instances, so it is called an instance provider. But another provider might support the retrieval of instances and also have built-in support for events. A WMI provider only has to be installed on the computer that you will manage. In essence, when you install the WMI Administration Provider for SQL Server on the SQL Server machine, you move all management requirements to that machine. Management operations on that machine use the WMI Provider, so it can theoretically be operated on from anywhere in the world.

The CIM Repository and CIM Object Manager

Part of Windows Management Service, the CIM Repository is a store of static management information. Normally, static class definitions and static instance data such as settings are kept in the CIM Repository. CIM stands for Common Information Model, a standard that evolved from the efforts of *Distributed Management Task Force* (DMTF).

Table 9.2 Types of WMI Providers

Provider	Description
Class Provider	Provides the means for retrieving and updating classes
Event Provider	Provides the means for generating events
Instance Provider	Provides the means for retrieving and updating instances of classes
Method Provider	Provides the means for invoking methods
Property Provider	Provides the means for reading and writing properties of a class

CIM is a model that is used to describe management environments. This model is object-oriented and hierarchical and can model managed objects as well as capture their dynamic nature and relationships between them and other managed objects. With Microsoft being an active party in DMTF, WMI has complied (and continues to comply) with today's future specifications of CIM and WBEM.

CIM uses the *Managed Object Format* (MOF) to create the blueprint of a managed environment. The blueprint is called a schema. This schema is saved as a Managed Object File (.mof) containing class definitions that are written down in MOF syntax. Classes are often referred to as templates for managed objects, which is a good way to look at them. A class declares features such as properties, methods, of a managed object. The properties contain the attributes, or characteristics, of the class and the methods that define the behavior of the class. For example, a service can be characterized by a unique ID, and the capability to start and stop a service encapsulates its behavior. Classes, properties, and methods also have qualifiers. Qualifiers are used to provide additional meta-information about classes, properties, and methods. A qualifier could, for example, state that PropertyX's access type is read only, or it could simply provide a textual description of PropertyX. Completed MOF files are compiled, and if the compilation is successful, the class definitions are written to and stored in the CIM Repository. Last, another aspect of classes are class instances. While the class itself is a template for a managed object, the class instance is the actual managed object. This object represents the concrete data that you will operate on through WMI.

Every class lives within the scope of the defined namespace in the CIM Repository. A management application that connects to a local or remote WMI host computer thus connects to a namespace on the WMI host computer. When the client requests a namespace, it is determined whether the namespace and the required permissions for accessing the namespace exist. If you manage to successfully log on, a pointer to the namespace is returned to you. The implementations of namespaces are hidden to you, but a good illustration of how they're organized is to visualize them as files and folders on a hard drive. The namespaces contain classes related to the managed environment. So behind the scenes, namespaces also protect class definitions from clashing with similar class definitions in other namespaces. For example, you cannot have two files of the same name in the same folder. Similarly, namespaces keep two classes from sharing the same name in a managed environment. That way, you will not get the wrong class and perform operations on the wrong object. In some cases, however, it might be desirable for one namespace to utilize classes from another namespace. This task can be done easily. The WMI View Provider is capable of virtually importing classes from one namespace into the other. Microsoft SQL Server is one managed environment that utilizes this feature.

Classes can be labeled as static or dynamic. Static refers to data that infrequently changes. This data can be safely stored in the CIM Repository, while dynamic data must be consistently looked up for up-to-date values. What happens when the management application requests a class is that the CIM Object Manager goes to the CIM Repository to see whether the class definition is static or dynamic. If a qualifier exists that indicates that the class is dynamic (note that the qualifier is simply named dynamic), and it means that the class is dynamically supplied by a WMI provider. Then, a Provider qualifier identifies which WMI provider is supplying it. Instances of dynamic classes are never written to or cached in the repository. Instead, the WMI Provider is used for all types of operations on dynamic instances. Static classes, on the other hand, supply instances that are stored in the CIM repository. Microsoft SQL Server supplies mostly dynamic classes. Only some settings are stored in the CIM Repository.

The WMI Provider is the software that carries out the operations you perform through the WMI Scripting API or WMI COM API. The WMI Provider for SQL Server 2000 makes all its calls to the underlying Distributed Management Objects API that ships with SQL Server. For example, let's say that you use the WMI Scripting API to enumerate all instances of databases in an instance of SQL Server. The call from the WMI Scripting API goes to the WMI SQL Server Provider. The provider makes the appropriate calls to DMO and then returns the result back to your management application.

About CIM

CIM is an object-oriented technology and a standard for modeling management environments. We will not discuss it thoroughly, however, because it is not the focus of this book. At the most basic level, however, CIM is considered a conceptual model that consists of three types of schemas:

- The Core Model is the design pattern for all management domains. This model is a relatively small set of definitions for managed objects.
- The Common Model is an extension of the Core Model. This model models more tangible, manageable objects (for example, physical and logical devices, computers and networks, and applications).
- It has technology-specific extensions. These are models for a particular technology, such as Microsoft SQL Server, and they must be implemented by a third party.

The Core Model and the Common Model are standard schemas, and they form the basis for modeling an environment by using CIM. Additionally, they are independent of platform, technology, and implementation. A number of founding classes are defined in CIM.

Classes and Instances

A class is a template for a managed object. Classes can be either abstract or non-abstract. Abstract classes can't have instances, such as managed objects. But abstract classes do have their use. Object-oriented programming supports the notion of inheritance. Inheritance allows a class to inherit the existing features of a particular class. So non-abstract, or concrete, classes that can have instances are often subclasses of an abstract class. The features of a class are properties and methods. Properties are the attributes of the managed object, and methods control the object's behavior.

A property has a data type, name, access type, and value. The data type specifies a type of data to which the value must conform, for example, integer, double, or string. The data type can also be tagged as an array. If it's an array, it means that the value is a list of values that conform to the data type. The property name is a textual name of the property. It typically indicates the meaning of the property's value, or, in other words, the particular attribute of the object that it defines. Consider an object that has a string type property named Description. That property's value contains a textual description of the object that gives you more information about it. So, with that in mind, the value defines the attribute represented by the property. It must conform to a data type specified by the property. What modifications you can do to the value depends on the access type. And the name is the descriptive name of the property.

Methods control the behavior of the object. Methods have a name, return type, and often parameters. Parameters are like properties in the sense that they each have a name and data type that helps define the value of the parameter. There are two kinds of parameters: input and output. Input parameters are data that the client passes to the method. Output parameters are placeholders for values returned by the method. A method can be seen as either a function or an operation. Functions are used to access values, and they typically produce no side-effects. For example, functions can return the status, name, or description of an object. Those types of calls should have no side-effect, such as data modification, in the object itself. Operations, on the other hand, do have side-effects. You use them to perform an operation, such as spawning a new process in Windows. These methods return a status code to the calling program, indicating the success or failure of the operation. Either the status is the actual return type of the method, or it's returned into an output parameter because, say, the return type is an object spawned from the method call. Input parameters are commonly passed to operational methods. The input parameters have a name and data type. You pass a value confirming to the data type of the parameter in order to provide additional information that will be used for the operation.

Classes, methods, and properties can have qualifiers. Qualifiers are meta-information. They are in some instances used for simple things such as providing a thorough description about a property, method, or class. However, qualifiers are also used for defining what type a class is, such as abstract, dynamic, or association class. Moreover, qualifiers define access type on properties and whether a parameter is an input or output parameter, to name a few of things. There are several types of standard qualifiers, and one very important qualifier is the key qualifier. A class can have one or more keys as well as none. And the key qualifier is attached to properties. These properties are then used to uniquely identify a managed object. Together with the class name, the key properties are what you use when locating a managed object.

Abstract Classes

Abstract classes cannot have instances. The common use of abstract classes is for other classes to inherit from them in order to model an area of management.

A class can declare itself as a subclass of an abstract class and then inherit its features. Inheritance in this context is only supported on a parent-child class level, however, so what is inherited is the data structure of the class. Finding a use for abstract classes is easy when you are creating new classes. For example, in Microsoft SQL Server, they often serve as generic data structures for classes that define permissions, settings, database objects, and so forth.

Although a subclass can inherit features, there are some rules that apply. For example, superclasses can keep class members private so that the subclass does not inherit them. Similarly, subclasses can redefine inherited class members if they are permitted to do so by the superclass. Redefining a class member is called overriding. A subclass commonly overrides an inherited property into a key property.

Non-Abstract Classes

Non-abstract classes can have instances that are managed objects. The properties that are declared in the class definition contain values that describe the instance. The methods that belong to the class can also be used to trigger its behavior.

Non-abstract classes contain some properties with a Key qualifier and are called *keys* for short. Keys uniquely identify instances for a class. So within the scope of a class, the keys make an instance unique. The combination of the class name and the unique keys makes an instance unique within a namespace. Concatenating the WMI host computer name, namespace, and class name with the name-value pairs of the keys, you get a valid path to a managed object. For example, you can use the object path to locate the SQL Server Windows Server and shut it down or fire it up. Keys used to be defined in CIM classes by DMTF. But it really became a problem since it forced subclasses to use those keys defined by DMTF. The best design is to let non-abstract classes define keys and keep abstract classes from it.

Associations

Associations are special types of classes. They can be either abstract or non-abstract, and their purpose is to model a relationship between classes. Associations are often described as modeling a relationship between two or more classes. I have, however, never seen a class related to more than two classes. And it can actually be less than two if an association relates a class to itself. There are five components to the association class:

- The association class itself
- Two or more references in the association class
- Two or more classes pointed to by the references

Associations can be read-only or writeable. The typical read-only association is bi-directional and is meant to be enumerated or traversed by your program. A writeable class is also bi-directional, but its instances are meant to be defined by the administrator. You can use writeable association classes to define attributes (such as permissions) in order for a user to access a particular object in the system.

The Security Model

WMI's security model lies at several levels. First, management applications can specify a DCOM ImpersonationLevel and AuthenticationLevel. The ImpersonationLevel is a DCOM setting that determines whether processes that are owned by WMI can see or use your security credentials when making calls to other processes. From a security point of view, this process ensures that the server acts like the client. The machine could have to use your security credentials when making calls to other objects, processes, or machines. The most common impersonation levels are Impersonate and Delegate, where the latter is the more powerful. Impersonation assures that the client cannot use WMI to access a management environment or host computer where he or she is unauthorized. Impersonation also only works as it is supposed to if it is used by both the client and the server, however. If the client does not specify a level, the machine-wide default DCOM setting will be used. The Impersonation levels are listed in Table 9.3.

Table 9.3 Windows NT/2000 DCOM Impersonation Levels

Moniker Name	Constant	Value	Description
Anonymous	wbemImpersonationLevelAnonymous	1	The server can't impersonate the client.
Identify	wbemImpersonationLevelIdentify	2	The server can identify the client and do access control lists (ACL) checks.
Impersonate	wbemImpersonationLevelImpersonate	3	The server can act as the client, but if it's a remote machine, it's limited to that server only. On a local machine, the client can access network-resources if the client has the appropriate rights.
Delegate	wbemImpersonationLevelDelegate	4	Server can act as client and access all permitted network resources on local and remote machines.

Authentication is a process of validating the client's rights to access a remote computer. When connecting to a remote machine, Microsoft Windows NT/2000 can verify the username and password if they are both passed along with the connection request. Otherwise, the machine will default to the current user. The different authentication levels that can be used are specified in Table 9.4.

The DCOM levels for your computer can be configured with the tool Dcom-Cnfg.exe in the System32 directory in your environment. Additionally, as seen in Figure 9.2, NT-level security can be assigned for each namespace. Through the Computer Management MMC snap-in, you can locate the WMI Control under Services and define this security.

When authenticated, you will be assigned permissions that determine what you can do within WMI. Some tasks, though, could require certain privileges, or you might want to revoke some privileges for the clients. WMI makes this task possible for Windows NT/2000 by enabling you to enable and disable the privileges as defined in the privilege constants of WMI. SQL Server WMI provider doesn't have any privilege requirements. Other things like the NT Event Log do. In short,

Table 9.4 Windows NT/2000 DCOM Authentication Levels

Moniker Name	Constant	Value	Description
Default	wbemAuthenticationLevelDefault	0	Default Windows Authentication Setting.
None	wbemAuthenticationLevelNone	1	No authentication.
Connect	wbemAuthenticationLevelConnect	2	Authenticates the credentials of the client only when the client establishes a relationship with the server.
Call	wbemAuthenticationLevelCall	3	Authentication occurs at the beginning of each call when the server received the request.
Pkt	wbemAuthenticationLevelPkt	4	Authenticates that all packets received are from the expected client.
PktIntegrity	wbemAuthenticationLevelPktIntegrity	5	Authenticates that none of the packets transferred between client and server has been modified.
PktPrivacy	wbemAuthenticationLevelPktPrivacy	6	Authenticates all previous levels and encrypts the packet with each remote procedure call.

there is the DCOM impersonation security, and there are security settings that determine whether you can connect to the requested namespace. That can be set independently of whether you are allowed to perform operations in that namespace. Finally, there's security that determines if you can execute the operations defined by the classes in the namespace. The latter is mostly driven by whether your credentials are good enough for the API that the WMI provider calls.

WMI and Microsoft SQL Server

Microsoft's WMI Administration Provider for SQL Server WMI has some distinct features. Here, we will take a tour of the managed environment, meet its

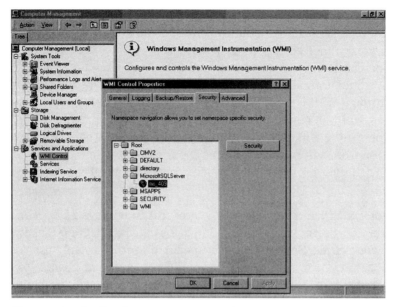

Figure 9.2 Configuring namespace security.

classes, see some methods, and learn about a couple of characteristics that are typical of Microsoft SQL Server.

The Provider

The WMI SQL Server Administration Provider is widely supported. This application runs on both Microsoft SQL Server 7.0 and 2000 and on every Windows platform where WMI is available. Furthermore, WMI is Microsoft's future strategy—not only for Windows, but also for upcoming releases of Microsoft SQL Server.

Microsoft SQL Server lives in its own namespace. When connecting to Microsoft SQL Server by using WMI, go through the Root namespace to the `Microsoft-SQLServer` namespace. To connect, you must have the following rights:

- *NT rights.* You must have NT logon rights for the WMI host machine.
- *WMI rights.* You must have the rights for connecting to the `MicrosoftSQLServer` namespace.
- *SQL rights.* You must pass either the standard or integrated SQL Server security levels.

With DCOM and WMI, either Impersonate or Delegate is the ideal DCOM ImpersonationLevel. Delegate is exclusively the most powerful level, because your credentials can be passed by a remote host machine to an unlimited number of host-machines. Impersonate, however, is fine for a single remote session, although you cannot go any further than the remote machine. Keep in mind that impersonation is a method in which the client cannot do more than what he or she would normally be allowed to do. In other words, the client that connected through WMI cannot wreak havoc by deleting a database or any other object to which the client already does not have access rights. As far as SQL Server goes, there isn't any use for delegation. Delegate is used if you ask for information from a third machine from the remote machine you are connected to. The SQL Server provider never talks to installations of SQL Server on other machines.

Then, there is SQL Server security. There are three ways to specify security through the SQL Server WMI Provider. First, you can use integrated security, which is the default setting. Second, you can specify a username and password in the `MSSQL_SQLServerConnectionSetting` class, and then change the `LoginSecure` property to false. Setting `LoginSecure` to false will disable integrated security, so the Login and Password properties of `MSSQL_SQLServerConnectionSetting` are not used when the client attempts a connection. You can specify different connection settings for each SQL Server instance if you're running multiple instances of SQL Server on the system. The `SettingID` property of `MSSQL_SQLServerConnectionSetting` defines the name of the SQL Server instance used for the settings. These settings stored in `MSSQL_SQLServerConnectionSetting` will be used by every incoming request to your SQL Server instance. Third, with every request you can pass a WMI context object containing the desired connection settings. Context objects override the settings in `MSSQL_SQLServerConnectionSetting`, so if you're using both, the settings in the context object are what will be used. The benefit of context objects is that they allow each operation to have a different security mode. In terms of security, the content of `MSSQL_SQLServerConnectionSetting` is—like all static instances in the repository—stored in clear text. The best practice is to use those settings for read-only access. WMI context objects should use COM security so that the client connection settings are encrypted before they are sent to the provider.

While we're talking about security, let's also mention that being an administrator has its privileges with Microsoft SQL Server. You will be able to see and start stopped instances of SQL Server. This functionality is not possible unless you are logged on as a member of the Administrators group, however.

MSSQL Classes

Slightly more than 150 classes exist in the `/Root/MicrosoftSQLServer` namespace. There are not only SQL Server classes in the namespace, though.

Several Windows classes are present, and some CIM classes from the Core and Common Model can be found there, as well. Distinguishing between these classes and Microsoft's SQL Server classes is easy.

Classes follow a naming scheme that is suggested in the CIM specification. Their names contain an abbreviation of the schema name, then an underscore, followed by the full class name: `CIM_Classname`, `Win32_Classname`, or `MSSQL_Classname`.

Windows classes and CIM classes lend their features to subclasses in the Microsoft SQL Server schema. Some Windows classes, though, provide features of their own—such as the capability to create and manage processes, user accounts, and services. The Windows classes are not delivered by the WMI SQL Provider. Instead, the WMI View Provider serves these classes through the `MicrosoftSQLServer` namespace.

Static and Dynamic Classes

Most MSSQL classes are dynamic. In other words, when you enumerate, create, delete, or modify instances, the WMI Provider does all of the work. It makes the calls to the underlying API and supplies the returned results to your application. A few classes, however, are static. Static classes represent data that rarely changes, for example, settings classes like the following:

- `MSSQL_SQLServerConnectionSetting`
- `MSSQL_BackupSetting`
- `MSSQL_BulkCopySetting`
- `MSSQL_RestoreSetting`
- `MSSQL_TransferSetting`

WMI lets you store static instances of the previous classes. For example, if you have some preference about the connection settings, you spawn an instance of `MSSQL_SQLServerConnectionSetting`, set your connection properties, and then put the instance in the repository. By doing so, those connection settings are used from there on. This often proves itself far more reusable passing your connection settings as twenty-something parameters in some method calls. Connection settings are rarely modified. For the other listed classes, you can set up your backup, bulk-copy, restore, and transfer settings. The latter classes are often spawned as instances and passed to a method that needs the information. You could, for example, spawn an instance of `MSSQL_BulkCopySetting`, define your bulk-copy settings by initializing the values of its properties, and then pass it as a parameter to either `ImportData()` or `ExportData()` of the `MSSQL_Table` class. Of course, you can also store a static instance of `MSSQL_BulkCopySetting` in the repository. In that case, you would get that instance from the repository and pass it to `ImportData()` or `ExportData()`. Examples in Chapter 12 will demonstrate how to use some of the static classes. A number of settings classes are dynamic in nature, as well. Therefore, if a class is about settings, that automatically does not mean that it is static.

Association Classes

Microsoft SQL Server uses a few types of associations—few as in "relative to the hundred-something known types of association classes in CIM." These association classes establish a variety of relationships. Some associations can be used for granting or denying a user or role the permissions to operate on a database object (see Figure 9.3).

Everyone benefits from association classes. Say, for example, that a third party has come up with a product for Microsoft SQL Server. The third party can either subclass or extend the existing Microsoft SQL Server schema, depending on its needs. If a third-party class has to be tightly knit to an existing class in the schema, it is often enough to add an association class definition describing their relationship. You do not have to rewrite any pre-existing code in the schema when you can add your own classes and associations that relate them to other classes. The object-oriented model in CIM is fully extensible, so it is less than bothersome to add new features to an existing WMI schema. Next, we will cover some of the more common associations in the Microsoft SQL Server management environment.

Aggregations

Aggregations are the types of associations that model a relationship where an instance of ClassA is made up of one or more instances of ClassB. It is essentially a part-of relationship where the parent in the association has one or more children of one type. Aggregations are used when modeling complex objects or when objects seem to be made up of other objects. In SQL Server, we can find some examples rather quickly:

■ *Aggregations are used to associate a table with one or more columns.* The `MSSQL_TableColumn` aggregation association class models the relationship between a table and a column contained in the table.

Figure 9.3 A simplified view of associations containing two references pointing to two different instances.

- *Aggregations are used to associate a database with one or more tables.* The MSSQL_DatabaseTable aggregation association class models the relationship between a database and a table contained in the database.

- *Aggregations are used to associate an SQL Server with one or more databases.* The MSSQL_SQLServerDatabase aggregation association class models the relationship between an SQL Server instance and a database that's part of the instance.

Think about one or more instances of ClassB as being core parts of ClassA's structure. As developers design a schema that fits into the CIM, a lot of the questions upon which they have had to agree relate to what type of association an association is (and more importantly, why it is an association and not another type). The reasoning behind aggregations is that they are both part of an object, and these parts are something that you can say describes the object primarily. For example, an instance of a table is on an aggregate relationship basis with one or more column instances. If you were to remove the columns, the table would be rendered useless. Similarly, tables are part of a database, and databases are part of an SQL Server instance. Remove databases from SQL Server, and the product is lost. An instance of an aggregation association class interrelates instances of ClassA and ClassB. Each aggregation has two properties, and each property plays an important role in the relationship. There are at least two properties of an aggregation association:

- *GroupComponent.* The parent component in the relationship
- *PartComponent.* The child component in the relationship

The properties value is set to the object path of the instance that is the parent (and respectively, the child) in the association. We will look at object paths in a moment. It is typical for associations to have properties that reference other instances via object paths, but there's nothing requiring it. In addition, there may be properties that describe the relationship in more detail.

Scope Associations

Relationships that are defined by scope can be confusing at first. For example, a stored procedure—although part of a database—is not related to the database through an aggregation relationship. When you first look at the stored procedure, it does not seem much different than what we have used in the aggregation relationship. We can find some basic similarities, such as the fact that they are both database objects of a particular database and that there can be several stored procedures in one database. Stored procedure objects also tend to look like a collection to the naked eye—which is similar to how tables appear to be a collection in a database. So, where do we draw the line? Well, a scoping relationship indicates that the scoped element, which is the stored procedure, must be unique within the scoping element or within the database. You will find two references in a scope association:

- *ScopingElement.* The logical element that defines the scope
- *ScopedElement.* The logical element within ScopingElement's scope

In the real world, a stored procedure does not belong anywhere else—but in a database, we cannot think of stored procedures as part of database tables (database columns). Stored procedures can operate on database tables, though, but it is not correct to think that a database is primarily a collection of stored procedures. A stored procedure must be unique within the scope of a database, just as a file must be unique within its containing directory. The stored procedure is an optional feature that you can use for operating on more vital parts of the database, such as on tables. With this fact in mind, we can find the following typical scoping relationships:

- *Associates a stored procedure with a database.* The `MSSQL_Database-StoredProcedure` association models the relationship between a database and a stored procedure that exists within the scope of the database.
- *Associates a user-defined function with a database.* The `MSSQL_DatabaseUserDefinedFunction` association models the relationship between a database and a user-defined function that exists within the scope of the database.
- *Associates a login with an SQL server.* The `MSSQL_SQLServerLogin` association models the relationship between an SQL Server instance and a login that exists within the scope of the SQL Server instance.

Dependencies

Dependency associations are used to express the fact that one class makes use of the features of another class. Class A, for example, depends on a device, software, or service provided by Class B. The properties that contain references to instances in this relationship are as follows:

- *Antecedent.* The independent object
- *Dependent.* The object that is dependent on the antecedent

Microsoft SQL Server has a number of dependent classes that will not operate without knowing their associations. Here are some examples:

- *Associates a user-defined data type with a system-defined data type on which it depends.* The MSSQL_BaseDataType models that relationship.

- *Associates a login with an SQL Server role on which it depends.* The MSSQL_MemberLogin association models that relationship.

- *Associates a table with a trigger that is defined for the table.* The MSSQL_TableTrigger association models that relationship.

When we first see dependencies, it sounds a bit harsh that "a table depends on a trigger." But such a relationship is only in effect when there is an instance of that association class. Until that point, it is a class definition that provides the means for such an instance (but in no way enforces it as something that applies to all of the tables).

Containment

Containment relationships indicate a relationship between ClassA as a container and ClassB as a contained object. The references in a Containment association are as follows:

- *Container.* The managed system element containing one or more other managed system elements

- *Containee.* The managed system element contained within another managed system element.

At this point, examples paint a clearer picture:

- *Associates an SQL Server instance to a database user contained in a database.* This relationship is modeled by the MSSQL_SQLServerUser class.

- *Associates a database to a login that is utilized by a user contained in the database.* This relationship is modeled by the MSSQL_DatabaseLogin class.

- *Associates between a database and a candidate key that is contained in a database table.* This relationship is modeled by the MSSQL_DatabaseCandidateKey class.

Configuration and Settings

When you configure, reconfigure, or traverse the settings of a managed object, you will use association classes. This action separates the configuration from the actual managed object, so if you have to switch configurations, you simply get rid of the current association and reassign a new association to the managed object. The references in these relationships typically are as follows:

- *Element.* The object for which the settings are defined
- *Setting.* The actual settings used by the element

In essence, settings associations are used to configure the managed element that is represented by ClassA by associating it with the settings that are defined in ClassB. Some examples of classes associating objects with settings are:

- The `MSSQL_DatabaseSetting` class associates a database with the operational settings for a database.
- The `MSSQL_SQLServerRegistry` class associates an SQL Server instance with its registry settings.
- The `MSSQL_SQLServerLanguageSetting` class associates an SQL Server instance with its language settings.

Statistics

Statistics associations are used to associate the managed element that is represented in ClassA with statistical information about the managed element that is represented in ClassB. The references are as follows:

- *Element.* The managed element
- *Stats.* Statistical information about the element

The only statistics class in the SQL Server namespace is the `MSSQL_IndexStatistics` class that associates an index for a table with statistical information for the index.

Identity

Identity relationships model the different aspects of a single entity. A managed object can be represented by other objects. These multiple objects are the different aspects of the underlying managed object. For example, a single object can have a logical aspect as well as a physical aspect, and these associations can be used to identify which aspect(s) the object possesses. Microsoft SQL Server uses this type of association to represent different aspects of logical elements. The references are as follows:

- *SystemElement.* One aspect of the underlying system entity
- *SameElement.* An alternate aspect of the underlying system entity

For example, the `FullTextWin32Service` association is used to represent an association between an instance of the Microsoft SQL Server `FullTextCatalogService` class and the corresponding instance that is running as a Windows service. Both instances are two aspects of the same underlying entity. Although CIM does not explicitly support multiple inheritance, this association provides a way to represent multiple-inheritance scenarios.

Extensions

An extension association declares the relationship between a managed element and an already defined class that extends that element. References are as follows:

- *ExtendedElement.* The system element to which the extension applies
- *Extension.* The extension that is used by `ExtendedElement`

When it is not possible or practical to subclass an existing class, the extensions classes are used. The most common use for these classes would be for third-party tools to integrate with the Microsoft SQL Server-managed environment.

Permissions

A common type of association to create and delete is one that applies to permissions. Every class that involves permissions is derived from `MSSQL_Permission`.

- *Element.* The object for which the permissions are defined
- *Grantee.* The object for whom the permissions to Element apply

Permission classes are used by the database administrator. It allows the administrator to define what privileges a user object has for working with a database object. You can, among other things, use the classes to grant a user only read-only access to a table, permit a user the privilege to create and own a new table, and give all privileges applicable to databases. Some examples of associations that deal with permissions are:

- The `MSSQL_UserStoredProcedurePermission` class that associates a user with the permissions the user has been granted or denied for a stored procedure.
- The `MSSQL_DatabaseRoleStoredProcedurePermission` class that associates a database role with the permissions the database role has been granted or denied for a stored procedure.
- The `MSSQL_DatabaseRoleTablePermission` class that associates a database role with the permissions the database role has been granted or denied for a table.

See Table 9.5 for a complete listing of the Microsoft SQL Server association classes.

Creating New Objects

When managing Microsoft SQL Server, you will want to create new objects. The standard way of creating new objects in WMI is to call the `SWbemObject.`

Table 9.5 Microsoft SQL Server Association Classes

Classname	Relationship	Abstract
CIM_Component	Aggregation	✔
CIM_Dependency	Dependency	✔
CIM_ElementSetting	Setting	✔
CIM_LogicalIdentity	Identity	✔
CIM_Statistics	Statistical	✔
MSSQL_BaseDatatype	Dependency	
MSSQL_ColumnDRIDefault	Dependency	
MSSQL_ColumnDatatype	Dependency	
MSSQL_ColumnDefault	Dependency	
MSSQL_ColumnRule	Dependency	
MSSQL_Containment	Containment	✔
MSSQL_DBMSObjectOwner	Dependency	
MSSQL_DatabaseCandidateKey	Containment	
MSSQL_DatabaseDatabaseRole	Scoping	
MSSQL_DatabaseDatabaseSetting	Setting	
MSSQL_DatabaseDatatype	Scoping	
MSSQL_DatabaseDefault	Scoping	
MSSQL_DatabaseFileDataFile	Extension	
MSSQL_DatabaseFileGroup	Dependency	
MSSQL_DatabaseFullTextCatalog	Dependency	
MSSQL_DatabaseLogin	Containment	
MSSQL_DatabaseOwnerLogin	Dependency	
MSSQL_DatabaseRoleDatabasePermission	Permission	
MSSQL_DatabaseRoleStoredProcedurePermission	Permission	
MSSQL_DatabaseRoleTablePermission	Permission	
MSSQL_DatabaseRoleUserDefined FunctionPermission	Permission	
MSSQL_DatabaseRoleViewPermission	Permission	
MSSQL_DatabaseRule	Scoping	
MSSQL_DatabaseStoredProcedure	Scoping	
MSSQL_DatabaseTable	Aggregation	
MSSQL_DatabaseTransactionLog	Dependency	

Table 9.5 (Continued)

Classname	Relationship	Abstract
MSSQL_DatabaseUserDefinedFunction	Scoping	
MSSQL_DatabaseUser	Scoping	
MSSQL_DatabaseView	Aggregation	
MSSQL_ErrorLogDataFile	Dependency	
MSSQL_ErrorLogErrorLogEntry	Aggregation	
MSSQL_Extends	Extension	✔
MSSQL_FileGroupDatabaseFile	Aggregation	
MSSQL_FullTextWin32Service	Identity	
MSSQL_IndexColumn	Dependency	
MSSQL_IndexFileGroup	Dependency	
MSSQL_IndexStatistics	Statistics	
MSSQL_KeyColumn	Aggregation	
MSSQL_KeyFileGroup	Dependency	
MSSQL_LoginDefaultDatabase	Dependency	
MSSQL_LoginWin32Group	Dependency	
MSSQL_LoginWin32UserAccount	Dependency	
MSSQL_MemberDatabaseRole	Dependency	
MSSQL_MemberLogin	Dependency	
MSSQL_MemberUser	Dependency	
MSSQL_Permission	Permission	✔
MSSQL_ReferencedKey	Dependency	
MSSQL_ReferencedTable	Dependency	
MSSQL_SQLServerBackupDevice	Dependency	
MSSQL_SQLServerConfigValue	Setting	
MSSQL_SQLServerDatabase	Aggregation	
MSSQL_SQLServerErrorLog	Dependency	
MSSQL_SQLServerIntegratedSecuritySetting	Setting	
MSSQL_SQLServerLanguageSetting	Setting	
MSSQL_SQLServerLogin	Scoping	
MSSQL_SQLServerRegistry	Setting	
MSSQL_SQLServerSQLServerConnectionSetting	Setting	
MSSQL_SQLServerServerRole	Scoping	

(continues)

Table 9.5 Microsoft SQL Server Association Classes (Continued).

Classname	Relationship	Abstract
MSSQL_SQLServerUser	Containment	
MSSQL_Scope	Scoping	✔
MSSQL_StoredProcedureStoredProcedure Parameter	Scoping	
MSSQL_TableCheck	Dependency	
MSSQL_TableColumn	Aggregation	
MSSQL_TableFileGroup	Dependency	
MSSQL_TableIndex	Dependency	
MSSQL_TableKey	Dependency	
MSSQL_TableTextFileGroup	Dependency	
MSSQL_TableTrigger	Dependency	
MSSQL_TransactionLogDataFile	Aggregation	
MSSQL_UserDatabasePermission	Permission	
MSSQL_UserDatatypeDefault	Dependency	
MSSQL_UserDatatypeRule	Dependency	
MSSQL_UserLogin	Dependency	
MSSQL_UserStoredProcedurePermission	Permission	
MSSQL_UserTablePermission	Permission	
MSSQL_UserUserDefinedFunctionPermission	Permission	
MSSQL_UserViewPermission	Permission	
Win32_GroupUser	Aggregation	

Put_() method. Similarly, to remove an object, there are the methods SWbem-Services.Delete_() and SWbemObject.Delete_().

In some cases, Microsoft SQL Server classes provide their own constructor and destructor. This feature is necessary when an object must go through additional processing or must provide parameters upon creation. Additionally, renaming instances is not possible in the native WMI, so the WMI Provider for SQL Server supplies an Instance.Rename() method when applicable.

Summary

This chapter has dealt with the basics of WMI. You have learned about the architecture behind WMI and the security model of WMI and have gained some fundamental knowledge about the WMI Provider for SQL Server. Next, we describe the programmatical interface to WMI (known as the Scripting API).

CHAPTER 10

The WMI Scripting API

S cript programmers can manage Microsoft SQL Server through the Scripting *Application Programming Interface* (API) for WMI. This Scripting API puts languages such as VBScript, JScript, REXX, Perl, and Python on a fast track toward building administration scripts.

Introduction

WMI makes administration easier. Some level of complexity has always been associated with writing scripts. Sometimes, this complexity is justified. But most of the time, it is nothing else than a myth that is keeping administrators from adopting script to their everyday projects. This situation is bad, because administrators at all levels can gain more control over the management environment by scripting WMI. Part of this situation comes from the fact that you have a single, common interface in order to instrument all management tasks within the enterprise.

As we mentioned earlier, it is easy to manage computers locally and remotely with WMI. A typical scenario is where you first set up a computer at a remote location. Then, some months later, a representative of the client contacts you about an issue and wants you to check out the SQL server that you installed. He or she probably wants you to reconfigure it as soon as humanly possible. One way to perform this task is to drive, fly, or take a train to that office. Another way is to utilize WMI. Log on to the remote computer's Microsoft SQL Server namespace from your home or office. Once you are connected, you can traverse class instances and inspect configurations in order to find out what is wrong with the machine. You can find out exactly as much from your own computer as you can at the remote location. You can walk through associations, see that everything is intact, search for missing instances, and possibly create new instances for missing associations. Even better, if you configured the machine with WMI at the beginning, just change the connection settings in your current script to the remote host computer and run the application again.

All networks can reap the benefits of WMI. Let's say that you are managing 1,000-something computers at a university when an incoming call alerts you that a particular security setting on all computers that are running, say, Microsoft Word, Internet Explorer, or Microsoft SQL Server is a risk. Your primary objective is to change the settings of all of the computers as fast as you can. While you could go out and pay a personal visit to each machine, a WMI script is more effective. You can write a tiny script to reconfigure every single machine while you go out for lunch.

TIP

The Active Directory provider, which is standard in Windows 2000, can be used to enumerate the computers on a network. This task is done through the `ds_computer` class under `root/directory/ldap`. You will receive a list of computers that are known to Active Directory (but not necessarily those that are live on the network).

The SWbemLocator Object

The `SWbemLocator` object gets you connected to WMI. Create an instance of the `SWbemLocator` object, and call the `SWbemLocator.ConnectServer()` method to make the connection. You have the option of including parameters that contain the host computer's name, the namespace, the username, the password, and so forth in the method call. If you connect to your local computer, you do not have to specify the host computer's name. Similarly, if you omit the namespace, the computer connects to the default namespace. You make your call to a remote computer by using the computer name, DNS name, or IP address. The WMI service on that host computer authenticates you. Then, if it finds the namespace in the CIM Repository, it returns an `SWbemServices` object.

```
' Create Locator-object
Set SWbemLocator = CreateObject("WbemScripting.SWbemLocator")
' Connect to local server and default namespace
Set SWbemServices = SWbemLocator.ConnectServer()
```

The `SWbemServices` object is your connection pointer to the namespace on the WMI host computer. It is the next object that we will look at in the Scripting

API, but before we do that, we should mention that the `GetObject()` function in your language can substitute the `SWbemLocator` object. In fact, the function `GetObject()` can make a connection *and* return the `SWbemServices` object, just like the `SWbemLocator` object.

```
Set SWbemServices = GetObject(strMoniker)
```

So, what is the `strMoniker` parameter? It is a variable that contains a WMI moniker. The moniker is a concatenated, textual string. Its value resolves to a host computer, to a namespace, and optionally extends to a specific class or instance within the namespace. Here is how to build a WMI moniker:

```
WinMgmts:" [securitySetting] "!" <objectPath>
```

The WMI moniker takes security settings and an object path. Forward slashes separate the namespace steps in the objectPath. For example, `root/Microsoft-SQLServer` Security involves the ImpersonationLevel and AuthenticationLevel. In addition to the namespace, the object path can point to a class or an instance of a class. Getting a class instead of a class instance enables you to perform operations like retrieving every instance of the class or creating a brand new instance of the class. Let's talk a little more about object paths. First, the Microsoft SQL Server namespace is a sibling of the Root namespace. It means only that it is registered under Root and that Root must be included in the object-path part of the moniker:

```
WinMgmts:{impersonationlevel=Impersonate}!root/MicrosoftSQLServer
```

Or, to connect to a remote computer, use the following command:

```
WinMgmts:{impersonationlevel=Impersonate}!//SERVER/root/MicrosoftSQLServer
```

Namespaces do not inherit anything from other namespaces. Although obvious, let's emphasize that the CD-ROM device or Microsoft SQL Server cannot from an inheritance perspective be accessed through the Internet Explorer 5 namespace or vice-versa. Another perspective is the WMI View Provider. It's used by various WMI providers, and it could allow a third-party WMI Provider views of the SQL Server classes. In fact, the view provider can get views on any class in any namespace. Back to the default namespace. If you want to, you can change the default namespace setting in the registry at:

```
HKEY_LOCAL_MACHINE\Software\Microsoft\WBEM\Scripting\Default Namespace
```

This setting can be a key that dedicated Microsoft SQL Server machines might want to change. For example, by setting the default namespace to `Root/MicrosoftSQLServer`, connections go straight into the SQL Server environment. Next, if you want to include an instance or a class in your object path, you must separate the namespace and class name by a single colon. This is what an object path to the `MSSQL_Database` class looks like:

```
Root/MicrosoftSQLServer:MSSQL_Database
```

As you may recall from the previous chapter, the combination of the class name and the unique keys makes an instance unique within a namespace. You'll use that knowledge to build an object path to an existing instance. The `MSSQL_Database` class contains two key properties: Name and SQLServerName. Name is the name of the database, and SQLServerName is the name of the SQL Server instance the database is part of. Now, let's say that you want to get the Northwind database from the SQL Server instance named mySQLServer. You then need to specify the values of Name and SQLServerName in the object path. You separate the class name from your list of keys by a single period. Multiple keys are separated from each other by commas, and a key's name and value is a separated by equals signs. Finally, the values of the keys are delimited by single quotes. The following object path points to the Northwind instance:

```
Root/MicrosoftSQLServer:MSSQL_Database.Name='Northwind',SQLServerName=
'mySQLServer'
```

You can use the object path when calling `GetObject()`. `GetObject()` is fine in lightweight situations. If you are going to make, say, two or more connections, however, the `SWbemLocator` object will scale better. If you need to pass a username and a password, go with the `SWbemLocator` object.

Overview: The SWbemLocator Object

Table 10.1 presents an overview of the Locator object and its members. As you can see, there is only one method and one property. Basically, this object is only used to connect to WMI and to get or set the security settings through the `SWbemLocator.Security_` property.

The definitions for `Security` can be found under the section on the `Swbem-Security` object.

Table 10.1 `SWbemLocator` Objects

Method	Return Type	Description
ConnectServer	SWbemServices	Connect to WMI Services
Property	**Data Type**	**Description**
Security_	SWbemSecurity	Security settings

ConnectServer( )

Use this method to connect to a namespace on a computer that is running WMI services. Specify the server by using the computer's name, DNS, or IP address in `strServer`. If you do not want to connect to the default namespace, specify one in the namespace parameter. `strUser` and `strPassword` are both information that you would need to pass a parameter to, say, a remote computer that requires that type of authentication or if you want to use other credentials than those you logged in with locally. Finally, `strLocale` can be set to the locale code that you want to use, or it can be left blank in order to use the current code. `strAuthority` can be an NT LAN Manager name, and `iSecurityFlags` is reserved by WMI.

```
SWbemServices ConnectServer (
    [BSTR strServer = "."]
    [BSTR strNamespace = ""]
    [BSTR strUser = ""]
    [BSTR strPassword = ""]
    [BSTR strLocale = ""]
    [BSTR strAuthority = ""]
    [long iSecurityFlags = 0]
    [objWbemNamedValueSet = Null]
)
```

`ConnectServer()` can run into problems if you try to connect through an ASP page in an Internet Information Services (IIS) Web server. The default account that runs IIS is `IUSR_Computername`, and this name is not recognized by WMI. It naturally declines your request for a connection as a result. If you need to execute scripts through an ASP page, either change the account that runs IIS to an account that can also run WMI or use the WMI Permission Editor (`wbemperm.exe`) on the default IIS account.

With SQL Server, the `objWbemNamedValueSet` parameter is used for passing a WMI context object with SQL Server connection settings, as discussed in Chapter 9. Demonstration of how it's used is shown in Chapter 12.

The SWbemServices Object

The `SWbemServices` object represents a connection to a namespace. Management applications use the `SWbemServices` object to access WMI services on the host computer.

The main type of operations that you will do through the `SWbemServices` object circulates around retrieving classes and instances. There is functionality to get and delete both classes and instances. `SWbemServices.Get()` returns a

`SWbemWbemObject` to the management applications, and that object can be used to create a new instance or to modify an existing instance.

In spite of get operations, the majority of methods that you can execute through the `SWbemServices` object return a collection object of classes or instances. These operations, however, can be done (and probably should be done) through *WMI Query Language* (WQL). WQL gives you more control over the data that is returned; therefore, you can improve performance both in the management application and on the network by slimming down the information about the classes or instances that you retrieve.

Finally, one of the most interesting portions of the `SWbemServices` object is its capability to bind an `SWbemEventSink` object in order to receive the notifications from an event query. Your management application can use this feature to implement event handlers for the events. That way, you can gain more control over your environment.

Get Instance or Class

The `SWbemServices.Get()` method is often used within WMI. There are two purposes to this method. First, you can use this method to get a specific managed object. This code gets you the Northwind database:

```
' Create the Locator-Instance
Set SWbemLocator = CreateObject("WbemScripting.SWbemLocator")
' Make the connection and get Services-Instance
Set SWbemServices = SWbemLocator.ConnectServer("YourServer", _
                             "root/MicrosoftSqlServer")
' Set impersonationlevel
SWbemServices.Security_.ImpersonationLevel = 3
' Build the objectPath to the Northwind-database
strObjectPath = "MSSQL_Database.Name='Northwind'," &_
             "SQLServerName='YourServer'"

' Get the instance of the Northwind-database
Set SWbemObject = SWbemServices.Get(strObjectPath)

' Echoes the disk-space available for the db-storage
WScript.Echo SWbemObject.SpaceAvailable
```

A returned instance of a `SWbemServices.Get()` call is a `SWbemObject` object. With it, you can do things such as cloning, deleting, or modifying the object. The second use for `SWbemServices.Get()` is to get the class definition that is needed to spawn a new managed object. For example, in order to create a new database column, use the following code:

```
' Get a class-definition
Set ClassDef = SWbemServices.Get("MSSQL_Column")
```

```
' Spawn a class-instance
Set SWbemObject = ClassDef.SpawnInstance_()

' Set some properties
...

' Write the new instance to your SQL Server
SWbemObject.Put_()
```

You can also use the shorthand approach that allows you to chain several method calls into a single line or two:

```
' Get a class and spawn a class-instance
Set SWbemObj = SWbemServices.Get("MSSQL_Column").SpawnInstance_()

' Set some properties
...

' Write the new column-instance
SWbemObject.Put_()
```

Enumerating Instances

The SWbemServices.InstancesOf() method is used to return all instances of a particular class. The following example enumerates all SQL Server instances (SQL Server 2000 can have up to 16 named instances on one machine) on the WMI host machine and prints name and version strings for each instance:

```
' Create the Locator-Instance
Set SWbemLocator = CreateObject("WbemScripting.SWbemLocator")
' Make the connection and get Services-Instance
Set SWbemServices = SWbemLocator.ConnectServer("SERVER", _
                    "root/MicrosoftSqlServer")
' Set impersonationlevel
SWbemServices.Security_.ImpersonationLevel = 3
Set SWbemObjectSet = SWbemServices.InstancesOf("MSSQL_SQLServer")
For Each SWbemObject In SWbemObjectSet
    WScript.Echo SWbemObject.Name & ": " &_
                 SWbemObject.VersionString
Next
```

Although these enumeration methods are common, it is preferable to use WQL to build your own enumeration queries. WQL enables you to decide for yourself what you want returned. These examples return all properties of each instance, while WQL can return just the properties that you need. This way, you do not get a lot of unconsumed data that you never intended to use (or did not want) at all.

Executing Queries

You call `SWbemServices.ExecQuery()` to execute a WMI Query Language statement over a namespace. A query like that commonly returns a collection object (as in the methods that we have seen so far). `SWbemServices.Exec-NotificationQuery()`, on the other hand, is used with the intention that the management application knows how to handle events. Notification queries set up the management application to poll for events, and it will return notification events as they occur. For example, you will be notified when an instance is created, deleted, or modified.

Overview: The SWbemServices Object

The `SWbemServices` object represents a connection pointer to a WMI namespace on a WMI host computer (see Table 10.2).

Get( )

Use this method to get a class or an instance:

```
SWbemObject Get (
    [BSTR strObjectPath = ""]
```

Table 10.2   Overview of the `SWbemServices` Object

Method	Return Type	Description
Get	SWbemObject	Get a class or instance
Delete		Delete a class or instance
InstancesOf	SWbemObjectSet	Enumerate instances of a class
SubclassesOf	SWbemObjectSet	Enumerate subclasses of a class
ExecQuery	SWbemObjectSet	Execute a query
AssociatorsOf	SWbemObjectSet	Enumerate Associators of a class or instance
ReferencesTo	SWbemObjectSet	Enumerate References to a class or instance
ExecNotificationQuery	SWbemEventSource	Execute a query for event-Notification
ExecMethod	SWbemObject	Execute a method
Property	**Data Type**	**Description**
Security_	SWbemSecurity	Security settings

```
      [long iFlags = 0]
      [objWbemNamedValueSet = Null]
   )
```

The `strObjectPath` parameter should be a valid objectPath that can be the full path to an instance or the name of a class within the current namespace. `iFlags` is reserved by WMI and should not be anything but 0.

GetAsync( )

Use this method to asynchronously get a class or an instance:

```
   void GetAsync (
      objWbemSink
      [BSTR strObjectPath = ""]
      [long iFlags = 0]
      [objWbemNamedValueSet = Null]
      [objWbemAsyncContext = Null]
   )
```

Pass the `objWbemSink` event sink with this call in order to receive a notification when the object is ready. Additionally, `iFlags` can be used to specify whether a status report is sent or not (by using `wbemFlagSendStatus` or `wbemFlagDontSendStatus`).

Delete( )

Use this method to delete the class or instance specified in `strObjectPath`:

```
   void Delete (
      BSTR strObjectPath
      [long iFlags = 0]
      [objWbemNamedValueSet = Null]
   )
```

`iFlags` is reserved by WMI.

DeleteAsync( )

Use this method to asynchronously delete the class or instance that is specified in `strObjectPath`:

```
   void DeleteAsync (
      objWbemSink
      BSTR strObjectPath
      [long iFlags = 0]
```

```
    [objWbemNamedValueSet = Null]
    [objWbemAsyncContext = Null]
)
```

Pass the event sink in order to receive the call results. The `iFlags` parameter is used to indicate whether the status should be sent during the operation (by using `wbemFlagSendStatus` or `wbemFlagDontSendStatus`).

InstancesOf( )

Use this method to return an enumerator of the instances of class `strClass`:

```
SWbemObjectSet InstancesOf (
    BSTR strClass
    [long iFlags = wbemFlagReturnImmediately]
    [objWbemNamedValueSet = Null]
)
```

The `iFlag` parameter is used to set `wbemFlagForwardOnly`, `wbemFlag-Bidirectional`, `wbemFlagReturnImmediately`, `wbemFlagReturnWhen-Complete`, `wbemQueryFlagShallow`, and `wbemQueryFlagDeep`.

InstancesOfAsync( )

Use this method to asynchronously receive each object from the query to the event sink until no more objects are in the queue:

```
void InstancesOfAsync (
    objWbemSink
    BSTR strClass
    [long iFlags = 0]
    [objWbemNamedValueSet = Null]
    [objWbemAsyncContext = Null]
)
```

The `iFlag` parameter is used as follows: `wbemFlagForwardOnly`, `wbem-FlagBidirectional`, `wbemQueryFlagShallow`, `wbemQueryFlagDeep`, `wbemFlagSendStatus`, and `wbemFlagDontSendStatus`.

SubclassesOf( )

Use this method to return an enumerator of the subclasses of superclass `strSuperClass`:

```
SWbemObjectSet SubclassesOf (
    [BSTR strSuperclass = ""]
    [long iFlags = wbemFlagReturnImmediately+wbemQueryFlagDeep]
```

```
      [objWbemNamedValueSet = Null]
  )
```

The `iFlag` parameter can be set to `wbemQueryFlagShallow`, `wbemQuery-FlagDeep`, `wbemFlagReturnImmediately`, or `wbemFlagReturnWhen-Complete`.

SubclassesOfAsync( )

Use this method to asynchronously receive each subclass from the query to the event sink until no more objects are in the queue:

```
void SubclassesOfAsync (
    objWbemSink
    [BSTR strSuperclass = ""]
    [long iFlags = wbemQueryFlagDeep]
    [objWbemNamedValueSet = Null]
    [objWbemAsyncContext = Null]
  )
```

The `iFlag` parameter can be set to `wbemQueryFlagShallow`, `wbemQuery-FlagDeep`, `wbemFlagSendStatus`, or `wbemFlagDontSendStatus`.

ExecQuery( )

Use this method to execute the WQL statement in `strQuery`:

```
SWbemObjectSet ExecQuery (
    BSTR strQuery
    [BSTR strQueryLanguage = "WQL"]
    [long iFlags = wbemFlagReturnImmediately]
    [objWbemNamedValueSet = Null]
  )
```

`iFlags` can be `wbemFlagForwardOnly`, `wbemFlagBiDirectional`, `wbem-FlagReturnImmediately`, `wbemFlagReturnWhenComplete`, and `wbem-QueryFlagPrototype`.

ExecQueryAsync( )

Use this method to asynchronously receive each class or instance from the WQL statement in `strQuery` to the event sink until no more objects are in the queue:

```
void ExecQueryAsync (
    objWbemSink
    BSTR strQuery
```

```
    [BSTR strQueryLanguage = "WQL"]
    [long iFlags = 0]
    [objWbemNamedValueSet = Null]
    [objWbemAsyncContext = Null]
)
```

The direction and status are set in `iFlags` through `wbemFlagBiDirectional`, `wbemFlagSendStatus`, `wbemFlagDontSendStatus`, and `wbemFlagQueryPrototype`.

AssociatorsOf( )

Use this method to return the associators of `strObjectPath`:

```
SWbemObjectSet AssociatorsOf (
    BSTR strObjectPath
    [BSTR strAssocClass = ""]
    [BSTR strResultClass = ""]
    [BSTR strResultRole = ""]
    [BSTR strRole = ""]
    [VARIANT_BOOL bClassesOnly = 0]
    [VARIANT_BOOL bSchemaOnly = 0]
    [BSTR strRequiredAssocQualifier = ""]
    [BSTR strRequiredQualifier = ""]
    [long iFlags = wbemFlagReturnImmediately]
    [objWbemNamedValueSet = Null]
)
```

The `iFlags` can be `wbemFlagForwardOnly`, `wbemFlagBidirectional`, `wbemFlagReturnImmediately`, or `wbemFlagReturnWhenComplete`.

AssociatorsOfAsync( )

Use this method to asynchronously receive each object from the query to the event sink until no more objects are in the queue:

```
void AssociatorsOfAsync (
    objWbemSink
    BSTR strObjectPath
    [BSTR strAssocClass = ""]
    [BSTR strResultClass = ""]
    [BSTR strResultRole = ""]
    [BSTR strRole = ""]
    [VARIANT_BOOL bClassesOnly = 0]
    [VARIANT_BOOL bSchemaOnly = 0]
    [BSTR strRequiredAssocQualifier = ""]
```

```
        [BSTR strRequiredQualifier = ""]
        [long iFlags = 0]
        [objWbemNamedValueSet = Null]
        [objWbemAsyncContext = Null]
    )
```

The iFlags can be wbemFlagForwardOnly, wbemFlagBidirectional, wbemFlagSendStatus, or wbemFlagDontSendStatus.

ReferencesTo( )

Use this method to get the references to strObjectPath:

```
SWbemObjectSet ReferencesTo (
    BSTR strObjectPath
    [BSTR strResultClass = ""]
    [BSTR strRole = ""]
    [VARIANT_BOOL bClassesOnly = 0]
    [VARIANT_BOOL bSchemaOnly = 0]
    [BSTR strRequiredQualifier = ""]
    [long iFlags = wbemFlagReturnImmediately]
    [objWbemNamedValueSet = Null]
)
```

Specify iFlags for wbemFlagForwardOnly, wbemFlagBidirectional, wbemFlagReturnImmediately, or wbemFlagReturnWhenComplete.

ReferencesToAsync( )

Use this method to asynchronously receive each object from the query to the event sink until no more objects are in the queue:

```
void ReferencesToAsync (
    objWbemSink
    BSTR strObjectPath
    [BSTR strResultClass = ""]
    [BSTR strRole = ""]
    [VARIANT_BOOL bClassesOnly = 0]
    [VARIANT_BOOL bSchemaOnly = 0]
    [BSTR strRequiredQualifier = ""]
    [long iFlags = 0]
    [objWbemNamedValueSet = Null]
    [objWbemAsyncContext = Null]
)
```

Specify iFlags for wbemFlagForwardOnly, wbemFlagBidirectional, wbemFlagSendStatus, or wbemFlagDontSendStatus.

ExecNotificationQuery( )

Use this method to execute a query in order to receive notification events:

```
SWbemEventSource ExecNotificationQuery (
    BSTR strQuery
    [BSTR strQueryLanguage = "WQL"]
    [long iFlags =
     wbemFlagReturnImmediately+wbemFlagForwardOnly]
    [objWbemNamedValueSet = Null]
)
```

You will use the returned SWbemEventSource object to receive them. The iFlags can be set as wbemFlagForwardOnly, wbemFlagBidirectional, wbemFlagReturnImmediately, or wbemFlagReturnWhenComplete.

ExecNotificationQueryAsync( )

Use this method to execute a query in order to asynchronously receive notification events through the event sink:

```
void ExecNotificationQueryAsync (
    objWbemSink
    BSTR strQuery
    [BSTR strQueryLanguage = "WQL"]
    [long iFlags =
     wbemFlagReturnImmediately+wbemFlagForwardOnly]
    [objWbemNamedValueSet = Null]
    [objWbemAsyncContext = Null]
)
```

You will use the returned SWbemEventSource object to receive them. The iFlags can be set as wbemFlagBidirectional, wbemFlagSendStatus, or wbemFlagDontSendStatus.

ExecMethod( )

Use this method to execute the method strMethodName on the object in strObjectPath:

```
SWbemObject ExecMethod (
    BSTR strObjectPath
    BSTR strMethodName
    [objWbemInParameters = Null]
    [long iFlags = 0]
    [objWbemNamedValueSet = Null]
)
```

The iFlags parameter is reserved by WMI.

ExecMethodAsync( )

Use this method to asynchronously execute a method on the object in `strOb-jectPath` in order to receive the result through the event sink:

```
void ExecMethodAsync (
    objWbemSink
    BSTR strObjectPath
    BSTR strMethodName
    [objWbemInParameters = Null]
    [long iFlags = 0]
    [objWbemNamedValueSet = Null]
    [objWbemAsyncContext = Null]
)
```

The `iFlags` parameter is reserved by WMI.

SWbemObject

The `SWbemObject` is a single class or an instance of a class. When single, it is typically the result of a `SWbemServices.Get()` call.

On the other hand, when you enumerate a class, you might have to navigate multiple `SWbemObjects`. To make that process easier, they are returned in an `SWbemObjectSet`.

Overview: The SWbemObjectSet

`SWbemobject` is a collection object that supports the common features that are found in an enumerator object (see Table 10.3).

NOTE

The `SWbemObjectSet.Item()` **method is** `Item(strObjectPath)`. **While some collections require an index or a name, this collection object expects an object path.**

Table 10.3 `SWbemObjectSet` Object

Method	Return Type	Description
Item	SWbemObject	Get an object from the collection
Count	long	Count objects in the collection
Property	**Data Type**	**Description**
Security_	SWbemSecurity	Security settings

The SWbemObject Object

When an instance is represented in an SWbemObject, the properties and methods that are exposed by the instance are available through the collection references Methods_ and Properties_. These are implemented as properties of the SWbemObject, but they support direct access. Thanks to direct access, you never need to explicitly go through the collection references in order to call a method or to read or write a property. It is enough for you to call a method, for example, as if the method were native to the class. For example, for the property MailSender, the following two statements are equivalent:

```
' Without Direct Access
obj.Properties_.Item("MailSender").Value
' With Direct Access
ObjInstance.MailSender
```

With the properties of the SWbemObject being few and named with a trailing underscore, chances are that a property of an instance will clash with the name of a property in the SWbemObject. The odds are slightly better (or worse) when it comes to methods. A method might have the same name in both SWbemObject and in a class instance—in which case you would go through the SWbemObject.ExecMethod_() method. The immediate difference between SWbemObject.Methods_ and SWbemObject.ExecMethod_() is that you use the former to execute the latter. You get an object through the Methods_ property's Item() method. The returned object has a property called InParameters. InParameters can be used to locate and set the desired values for parameters that are passed with the method call and then to call SWbemObject.ExecMethod_() with the object representing the method in the parameter call. SWbemObject.ExecMethod_() is the most useful with languages that do not support output parameters. They would use the OutParameters property to locate the output parameters from the executed method.

The SWbemObject can be used in three ways to create a new managed object. First, we will use SWbemServices.Get() to retrieve the class for the managed object, and then we will call SWbemObject.SpawnInstance_() for a new instance. Then, we will set the key properties of the class, and SWbemObject.Put_() will be the instance. Please note that we are ignoring any other error checking than what will be trapped and reported by default in Windows Script Host.

```
' Get a services object
Set SWbemServices = _
GetObject("Winmgmts://myServer/Root/MicrosoftSQLServer")
' Set impersonationlevel
```

```
SWbemServices.Security_.ImpersonationLevel = 3
' Get the class
Set clsDef = SWbemServices.Get("MSSQL_Login")
' Spawn a class-instance
Set objSQLLogin = clsDef.SpawnInstance_()
' Set the Name-property
objSQLLogin.Name = "SomeNewLogin"
' Set the SQLServerName-property
objSQLLogin.SQLServerName = "myServer"
' Write the instance
objSQLLogin.Put_()
```

The second approach to creating a new login requires an existing login. This example is built on the fact that changing a key property and calling `SWbemObject.Put_()` does not update an object. Because WMI only sees an instance that has new key properties at `SWbemObject`, `Put_()`, it creates a new instance.

```
' Placeholder for the instance
Dim objSQLLogin
' For cosmetic purposes only
Dim strPath, strNS
' WMI host computer and namespace
strNS = "Winmgmts://myServer/Root/MicrosoftSQLServer"
' Path to the managed object
strPath = "MSSQL_Login.Name='SomeNewLogin',SQLServerName='myServer'"
' objSQLLogin is a SWbemObject
Set objSQLLogin = GetObject(strNS & ":" & strPath)
' Let's change the name
objSQLLogin.Name = "SomeOtherLogin"
' And Put_() the object
objSQLLogin.Put_()
```

Finally, some classes do not support creation through `SWbemObject.Put_()`. Because a class sometimes needs additional information before it can create an instance, that certain class implements a constructor. In such cases, the constructor is `Instance.Create()`.

`SWbemObject` has its own methods and properties. Furthermore, managed objects expose their own properties (and sometimes methods). As previously mentioned, you can access them as if they were native to `SWbemObject`, and that functionality is called Direct Access. Let's illustrate the point by using our little login from the earlier example:

```
...
Set objSQLLogin = GetObject(strNS & ":" & strPath)
' Print the number of properties
WScript.Echo objSQLLogin.Properties_.Count
' Print name and value of each property
For Each objProperty In objSQLLogin.Properties_
```

```
        WScript.Echo objProperty.Name & "=" & objProperty.Value
    Next
    ...
```

Several properties are echoed to the screen. Not all of them have values, though. They are the properties that belong to the class. When accessing individual properties, you can omit `Properties_` and they will still be available. Because the `SWbemObject` is primarily not a collection of properties, however, the following code is invalid:

```
' ! Error !
For Each objProperty In objSQLLogin
    WScript.Echo objProperty.Name & "=" & objProperty.Value
Next
```

Enumerating several instances returns a bunch of `SWbemObjects` in an `SWbemObjectSet`. Properties are contained in an `SWbemPropertySet` object, so these properties actually exist in the same location from which they are accessed when you iterate the collection (see Table 10.4).

Overview: The SWbemObject Object

`Put_()`

Use this method to put the current class or instance:

```
SWbemObjectPath Put_ (
    [long iFlags = wbemChangeFlagCreateOrUpdate]
    [objWbemNamedValueSet = Null]
)
```

The `iFlags` parameter can be used to specify `wbemChangeFlagUpdateCompatible`, `wbemChangeFlagUpdateSafeMode`, `WbemChangeFlagUpdateForceMode`, `wbemChangeFlagCreateOrUpdate`, `wbemChangeFlagCreateOnly`, `wbemChangeFlagUpdateOnly`, `wbemFlagReturnImmediately`, and `wbemFlagReturnWhenComplete`.

PutAsync_()

Use this method to asynchronously put the current class or instance and to receive a notification through the event sink:

```
void PutAsync_ (
    objWbemSink
    [long iFlags = wbemChangeFlagCreateOrUpdate]
    [objWbemNamedValueSet = Null]
    [objWbemAsyncContext = Null]
)
```

Table 10.4   SWbemObject Object

Method	Return Type	Description
Put_	SwbemObjectPath	Write current object
Delete_		Delete current object
Instances_	SwbemObjectSet	Enumerate instances of current object
Subclasses_	SwbemObjectSet	Enumerate subclasses of current class
Associators_	SwbemObjectSet	Enumerate Associators of current object
References_	SwbemObjectSet	Enumerate References to current object
ExecMethod_	SWbemObject	Execute a method of current object
Clone_	SWbemObject	Clone current object
GetObjectText_	Bstr	Retrieve MOF representation of object
SpawnDerivedClass_	SWbemObject	Spawn a subclass of current object
SpawnInstance_	SWbemObject	Spawn an instance of current object
CompareTo_	Boolean	Compare current object with another object
Derivation_	Variant	Array containing the inheritance tree
Property	**Data Type**	**Description**
Qualifiers_	SwbemQualifierSet	Qualifiers collection
Properties_	SwbemPropertySet	Properties collection
Methods_	SwbemMethodSet	Methods collection
Path_	SwbemObjectPath	Path information
Security_	SwbemSecurity	Security settings

The iFlags parameter can be set to wbemChangeFlagUpdateCompatible, wbemChangeFlagUpdateSafeMode, WbemChangeFlagUpdateForceMode, wbemChangeFlagCreateOrUpdate, wbemChangeFlagCreateOnly, wbemChangeFlagUpdateOnly, wbemFlagReturnImmediately, wbemFlagReturnWhenComplete, wbemFlagSendStatus, or wbemFlagDontSendStatus.

Delete_( )

Use this method to delete the current class or instance:

```
void Delete_ (
    [long iFlags = 0]
    [objWbemNamedValueSet = Null]
)
```

iFlags is reserved by WMI.

DeleteAsync_( )

Use this method to asynchronously delete the current class or instance and to receive a notification through the event sink:

```
void DeleteAsync_ (
    objWbemSink
    [long iFlags = 0]
    [objWbemNamedValueSet = Null]
    [objWbemAsyncContext = Null]
)
```

The iFlags parameter can be wbemFlagSendStatus or wbemFlag-DontSendStatus.

Instances_( )

Use this method to return an enumerator of the instances of the current class:

```
SWbemObjectSet Instances_ (
    [long iFlags = wbemFlagReturnImmediately]
    [objWbemNamedValueSet = Null]
)
```

The iFlag parameter is reserved by WMI.

InstancesAsync_( )

Use this method to asynchronously receive each instance of the current class to the event sink until no more objects are in the queue:

```
void InstancesAsync_ (
    objWbemSink
    [long iFlags = 0]
    [objWbemNamedValueSet = Null]
    [objWbemAsyncContext = Null]
)
```

The iFlag parameter can be set to wbemFlagSendStatus or wbemFlag-DontSendStatus.

Subclasses_( )

Use this method to return the subclasses of the current class or instance:

```
SWbemObjectSet Subclasses_ (
    [long iFlags = wbemFlagReturnImmediately+wbemQueryFlagDeep]
    [objWbemNamedValueSet = Null]
)
```

The `iFlags` parameter can be `wbemQueryFlagDeep`, `wbemQueryFlagShallow`, `wbemFlagReturnImmediately`, or `wbemFlagReturnWhenComplete`.

SubclassesAsync_( )

Use this method to asynchronously receive each subclass from the query to the event sink until no more subclasses are in the queue:

```
void SubclassesAsync_ (
    objWbemSink
    [long iFlags = wbemQueryFlagDeep]
    [objWbemNamedValueSet = Null]
    [objWbemAsyncContext = Null]
)
```

The `iFlags` parameter can be `wbemQueryFlagDeep`, `wbemQueryFlagShallow`, `wbemFlagSendStatus`, or `wbemFlagDontSendStatus`.

Associators_( )

Use this method to return the associators of the current class or instance:

```
SWbemObjectSet Associators_ (
    [BSTR strAssocClass = ""]
    [BSTR strResultClass = ""]
    [BSTR strResultRole = ""]
    [BSTR strRole = ""]
    [VARIANT_BOOL bClassesOnly = 0]
    [VARIANT_BOOL bSchemaOnly = 0]
    [BSTR strRequiredAssocQualifier = ""]
    [BSTR strRequiredQualifier = ""]
    [long iFlags = wbemFlagReturnImmediately]
    [objWbemNamedValueSet = Null]
)
```

The `iFlags` parameter can be `wbemFlagForwardOnly`, `wbemFlagBidirectional`, `wbemFlagReturnImmediately`, or `wbemFlagReturnWhenComplete`.

AssociatorsAsync_( )

Use this method to asynchronously receive the associators of the class or instance:

```
void AssociatorsAsync_ (
    objWbemSink
    [BSTR strAssocClass = ""]
    [BSTR strResultClass = ""]
```

```
        [BSTR strResultRole = ""]
        [BSTR strRole = ""]
        [VARIANT_BOOL bClassesOnly = 0]
        [VARIANT_BOOL bSchemaOnly = 0]
        [BSTR strRequiredAssocQualifier = ""]
        [BSTR strRequiredQualifier = ""]
        [long iFlags = 0]
        [objWbemNamedValueSet = Null]
        [objWbemAsyncContext = Null]
    )
```

The `iFlags` parameter can be `wbemFlagForwardOnly`, `wbemFlagBidi-rectional`, `wbemFlagSendStatus`, or `wbemFlagDontSendStatus`.

References_( )

Use this method to return the references that are pointing to the current class or instance:

```
    SWbemObjectSet References_ (
        [BSTR strResultClass = ""]
        [BSTR strRole = ""]
        [VARIANT_BOOL bClassesOnly = 0]
        [VARIANT_BOOL bSchemaOnly = 0]
        [BSTR strRequiredQualifier = ""]
        [long iFlags = wbemFlagReturnImmediately]
        [objWbemNamedValueSet = Null]
    )
```

The `iFlags` parameter can be `wbemFlagForwardOnly`, `wbemFlagBidi-rectional`, `wbemFlagReturnImmediately`, or `wbemFlagReturnWhen-Complete`.

ReferencesAsync_( )

Use this method to asynchronously receive the references of the current class or instance:

```
    void ReferencesAsync_ (
        objWbemSink
        [BSTR strResultClass = ""]
        [BSTR strRole = ""]
        [VARIANT_BOOL bClassesOnly = 0]
        [VARIANT_BOOL bSchemaOnly = 0]
        [BSTR strRequiredQualifier = ""]
        [long iFlags = 0]
```

```
    [objWbemNamedValueSet = Null]
    [objWbemAsyncContext = Null]
)
```

The iFlags parameter can be wbemFlagForwardOnly, wbemFlagBidi-rectional, wbemFlagSendStatus, or wbemFlagDontSendStatus.

ExecMethod_( )

Use this method to execute a method on the object:

```
SWbemObject ExecMethod_ (
    BSTR strMethodName
    [objWbemInParameters = Null]
    [long iFlags = 0]
    [objWbemNamedValueSet = Null]
)
```

In strObjectPath, the iFlags parameter is reserved by WMI.

ExecMethodAsync_( )

Use this method to asynchronously execute a method on the object in strObjectPath and to receive the result through the event sink:

```
void ExecMethodAsync_ (
    objWbemSink
    BSTR strMethodName
    [objWbemInParameters = Null]
    [long iFlags = 0]
    [objWbemNamedValueSet = Null]
    [objWbemAsyncContext = Null]
)
```

The iFlags parameter can be set to wbemFlagSendStatus or wbemFlag-DontSendStatus.

GetObjectText_( )

Use this method to return the MOF representation of the current object:

```
BSTR GetObjectText_ (
    [long iFlags = 0]
)
```

iFlags is reserved by WMI.

SpawnDerivedClass_( )

Use this method to create a new derived class from the object:

```
SWbemObject SpawnDerivedClass_ (
    [long iFlags = 0]
)
```

`iFlags` is reserved by WMI.

SpawnInstance_( )

Use this method to create a new instance of a class:

```
SWbemObject SpawnInstance_ (
    [long iFlags = 0]
)
```

`iFlags` is reserved by WMI.

CompareTo_( )

Use this method to compare the current object against `objWbemObject`:

```
VARIANT_BOOL CompareTo_ (
    objWbemObject
    [long iFlags = wbemComparisonFlagIncludeAll]
}
```

`iFlags` specifies the type of comparison by using a `wbemComparisonEnum`.

The SWbemSink Object

The `SWbemSink` object forwards event notifications to your management applications. WMI supports events quite widely, so with Windows Script Host, you can easily integrate event handling into your code. The majority of popular scripting languages support Windows Script Host, but although Perl and Python (for example) support Windows Script Host, they also have native support for events. Essentially, how your code handles events depends on what language you are using and how you decide to implement that language. The only sure thing that I can say is that if the scripting language does not have native support for events, you will be using Windows Script Host.

Events are the results of asynchronous operations in WMI. Each method in the Scripting API has an asynchronous counterpart. These methods can be passed a `SWbemSink` object in order to notify your management applications of events. The events in WMI fire at different occasions, such as when the status of a call completes or when a call completes. SWbemSink supplies four events with which your script code can interact. It is as easy as implementing subroutines that are executed due to the events, and for this reason, Windows Script Host provides a special parameter in its CreateObject() method. While SWbemSink names the events, your application can make local subroutines that have the same names as the events (but with a prefix). By informing Windows Script Host of the prefix, the implemented events will be called as they are fired. The four events of SWbemSink are listed in Table 10.5.

Overview: The SWbemSink Object

The SWbemSink object provides a **Cancel()** method that is used to cancel any further event notifications. After calling this method, you need to destroy the object by undefining it with *nothing* or with an empty VT_DISPATCH variant if you are using a language other than VBScript. Finally, events do not just fire. They pass parameters that enable further interaction with the managed objects that are being operated on, so let's look at them in detail.

OnCompleted

OnCompleted can be used to notify the client of a successful operation that has completed or to notify the client of an error that occurred during processing. If it completes all of the processing, you can use it to clean up the garbage and to free memory that has been allocated for the management application:

```
OnCompleted (
    WbemErrorEnum iHResult,
    SWbemObject objWbemErrorObject,
    SWbemNamedValueSet objWbemAsyncContext
)
```

Table 10.5 SWbemSink Object

Method	Description
Cancel	Cancels asynchronous operations
Event	**Fires**
OnCompleted	When an asynchronous call is complete
OnObjectPut	When an asynchronous put operation is complete
OnObjectReady	When an asynchronous operation returns an object
OnProgress	When an asynchronous operation returns the status of a call in progress

`Hresult` contains an integer value that represents the COM return value. A value of zero means that no errors occurred and that anything is an error code. `SWbemLastError` is an error object that you can use to examine an error more in depth, and the `SWbemNamedValueSet` can be used to locate the origin of the asynchronous call in case it was made in a series of multiple calls.

OnObjectPut

Because `OnObjectPut` fired when an instance was put, you can use it to notify the client that the operation was a success. In case you need to do further processing on the object, such as creating an association, you can use the returned object path to point the reference in the association class to your newly created instance:

```
OnObjectPut (
    SWbemObjectPath objWbemObjectPath,
    SWbemNamedValueSet objWbemAsyncContext
)
```

`SWbemObjectPath` is an object of the same name, and it can be used to extract the object path or WMI moniker to the just-created instance or class. The `SWbemNamedValueSet` can be used to locate the origin of the asynchronous call in case it was made in a series of multiple calls.

OnObjectReady

`OnObjectReady` can encapsulate the logic that is used to do the operations for which the requested object was fetched:

```
OnObjectPut (
    SWbemObject objWbemObject,
    SWbemNamedValueSet objWbemAsyncContext
)
```

`SWbemObject` contains the object that was the result of an asynchronous operation. It is a ready object, and when a set of objects is returned, `OnObjectReady` is called for each object as it is returned from the asynchronous call. The `SWbemNamedValueSet` can be used to locate the origin of the asynchronous call in case it was made in a series of multiple calls.

OnProgress

`OnProgress` can be used to implement a system in which the management application notifies the client of the current status, how much is left to do, what is currently being done, and so on. This event is the only event that you must flag for, so by setting the `wbemFlagSendStatus` (0x80) flag in your asynchronous call, you will receive status notifications unless the WMI Provider has not implemented it.

```
OnProgress (
    long iUpperBound,
    long iCurrent,
    BSTR strMessage,
    SWbemNamedValueSet* objWbemAsyncContext
)
```

The `UpperBound` parameter is the total number of tasks to complete, and `CurrentIndex` is the current position in the task queue. `Message` is a textual description of the task that is being processed, and `SWbemNamedValueSet` can be used to locate the origin of the asynchronous call in case it was made in a series of multiple calls.

The SWbemMethod and SWbemProperty Objects

A method is part of a MethodSet. There are two purposes for `SWbemMethod`. The first one is to provide a way for examining a method definition. The second is to allow script languages that do not support output parameters to retrieve these parameters. The attribute counterpart to `SWbemMethod` is `SWbemProperty`. This property is contained within an `SWbemPropertySet` and is used to read or write a property—although it is unrealistic that you would write a property when you have direct access. Refer to Tables 10.6 through 10.9.

Table 10.6 SWbemMethodSet Object

Method	Return Type	Description
Item	SWbemMethod	Get object from the collection
Count	long	Count objects in the collection

Table 10.7 SWbemMethod Object

Property	Data Type	Description
Name	Bstr	The name of the method
Origin	Bstr	Originating class of the method
InParameters	SWbemObject	Input-parameters of the method
OutParameters	SWbemObject	Output-parameters for the method
Qualifiers_	SWbemQualifierSet	Qualifiers-collection

Table 10.8 SWbemPropertySet Object

Method	Return Type	Description
Item	SWbemProperty	Get an object from the collection
Count	long	Count objects in the collection
Add	SWbemProperty	Add an object to the collection
Remove		Remove an object from the collection

Table 10.9 SWbemProperty Object

Property	Data Type	Description
Value	Variant	Value of the property
Name	Bstr	Name of the property
IsLocal	Boolean	Boolean for whether property is local to the class
Origin	Bstr	Originating class of the property
CIMType	WbemCimTypeEnum	CIM-type of the property
Qualifiers_	SWbemQualifierSet	Qualifiers-collection
IsArray	Boolean	Boolean for whether property is an array

Overview: The SWbemMethodSet Collection, SWbemMethod Object SWbemPropertySet Collection, and SWbemProperty Objects

The Item() method returns a SWbemMethod object, and the Count() method returns the number of SWbemMethod objects in the SWbemMethodSet. This item( ) method takes the name of the method you want to access.

Item( )

```
SWbemMethod Item (
   BSTR strName
   [long iFlags = 0]
)
```

For the SwbemPropertySet, the Item() method returns a SWbemProperty object. The Add() and Remove() methods are used to add a property and remove a property respectively from the SwbemPropertySet collection object.

Item( )

```
SWbemProperty Item (
    BSTR strName
    [long iFlags = 0]
)
```

Add( )

```
SWbemProperty Add (
    BSTR strName =
    WbemCimtypeEnum iCimType =
    [VARIANT_BOOL bIsArray = 0]
    [long iFlags = 0]
)
```

Remove( )

```
void Remove (
    BSTR strName
    [long iFlags = 0]
)
```

The SWbemPrivilegeSet Object

The `PrivilegeSet` is a collection object of Windows NT/2000 privileges. You can either add a privilege by using the `Add()` method (in which case you use a `WbemPrivilegeEnum` constant), or by using `AddAsString()` (which is a textual representation of the enumerated constants). You can find out the textual representation by removing the `WbemPrivilege` part of a constant and replacing it with `Se`. Then, you add a trailing `Privilege` to it, and you have a string that looks like, say, `SeCreateTokenPrivilege`. You can gain more information about Privileges from the `SWbemPrivilegeObject` and from Table 10.10.

Overview: The SwbemPrivilegeSet Collection Object

The `Item()` method returns a `SWbemPrivilege` object from the collection. You can use the `SWbemPrivilegeSet` and the `Item()` method to explore the privileges you've been granted. `Add()` will put a new `SWbemPrivilege` object in the collection. For adding privileges that way, you need to use a `WbemPrivilege-Enum`. Some people will prefer `AddAsString()`, which does the same thing as

Table 10.10 SWbemPrivilegeSet Object

Method	Return Type	Description
Item	SWbemPrivilege	Get an object from the collection
Count	long	Count objects in the collection
Add	SWbemPrivilege	Add an object to the collection
Remove		Remove an object from the collection
DeleteAll		Delete all object in the collection
AddAsString	SWbemPrivilege	Add an object to the collection

Add(), because it takes an easy to read privilege string. Remove() removes a single object from the collection, and DeleteAll() will get rid of all objects.

Item( )

```
SWbemPrivilege Item (
    WbemPrivilegeEnum iPrivilege
)
```

Add( )

```
SWbemPrivilege Add (
    WbemPrivilegeEnum iPrivilege
    [VARIANT_BOOL bIsEnabled = -1]
)
```

Remove( )

```
void Remove (
    WbemPrivilegeEnum iPrivilege
)
```

AddAsString( )

```
SWbemPrivilege AddAsString (
    BSTR strPrivilege
    [VARIANT_BOOL bIsEnabled = -1]
)
```

You can use IsEnabled for each SWbemPrivilege object in order to enable and disable privileges. DisplayName provides a textual description of the

Table 10.11 SWbemPrivilege Object

Property	Data Type	Description
IsEnabled	Boolean	Enables the object
Name	Bstr	The name of the object
DisplayName	Bstr	The display name of the object
Identifier	WbemPrivilegeEnum	The object identifier constant

object, and Name and Identifier can be used to address the privilege at this time or at another time, respectively. Refer to Table 10.11.

The SWbemObjectPath Object

The SWbemObjectPath object is referenced through the Path_ property of SWbemObject object. Refer to Table 10.12.

Table 10.12 SWbemObjectPath Object

Method	Return Type	Description
SetAsClass		Set current path to a class
SetAsSingleton		Set current path to an instance
Property	**Data Type**	**Description**
Path	Bstr	Full path to object
RelPath	Bstr	Relative path to object
Server	Bstr	Name of the server
Namespace	Bstr	Namespace path
ParentNamespace	Bstr	Parent namespace path
DisplayName	Bstr	Display name for this path
Class	Bstr	Name of the class
IsClass	Boolean	Path leads to a class
IsSingleton	Boolean	Path leads to an instance
Keys	SWbemNamedValueSet	Key name-value pairs
Security_	SWbemSecurity	Security settings
Locale	Bstr	Locale portion
Authority	Bstr	Authentication portion

Table 10.13 SWbemLastError Object

Method	Return Type	Description
Put_	SWbemObjectPath	Write current object
Delete_		Delete current object
Instances_	SWbemObjectSet	Enumerate instances of current object
Subclasses_	SWbemObjectSet	Enumerate subclasses of current class
Associators_	SWbemObjectSet	Enumerate Associators of current object
References_	SWbemObjectSet	Enumerate References to current object
ExecMethod_	SWbemObject	Execute a method of current object
Clone_	SWbemobject	Clone current object
GetObjectText_	Bstr	Retrieve MOF-definition of object
SpawnDerivedClass_	SWbemObject	Spawn a subclass of current object
SpawnInstance_	SWbemObject	Spawn an instance of current object
CompareTo_	Boolean	Compare current object with another object
Derivation_	Variant Array	The inheritance tree as an array
Property	**Data Type**	**Description**
Qualifiers_	SWbemQualifierSet	Qualifiers-collection
Properties_	SWbemPropertySet	Properties-collection
Methods_	SWbemMethodSet	Methods-collection
Path_	SWbemObjectPath	Path information
Security_	SWbemSecurity	Security Settings

Overview: The SWbemLastError Object

The SWbemLastError object contains error information from a failed method call. Refer to Table 10.13.

See SWbemObject for the methods.

The SWbemNamedValueSet Object

This object is a collection of named values. SWbemNamedValue objects are used to send additional information to a WMI provider. These objects are often called WMI context objects. You fill them with the additional information a management source requires, and pass it with your method call. WMI context objects offer one way of specifying SQL Server security through the provider, such as your username, password, and other connection settings. You'd fill a context object with the SQL Server security information and pass it with your call to ConnectServer(). Refer to Table 10.14.

Overview: The SWbemNamedValueSet Collection Object

Item( )

```
SWbemNamedValue Item (
    BSTR strName
    [long iFlags = 0]
)
```

Add( )

```
SWbemNamedValue Add (
    BSTR strName
    VARIANT varValue
    [long iFlags = 0]
)
```

Remove( )

```
void Remove (
    BSTR strName
    [long iFlags = 0]
)
```

Table 10.14 SWbemNamedValueSet Object

Method	Return Type	Description
Item	SWbemNamedValue	Get object from the collection
Count	long	Count objects in the collection
Add	SWbemNamedValue	Add object to the collection
Remove		Remove object from the collection
Clone	SWbemNamedValueSet	Clone the collection
DeleteAll		Delete all objects in the collection

The SWbemNamedValue Object

This object contains a user-defined, named value (see Table 10.15, SWbem-NamedValue objects).

The SWbemEventSource Object

The SWbemEventSource object is returned after a call to SWbemServices.ExecNotificationQuery. Applications use the object to control the retrieval of events. Refer to Table 10.16.

Overview: The SWbemEventSource Object

NextEvent( )

Use this method to fetch the next event:

```
SWbemObject NextEvent (
    [long iTimeoutMs = -1]
)
```

This method fetches the next event either immediately or waits for the milliseconds that are specified in iTimeoutMs milliseconds before fetching the event.

Table 10.15 SWbemNamedValue **Object**

Method	Return Type	Description
Value	Variant	The value of the object
Name	Bstr	The name of the object

Table 10.16 SWbemEventSource **Object**

Method	Return Type	Description
NextEvent	SWbemObject	Fetch the next event
Property	**Data Type**	**Description**
Security_	SWbemSecurity	Security settings

Method Return Values

The WMI provider for SQL Server often returns a particular object from a method call. This object contains status information, so it can be examined to see whether the underlying API method call was successful or not.

The object is an instance of MSSQL_MethodRtnVal and is not involved with the WMI API's error handling. Instead, it reports the return code from the API that is called by the WMI provider. An error that occurs in the WMI API is reported by an SWbemLastError object unless your language catches it and throws an error. Now, you should understand that the WMI Provider supplies this particular object because errors will not be caught and thrown automatically unless your code does the error checking for MSSQL_MethodRtnVal instances.

We will illustrate the use of this object by intentionally calling SetPassword() with faulty parameters on an instance of MSSQL_Login. SetPassword() expects the old password of a login as its first parameter and the new login as its second parameter. Because everyone has the sa login by default, we will settle for that one:

```
Dim objWbemSvc, objRtnVal
Dim strSqlServer, strPath
' Object-path to Login-instance
strPath = "MSSQL_Login.Name='sa',SQLServerName='" & strSqlServer &
"thebox'"
' Get services
Set objWbemSvc = GetObject("Winmgmts:\\.\root\MicrosoftSQLServer")
' The returned object
Set objRtnVal = objWbemSvc.Get(strPath).SetPassword("xxx",_
                                                    "blah")
' Says no changes were made due to incorrect password
WScript.Echo objRtnVal.ReturnValue & "=" &_
            objRtnVal.Description
' Says that Microsoft SQL DMO is where the error occured
WScript.Echo objRtnVal.Source
```

The properties of objRtnVal contain the error information. If no errors occurred, the ReturnValue property would have been equal to zero. Ideally, you wrap up error checking in a conditional statement that is inside or outside a subroutine, depending on how frequently you use error checking.

```
If Not objRtnVal.ReturnValue = 0 Then
    ' Says no changes were made due to incorrect password
    WScript.Echo objRtnVal.ReturnValue & "=" &_
            objRtnVal.Description
```

```
        ' Microsoft SQL DMO is where the error occured
        WScript.Echo objRtnVal.Source
        ' Stop execution
        WScript.Quit
    End If
```

Languages and Output Parameters

We are focusing on VBScripts example wise, which do not support output parameters. If you are using a version of Jscript that does not support output parameters, however, here is a sample for you:

```
// Object-path
var strPath =
"MSSQL_Database.Name='Northwind',SQLServername='myServer'";
// Locator-object
var objLoc = new ActiveXObject("WbemScripting.SWbemLocator");
// Connect to WMI
var objSvc = objLoc.ConnectServer(".", "Root/MicrosoftSQLServer");
// Impersonate
objSvc.Security_.ImpersonationLevel=3;
// Get instance
var objInst = objSvc.Get(strPath);
// Method to execute
var objMethod = objInst.Methods_("EnumerateStoredProcedures");
// Parameters to pass
var objInParam = objMethod.InParameters.SpawnInstance_();
// Text in stored procedure to match
objInParam.Str = "SELECT";
// Output parameters returned
var objOutParams = objInst.ExecMethod_("EnumerateStoredProcedures",
objInParam);
// Convert it to array
var varArray = objOutParams.Properties_.Item("SP").Value.toArray();
// Echo each item
for (var i = 0; i < varArray.length; i++) {
    WScript.Echo(varArray[i]);
}
```

The outparameter in `EnumerateStoredProcedures()` is SP. It receives the
names of the stored procedures whose Text property contains the string in the
input parameter `Str`. Because the array is passed through the COM, we need to
explicitly convert it to a Jscript array.

About Output Parameters and VBScript

Output parameters are a common notion in programming. If you have used
anything COM-related before, chances are that you have used output parameters. They are essentially parameters that receive values. An output parameter

is passed by a reference in the parameter list in VBScript and is then initialized to a value by the method.

The WMI SQL Server provider, among many others, uses output parameters on several occasions. Here is how to use the `EnumerateStoredProcedures()` method of `MSSQL_Database` in VBScript:

```
...
' Name of database to scan
strDatabase  = "Northwind"
' Name of SQL Server Instance
strSQLServer = "myServer"
' String to match
strMatch     = "SELECT"
' Put together a valid object-path
strPath = "MSSQL_Database.Name='" & strDatabase  & "'" & _
          ",SQLServerName='"       & strSQLServer & "'"
...
' Get the Instance
Set objDB = objWmiSvc.Get(strPath)
' Get the stored procedures
Set objRetVal = objDB.EnumerateStoredProcedures(strMatch, _
                                                0,arrSP)
' Make sure we were successful, or else ...
If objRtnVal.ReturnValue = 0 Then
    For Each StoredProcedure In arrSP
        WScript.Echo StoredProcedure
    Next
Else
    WScript.Echo objRtnVal.Description
End If
```

Scripting Languages and Variants

Sometimes it is necessary to know the corresponding variant data type of a parameter or return value. A language such as Perl must (with some variants) know the type and create an explicit variant of that type in order for the code to work. In some instances, the conversion from variant to a language's native data type (or vice-versa) does not work. This problem is not an issue in VBScript, though, because its native data type is a variant.

Table 10.17 aids you in understanding the conversion, but please notice that the scripting layer of WMI can sometimes do some typecasting of its own (especially true when you are expecting to receive an array such as `VT_BSTR | VT_ARRAY`). Because some scripting languages handle `VT_VARIANT | VT_ARRAY` better than the former type, it is not uncommon for you to have to watch out for it being sent as a `VT_VARIANT | VT_ARRAY` before the scripting layer passes it to the management application.

Table 10.17   Data Type Mapping

Verbose	Data-type	Variant
Boolean	Boolean	VT_BOOL
Date-time	DateTime	VT_BSTR
Signed 8-bit Integer	Sint8	VT_I2
Signed 16-bit Integer	Sint16	VT_I2
Signed 32-bit Integer	Sint32	VT_I4
Signed 64-bit Integer as String	Sint64	VT_BSTR
Eight-byte Floating Point (IEEE)	Real8	VT_R8
Four-byte floating point (IEEE)	Real32	VT_R4
Eight-byte Floating Point	Real64	VT_R8
Unsigned 8-bit Integer	Uint8	VT_UI1
Unsigned 16-bit Integer	Uint16	VT_I4
Unsigned 32-bit Integer	Uint32	VT_I4
Unsigned 64-bit Integer as String	Uint64	VT_BSTR
Reference	ref	VT_BSTR
Single 16-bit Unicode Character	Char16	VT_I2
Unicode Character String	String	VT_BSTR
Array	Array	VT_TYPE	VT_ARRAY

Common WMI Enumerated Constants

WMI includes a set of enumerated constants in its type library. You can use the constants to trigger certain behaviors of methods that support them. When a method supports a constant, it can be passed as a parameter. Additionally, some parameters can be the combined values of several constants. In any event, Tables 10.18 through 10.22 list the constants that are most commonly used in WMI.

wbemErrorEnum represents an error by WMI. By default, Windows Script Host, which is used in this book's examples, will notify you of an error. The error code is hexadecimal, and you can look it up in the wbemErrorEnum table (see Table 10.23).

Table 10.18   wbemTimeout

Constant	Value
wbemTimeoutInfinite	0xffffffff

Table 10.19 wbemComparisonFlagEnum

Constant	Value
wbemComparisonFlagIncludeAll	0
wbemComparisonFlagIgnoreQualifiers	1
wbemComparisonFlagIgnoreObjectSource	2
wbemComparisonFlagIgnoreDefaultValues	4
wbemComparisonFlagIgnoreClass	8
wbemComparisonFlagIgnoreCase	16
wbemComparisonFlagIgnoreFlavor	32

Table 10.20 wbemTextFlagEnum

Constant	Value
wbemTextFlagNoFlavors	1

Table 10.21 wbemQueryFlagEnum

Constant	Value
wbemQueryFlagDeep	0
wbemQueryFlagShallow	1
wbemQueryFlagPrototype	2

Table 10.22 wbemFlagEnum

Constant	Value
wbemFlagReturnImmediately	16
wbemFlagReturnWhenComplete	0
wbemFlagBidirectional	0
wbemFlagForwardOnly	32
wbemFlagNoErrorObject	64
wbemFlagReturnErrorObject	0
wbemFlagSendStatus	128
wbemFlagDontSendStatus	0
wbemFlagUseAmendedQualifiers	0x00020000

The wbemPrivilegeEnums can be used with the SWbemPrivilege object to enable and disable certain privileges. Refer to Table 10.24.

Table 10.23 wbemErrorEnum

Constant	Value
wbemNoErr	0
wbemErrFailed	0x80041001
wbemErrNotFound	0x80041002
wbemErrAccessDenied	0x80041003
wbemErrProviderFailure	0x80041004
wbemErrTypeMismatch	0x80041005
wbemErrOutOfMemory	0x80041006
wbemErrInvalidContext	0x80041007
wbemErrInvalidParameter	0x80041008
wbemErrNotAvailable	0x80041009
wbemErrCriticalError	0x8004100a
wbemErrInvalidStream	0x8004100b
wbemErrNotSupported	0x8004100c
wbemErrInvalidSuperclass	0x8004100d
wbemErrInvalidNamespace	0x8004100e
wbemErrInvalidObject	0x8004100f
wbemErrInvalidClass	0x80041010
wbemErrProviderNotFound	0x80041011
wbemErrInvalidProviderRegistration	0x80041012
wbemErrProviderLoadFailure	0x80041013
wbemErrInitializationFailure	0x80041014
wbemErrTransportFailure	0x80041015
wbemErrInvalidOperation	0x80041016
wbemErrInvalidQuery	0x80041017
wbemErrInvalidQueryType	0x80041018
wbemErrAlreadyExists	0x80041019
wbemErrOverrideNotAllowed	0x8004101a
wbemErrPropagatedQualifier	0x8004101b
wbemErrPropagatedProperty	0x8004101c
wbemErrUnexpected	0x8004101d
wbemErrIllegalOperation	0x8004101e
wbemErrCannotBeKey	0x8004101f
wbemErrIncompleteClass	0x80041020

Table 10.23 (Continued)

Constant	Value
wbemErrInvalidSyntax	0x80041021
wbemErrNondecoratedObject	0x80041022
wbemErrReadOnly	0x80041023
wbemErrProviderNotCapable	0x80041024
wbemErrClassHasChildren	0x80041025
wbemErrClassHasInstances	0x80041026
wbemErrQueryNotImplemented	0x80041027
wbemErrIllegalNull	0x80041028
wbemErrInvalidQualifierType	0x80041029
wbemErrInvalidPropertyType	0x8004102a
wbemErrValueOutOfRange	0x8004102b
wbemErrCannotBeSingleton	0x8004102c
wbemErrInvalidCimType	0x8004102d
wbemErrInvalidMethod	0x8004102e
wbemErrInvalidMethodParameters	0x8004102f
wbemErrSystemProperty	0x80041030
wbemErrInvalidProperty	0x80041031
wbemErrCallCancelled	0x80041032
wbemErrShuttingDown	0x80041033
wbemErrPropagatedMethod	0x80041034
wbemErrUnsupportedParameter	0x80041035
wbemErrMissingParameter	0x80041036
wbemErrInvalidParameterId	0x80041037
wbemErrNonConsecutiveParameterIds	0x80041038
wbemErrParameterIdOnRetval	0x80041039
wbemErrInvalidObjectPath	0x8004103a
wbemErrOutOfDiskSpace	0x8004103b
wbemErrBufferTooSmall	0x8004103c
wbemErrUnsupportedPutExtension	0x8004103d
wbemErrUnknownObjectType	0x8004103e
wbemErrUnknownPacketType	0x8004103f
wbemErrUnknownObjectType	0x8004103e
wbemErrUnknownPacketType	0x8004103f

(continues)

Table 10.23 wbemErrorEnum (Continued)

Constant	Value
wbemErrMarshalVersionMismatch	0x80041040
wbemErrMarshalInvalidSignature	0x80041041
wbemErrInvalidQualifier	0x80041042
wbemErrInvalidDuplicateParameter	0x80041043
wbemErrTooMuchData	0x80041044
wbemErrServerTooBusy	0x80041045
wbemErrInvalidFlavor	0x80041046
wbemErrCircularReference	0x80041047
wbemErrUnsupportedClassUpdate	0x80041048
wbemErrCannotChangeKeyInheritance	0x80041049
wbemErrCannotChangeIndexInheritance	0x80041050
wbemErrTooManyProperties	0x80041051
wbemErrUpdateTypeMismatch	0x80041052
wbemErrUpdateOverrideNotAllowed	0x80041053
wbemErrUpdatePropagatedMethod	0x80041054
wbemErrMethodNotImplemented	0x80041055
wbemErrMethodDisabled	0x80041056
wbemErrRefresherBusy	0x80041057
wbemErrUnparsableQuery	0x80041058
wbemErrNotEventClass	0x80041059
wbemErrMissingGroupWithin	0x8004105a
wbemErrMissingAggregationList	0x8004105b
wbemErrPropertyNotAnObject	0x8004105c
wbemErrAggregatingByObject	0x8004105d
wbemErrUninterpretableProviderQuery	0x8004105f
wbemErrBackupRestoreWinmgmtRunning	0x80041060
wbemErrQueueOverflow	0x80041061
wbemErrPrivilegeNotHeld	0x80041062
wbemErrInvalidOperator	0x80041063
wbemErrLocalCredentials	0x80041064
wbemErrLocalCredentials	0x80041064
wbemErrCannotBeAbstract	0x80041065
wbemErrAmendedObject	0x80041066

Table 10.23 (Continued)

Constant	Value
wbemErrRegistrationTooBroad	0x80042001
wbemErrRegistrationTooPrecise	0x80042002
wbemErrTimedout	0x80043001
wbemErrResetToDefault	0x80043002

Table 10.24 wbemPrivilegeEnum

Privilege String	Constant	Value
SeCreateTokenPrivilege	wbemPrivilegeCreateToken	1
SeAssignPrimaryTokenPrivilege	wbemPrivilegePrimaryToken	2
SeLockMemoryPrivilege	wbemPrivilegeLockMemory	3
SeIncreaseQuotaPrivilege	wbemPrivilegeIncreaseQuota	4
SeMachineAccountPrivilege	wbemPrivilegeMachineAccount	5
SeTcbPrivilege	wbemPrivilegeTcb	6
SeSecurityPrivilege	wbemPrivilegeSecurity	7
SeTakeOwnershipPrivilege	wbemPrivilegeTakeOwnership	8
SeLoadDriverPrivilege	wbemPrivilegeLoadDriver	9
SeSystemProfilePrivilege	wbemPrivilegeSystemProfile	10
SeSystemtimePrivilege	wbemPrivilegeSystemtime	11
SeProfileSingleProcessPrivilege	wbemPrivilegeProfileSingleProcess	12
SeIncreaseBasePriorityPrivilege	wbemPrivilegeIncreaseBasePriority	13
SeCreatePagefilePrivilege	wbemPrivilegeCreatePagefile	14
SeCreatePermanentPrivilege	wbemPrivilegeCreatePermanent	15
SeBackupPrivilege	wbemPrivilegeBackup	16
SeRestorePrivilege	wbemPrivilegeRestore	17
SeShutdownPrivilege	wbemPrivilegeShutdown	18
SeDebugPrivilege	wbemPrivilegeDebug	19
SeAuditPrivilege	wbemPrivilegeAudit	20
SeSystemEnvironmentPrivilege	wbemPrivilegeSystemEnvironment	21
SeChangeNotifyPrivilege	wbemPrivilegeChangeNotify	22
SeRemoteShutdownPrivilege	wbemPrivilegeRemoteShutdown	23
SeUndockPrivilege	wbemPrivilegeUndock	24
SeSyncAgentPrivilege	wbemPrivilegeSyncAgent	25
SeEnableDelegationPrivilege	wbemPrivilegeEnableDelegation	26

Summary

This chapter gave an introduction to WMI and the WMI Scripting API. In the next chapter, we're going to look at the WMI query language.

CHAPTER 11

WMI Query Language

W MI Query Language is a core part of WMI. WQL is a subset of *Structured Query Language* (SQL) that provides the means for data access. WQL supports the necessary features of SQL that are used to retrieve and report data. In this chapter, we will look at the features that are supported by WQL and examine how to incorporate events into management applications.

Introduction

WQL is meant for enumerating, exploring, and reporting about the ongoings of a managed environment. Unlike traditional SQL, WQL is a pure query language and is not designed for updating, deleting, or inserting data. The means for such operations are instead supported through the scripting *Application Programming Interface* (API). WQL supports three types of queries:

Data queries   Used by management applications that have to select instances and data associations about instances.

Event queries   Used by management applications that implement event handling. Events are fired within your management application to notify you of changes such as the creation, deleting, or modification of a database. These queries register the management application for event notifications.

Schema queries   Similar to data queries, but these return meta information instead of actual instances.

These three types of queries will be covered next, and we will give suggestions as to where they can be used. We will also present tips on how they can be optimized.

Data Queries

Management applications that operate on instances within a management environment find the most uses for data queries. These types of queries are executed by the `ExecQuery()` method (or its asynchronous counterpart), and the statements are extremely similar to that of standard SQL.

SELECT Statements

The first statement that we will look at is `SELECT`. This statement is used to retrieve data from a namespace. As you build a statement, you can define one class that you are querying and several properties, or you can asterisk all properties that you want returned with the instances. For example, the following code queries all instances of the Database class and then echoes all properties that were returned per object:

```
' Do some stuff
...
' Build the WQL-query
strWQL = "SELECT * FROM MSSQL_Database"
' Set impersonationlevel
SWbemServices.Security_.ImpersonationLevel = 3
' Return a set of all database-Instances
Set objSet = SWbemServices.ExecQuery(strWQL)
' For each instance
For Each objDB In objSet
    ' Empty this string for a new instance
    strEcho = ""
    ' For each property
    For Each pty In objDB.Properties_
        ' Build a string of all properties
        strEcho = strEcho & pty.Name & "=" & pty.Value & vbNewLine
    Next
    ' Echo database-name and strEcho
    Wscript.Echo objDB.Name & vbNewLine & strEcho
Next
```

If you only want a few properties, do not use the asterisk. Enter the properties that you want to return, which means changing the query to the following:

```
strWQL = "SELECT SpaceAvailable FROM MSSQL_Database"
```

As a result, the `Name`, `SpaceAvailable`, and `SQLServerName` properties are populated and returned. By design, `Name` and `SQLServerName` are key properties, so they come automatically.

You do not have to grab all instances of a class. By specifying a `WHERE` clause, it is possible to get a specific instance. Here, you can select the names of all instances where `SpaceAvailable` properties (measured in kilobytes [KB]) is less than 500 (see Table 11.1):

```
SELECT Name FROM MSSQL_Database
WHERE SpaceAvailable < 500
```

Or, you can select all properties from the Northwind database:

```
SELECT * FROM MSSQL_Database
WHERE Name='northwind'
```

The previous example may return more than one instance if there is more than one Northwind database on the system. This would happen where you use multiple instances of SQL Server because the query will look in all SQL Server instances. For the same reason, the query would not be very performant.

On a final note, WQL queries are case-insensitive—just like everything else in WMI. The exact use of the ISA operator varies per context. In a data query, it works just like a `SELECT . . . WHERE` statement, in which `Embedded-Property ISA "Superclass"` is used to return objects that are derived from `Superclass` that are embedded in `EmbeddedProperty`.

Table 11.1 Supported WQL Operators

Operator	Meaning
=	Equal to
<	Less than
>	Greater than
<=	Less than or equal to
>=	Greater than or equal to
!=	Not equal to
<>	Not equal to
IS	Use as SELECT ... WHERE Property IS NULL
IS NOT	Use as SELECT ... WHERE Property IS NOT NULL
ISA	Use as SELECT ... ISA "Superclass"

ASSOCIATORS OF

ASSOCIATORS OF selects the associators of an instance. The associators are instances that are associated to a source class by way of an association class, so this functionality enables the dynamic discovery and traversal of schema relationships.

WMI uses the information in the schema to find out which classes are related to the instance you're querying about. With the classes it finds, WMI creates the WQL queries that return the actual associators.

The syntax for an ASSOCIATORS OF query is slightly more complex than the SELECT statement (see Table 11.2):

```
ASSOCIATORS OF {SourceObjectPath}
WHERE AssocClass = AssocClassName
      ClassDefsOnly
      RequiredAssocQualifier = QualifierName
      RequiredQualifier = QualifierName
      ResultClass = ClassName
      ResultRole = PropertyName
      Role = PropertyName
```

The best way to start querying associators is with something familiar. The Northwind database will do well for this example, so here is a query that gets all instances that are associated with the Northwind database:

Table 11.2 ASSOCIATORS OF

Keyword	Meaning
AssocClass	The instances must be associated through this class or one of its derivatives.
ClassDefsOnly	It returns class-definitions only; no instances are returned.
RequiredAssocQualifier	The instances must be associated through a class with the specified qualifier in its qualifier-list.
RequiredQualifier	The instances must include the specified qualifier in its qualifier-list.
ResultClass	The instances must belong to the specified class or a derivative of the specified class.
ResultRole	The instances must be playing the specified role as defined in the references of the association class.
Role	The source object is related to the instances through the specified role.

```
ASSOCIATORS OF
{MSSQL_Database.Name='northwind',SQLServerName='yourserver'}
```

This code handles the returned instances:

```
For Each objDB In objSet
    WScript.Echo objDB.Path_.DisplayName
Next
```

With `ASSOCIATORS OF`, we're returning instances associated to the one specified in the query. The association instances themselves are not returned. In the previous example we echoed the display name, which is a WMI moniker, to the screen. The query that we just executed previously returns quite a set of instances, so you probably do not want to suffer through the whole process for each. A more specific query is one that gets all tables that are associated with the Northwind database:

```
ASSOCIATORS OF
{MSSQL_Database.Name='northwind',SQLServerName='yourserver'}
WHERE AssocClass=MSSQL_DatabaseTable
```

The `WHERE` clause and keywords are optional. And `ASSOCIATORS OF` can not use the logical operators AND and OR. With keywords, such as `AssocClass`, the equals sign is the only valid operator. The next example is one that selects the logins whose instances have `sysadmin` rights:

```
ASSOCIATORS OF
{MSSQL_SQLServerRole.Name='sysadmin',SQLServerName='yourserver'}
WHERE AssocClass = MSSQL_MemberLogin
```

Administrators will find `ASSOCIATORS OF` useful because they do not have to know the name of an association that relates two classes. All the administrator needs to know is that ClassA is related to ClassB. Similarly, applications that dynamically discover which objects are related to ClassA can use `ASSOCIATORS OF`, because instances of associated classes, new association classes can be added at any time.

REFERENCES OF

`REFERENCES OF` returns the association class instances that point to a defined source instance. The syntax is as follows:

```
REFERENCES OF {SourceObject} WHERE
    ClassDefsOnly
    RequiredQualifier = QualifierName
    ResultClass = ClassName
    Role = PropertyName
```

The WHERE clause and keywords are optional. REFERENCES OF can not use logical operators like AND and OR. Additionally, the equals sign is the only valid operator for the keywords.

Event Queries

Event queries are written to receive event notifications. Event queries are similar to what we have just seen with data queries (except for the use of some additional clauses). Event queries for scripted management applications are considered temporary queries because they last only as long as the script is in a running state.

Management applications can be notified of events in two ways. The underlying system that you're managing may have an eventing system. If so, it will notify your application of occurred events. This is the case of the NT Event Log provider. It is a native event provider with a callback routine that notifies your application when an event occurs. When there is no underlying eventing system, WMI polls for events. In that case, WMI sends event notifications to your management application.

Event queries are the results of asynchronous method calls of the scripting *Application Programming Interface* (API). When you decide where you want to monitor for events, you must figure out for what and, when there is no underlying eventing system, how often your script will poll. SQL Server has no eventing system, so WMI provides three main classes for events. These classes are listed in Tables 11.3 through 11.5.

The classes with a leading double-underscore are called "System Classes." Those are provided by WMI itself and not compiled in via MOF. They also exist

Table 11.3 __ClassOperationEvent

Event	Fires
__ClassCreationEvent	When a class is created
__ClassDeletionEvent	When a class is deleted
__ClassModificationEvent	When a class if modified

Table 11.4 __InstanceOperationEvent

Event	Fires
__InstanceCreationEvent	When an instance is created
__InstanceDeletionEvent	When an instance is deleted
__InstanceModificationEvent	When an instance is modified

Table 11.5   `__NamespaceOperationEvent`

Event	Fires
__NamespaceCreationEvent	When a namespace is created
__NamespaceDeletionEvent	When a namespace is deleted
__NamespaceModificationEvent	When a namespace is modified

in all namespaces. You can poll a base class for the events that are provided by its derivatives. For example, polling `__InstanceOperationEvent` will return notifications on `__InstanceCreationEvent`, `__InstanceDeletionEvent`, and `__InstanceModificationEvent`. You can also be more direct and poll only `__InstanceCreationEvent` or any other derivative of an event class. Finally, it's worth mentioning that you won't use namespace events with SQL Server. Nothing is done to the SQL Server namespace once it's created.

The most common types of events within Microsoft SQL Server's namespace are those that relate to instances. You can poll for new server instances, database objects, errors, changes in server state, or for any other instance-related event.

Furthermore, every event base class provides subclasses with an object. The `__ClassOperationEvent` class contains a `TargetClass` object. Similarly, `__InstanceOperationEvent` and `__NamespaceOperationEvent` propagate `TargetInstance` and `TargetNamespace`. Depending on the context of the operation, the type of object that is passed to the subclass varies. Creation events pass a copy of the newly created object; Deletion events pass a copy of the just-deleted object; and Modification events pass the instance after modification. Moreover, Modification events pass the instance before modification as well, and the instance becomes available as either `PreviousInstance`, `PreviousClass`, or `PreviousNamespace`.

To query for events, you must tell WMI how often it should poll. This action is performed by specifying a delay interval in seconds. The more frequent the polling, the more processing power is used. These types of temporary event consumers that script use are not bulletproof, either. It is possible that an instance is created and deleted while your script is not polling for events; thus, you will never know about it. With Microsoft SQL Server, that will hardly matter—but in other scenarios, it might be of a bigger magnitude.

When polling for events, what happens is that the WMI provider on each interval enumerates the instances of the polled class to see whether any changes have occurred. If an instance has been created, deleted, or modified since it was last checked, the management application is sent a notification. The syntax of an event query looks similar to the following:

```
SELECT <PropertyList> FROM EventClass
WITHIN SecInterval
[WHERE Property=Value]
```

The `PropertyList` represents the properties that you want to select; `Event-Class` specifies the class to poll; and `SecInterval` indicates the number of seconds between each poll.

NOTE

`WITHIN` is used with events that are provided by WMI. It is not necessary to poll true event providers.

Moreover, event queries can be grouped using the `GROUP` clause. The syntax for that clause is:

```
SELECT <PropertyList> FROM EventClass
[WHERE Property=Value]
GROUP WITHIN SecInterval
[BY PropertyList]
[HAVING NumberOfEvents Operator IntegerValue]
```

`GROUP` generates one event notification for a group of events. The NT Event Log, which is an event provider, can be used with the `GROUP` clause. You can, for example, sign up for receiving a grouped event every 30 seconds:

```
SELECT * FROM __InstanceCreationEvent WHERE TargetInstance ISA
'Win32_NTLogEvent' GROUP WITHIN 30
```

The BY argument of the `GROUP` clause allows you to group your events by specific properties. You can, for example, group the events by the user property of the NT Event Log class:

```
SELECT * FROM __InstanceCreationEvent WHERE TargetInstance ISA
'Win32_NTLogEvent' GROUP WITHIN 30 BY User
```

Lastly, the `HAVING` clause and `NumberOfEvents` keyword allows you to receive events in a more specific manner. The following uses `HAVING` and `NumberOf-Events` to receive a notification if the number of events have exceeded 10 every 30 seconds:

```
SELECT * FROM __InstanceCreationEvent WHERE TargetInstance ISA
'Win32_NTLogEvent' GROUP WITHIN 30 HAVING NumberOfEvents > 10
```

The grouped events result in an object containing two properties: `NumberOf-Events` and Representative. `NumberOfEvents` is a property containing the number of events that occurred, and Representative is an embedded object. From the previous example, that embedded object contains one of the instances created during the event interval.

Schema Queries

Schema queries get meta information. The syntax is roughly similar to other WQL queries:

```
SELECT * FROM meta_class
```

The meta class tells the parser that the query is a schema query. You can then use additional keywords such as the __this property or __Class property. The __this property identifies the target class of the query:

```
SELECT * FROM meta__class
WHERE __this ISA 'MSSQL_SQLServer'
```

The __Class property tells the parser to return a class definition. You can then use the returned class definition to spawn a new instance of the class (or anything else).

Query Optimization

In order to optimize WQL queries, some of the same idioms that apply to relational databases can be applied when thinking in WMI.

Execute queries for forward-only enumerators as often as possible. The software keeps less information in memory because it only needs to keep the current position and the position of the next object to return in memory, which is a better enumerator than the bidirectional enumerator:

```
SWbemServices.ExecQuery(strWQL, "WQL", wbemFlagForwardOnly)
```

Forward-only enumerators are typically used when you do a one-shot loop through the return objects. It will not enable you to move backward, clone, or reset the enumerator. A bidirectional enumerator, however, which would provide more freedom, keeps the previous, current, and next position to return in memory. It is a lot more data for it to handle.

Next, sometimes schema queries can be useful. There is no need to allocate memory for objects unless you absolutely must. When you need to retrieve instances, use a query that specifies the properties that you want to access. Relational databases do not perform well when passed the asterisk instead of column names, and the same goes for WMI. The best query performance is achieved when specifying actual column names for which it can search:

```
SELECT Name, SQLServerName FROM SomeClass
```

Another benefit of specifying the properties is that you only get the data that you need. This feature reduces the amount of data that is transferred over the network, and the query is speedier.

A tenet of WQL queries is that the more key properties that you can match in your statement, the better the performance. For example, in the previous query, by adding a `WHERE` clause to match one key property name and value match, you would return the results faster:

```
SELECT Name, SQLServerName FROM SomeClass
WHERE Name='BobsBox'
```

Additionally, if you were to locate and match all key properties, it will be even faster. These query statement-specific optimizations are enabled by the WMI provider. Consider using WQL as often as you can. Queries can do everything `GetObject()` and the enumeration methods can. They will also get you in the habit of optimizing your request for exactly what you want rather than asking for everything.

Programming with Events

Because we have covered the major objects and WQL, it is time to see how they can interact with events. Events are supported through notification queries and asynchronous operations.

Here is a simple template for handling the events:

```
Sub myOnObjectReady (oObject, oContext)
WScript.Echo "Hello from OnObjectReady!"
End Sub
Sub myOnCompleted (iHResult, oError, oContext)
WScript.Echo "Hello from OnCompleted!"
End Sub
Sub myOnObjectPut  (oPath,  oContext)
WScript.Echo "Hello from OnObjectPut!"
End Sub
Sub myOnProgress  (iUBound, iCurrent, strMsg, oContext)
WScript.Echo "Hello from OnProgress!"
End Sub
```

Also, we can add some code that fires the events when you start, stop, pause, and continue the Microsoft SQL Server server. The following code belongs to the same file and is what receives the events as they come:

```
' Create instance of sink and define the prefix to use for
' subroutines that are fired for events of the same name (but
' without the prefix)
'
Set objWbemSink = WScript.CreateObject("WbemScripting.SWbemSink", _
"my")
' Locator object
Set objWbemLoc= WScript.CreateObject("WbemScripting.SWbemLocator")
' Services object
```

```
Set objWbemSvc = objWbemLoc.ConnectServer(".", _
"root/MicrosoftSQLServer")
' Set impersonationlevel
objWbemSvc.Security_.ImpersonationLevel = 3
' Build WQL-query
myQuery = "SELECT * FROM __InstanceOperationEvent WITHIN 1" _
        & "WHERE TargetInstance ISA 'Win32_Service' " _
        & "AND   TargetInstance.Name='MSSQLSERVER'"
' Execute query
objWbemSvc.ExecNotificationQueryAsync objWbemSink, myQuery
' Wait for events
WScript.Echo "Polling for Events"
```

Since the query specifies a key value—the Name property—WMI is going to monitor only that particular instance. No other service instances will be polled. You could register for all different types of events with WMI. For example, to be notified when a database is created, implement a subroutine that handles `onObjectReady` events and use the following query:

```
SELECT * FROM __InstanceCreationEvent WITHIN 15
WHERE TargetInstance ISA 'MSSQL_Database'
AND   TargetInstance.SQLServerName='YourServer'
```

Because WMI runs on the host computer, the event polling is run on that computer. In other words, you can receive event notifications from a remote computer without your machine doing the polling.

Summary

We've looked at the *WMI Query Language* (WQL). It can be used to enumerate instances and further explore the schema with exploring associations and references. Also touched upon was how you can use WQL to poll for events.

Common Management Tasks

T he WMI SQL Server provider makes numerous administration tasks easy to automate. The intention of this chapter is not to provide full coverage of what Microsoft SQL Server can be programmed to do. Instead, this chapter aims at providing the foundation that is needed to understand how to program the classes and instances that are served by the WMI Administration Provider for Microsoft SQL Server.

Creating a New Database

A database is an organized collection of objects. When you have created a database, you can add tables, stored procedures, users, and other associated objects to it through WMI. The only way of creating a new database makes use of the class's constructor. Put_() cannot provide enough information for creating an instance, so Create() is provided as a class method:

```
Option Explicit

' Our variables
Dim objWbemLoc, objWbemSvc

' Name of SQL Server
strSQLserver = "THEBOX"
```

```
' Name of the database to create
strDBname = "WMISampleDB"

' The namespace to connect
strNS = "root/MicrosoftSQLServer"

' Create instance of Locator-object
Set objWbemLoc = CreateObject("wbemscripting.swbemlocator")

' Create instance of Services-object
Set objWbemSvc = objWbemLoc.ConnectServer(".", strNS)

' Set impersonationlevel
objWbemSvc.Security_.ImpersonationLevel = 3

' Get the DatabaseFile class
Set objDBFile = objWbemSvc.Get("MSSQL_DatabaseFile")

' Get the Database ckass
Set objDB  = objWbemSvc.Get("MSSQL_Database")

' Get a fresh DatabaseFile-instance
Set objNewFile = objDBFile.SpawnInstance_()

' Name of this new instance
objNewFile.Name = "WMISampleFile"

' Database the instance is part of
objNewFile.DatabaseName = strDBname

' Full path to operating system file
objNewFile.PhysicalName = "C:\WMISampleFile.dat"

' Set growth to be measured in percent
objNewFile.FileGrowthType = 1

' Grow by 10 percent
objNewFile.FileGrowth  = 10

' As big as it wants to be
objNewFile.MaximumSize = 100

' Create the database; 25 is initialsize in MB
Set objRtnVal = objDB.Create(strDBname, strSQLserver, objNewFile, 25)

If objRtnVal.ReturnValue = 0 Then
    WScript.Echo "Database Created!"
Else
    WScript.Echo objRtnVal.Description
End If
```

Creating a New Table

A table is the primary object of a database. The table is made up of columns, where each column has its own name, data type, and rules bound to it. A new entry in the database table is a record. A record is a row where all columns have a value. The table generally models a real-world object, such as a department, a products line, and so on. In this example, the `WMISampleTable` table is created in the `WMISampleDB` database. `WMISampleID` and `WMISample-Name` are the columns that are associated with the table:

```
Option Explicit

Dim objWbemLoc, objWbemSvc
Dim objTable, objColumn, objNewColumn
Dim strColumnName1, strColumnName2, strTableName, strSQLserver
Dim strDBname
Dim arrColumns(1)

    strTableName   = "WMISampleTable"
    strSQLServer   = "THEBOX"
    strDBname      = "WMISampleDB"
    strColumnName1 = "WMISampleID"
    strColumnName2 = "WMISampleName"

    Set objWbemLoc = CreateObject("wbemscripting.swbemlocator")
    Set objWbemSvc = objWbemLoc.ConnectServer(".", _
    "root\MicrosoftSqlServer")

    objWbemSvc.Security_.ImpersonationLevel = 3

    Set objColumn = objWbemSvc.Get("MSSQL_Column")

    Set objNewColumn = objColumn.SpawnInstance_
        objNewColumn.Name         = strColumnName1
        objNewColumn.Datatype     = "int"
        objNewColumn.AllowNulls = 0
        objNewColumn.Identity     = 1
        objNewColumn.IdentityIncrement = 1
    Set arrColumns(0) = objNewColumn

    Set objNewColumn = objColumn.SpawnInstance_
        objNewColumn.Name         = strColumnName2
        objNewColumn.Datatype   = "char"
        objNewColumn.Length     = 50
        objNewColumn.AllowNulls = 0
    Set arrColumns(1) = objNewColumn
```

```
Set objTable = objWmiSvc.Get("MSSQL_Table")

objTable.Create strTableName, strSQLserver, strDBname, arrColumns
```

This class is another class in which a `Create()` method is needed to write a new instance to the Microsoft SQL Server. When you are ready to delete the table, use the following code:

```
strPath = "MSSQL_Table.Name='" & strTableName & "',DatabaseName='" &
strDBname & "',SQLServerName='" & strSQLserver & "'"

Set objTable = objWbemSvc.Get(strPath)

objTable.Delete_()
```

Adding a New Column

The column is the primary object of a database table. Typically, two or more columns make up the structure of a database table. A column is assigned a name and a data type that it can store, and special characteristics can be attributed to it (such as whether it is an identity column). The `MSSQL_Column` class is associated with the `MSSQL_Table` class as the `PartComponent` in the aggregation relationship that is modeled by the `MSSQL_TableColumn` association. Here is a code-fragment of how you would add a column to an existing table:

```
Set objColumn = objWbemSvc.Get("MSSQL_Column").SpawnInstance_()

    With objColumn
        .Name = "myColumn"
        .AllowNulls = 1
        .Datatype = "int"
        .DatabaseName = strDBname
        .TableName = strTableName
        .SQLServerName = strSQLserver
        .Put_()
    End With
```

As you can see in the code, it uses the `Put_()` method to create a column. This is a change compared to the previous two examples. The reason is that `MSSQL_Table` and `MSSQL_Database` don't support creation through `Put_()`. `Put_()` takes no parameters, thus the `Create()` method is provided by the class. `MSSQL_Column`, on the other hand, doesn't require anything above what the WMI can provide with its native methods.

Creating a New Login

A standard SQL server or NT authentication login can be created in SQL Server through `MSSQL_Login`:

```
Set clsLogin = objWbemSvc.Get("MSSQL_Login")

Set objNewLogin = clsLogin.SpawnInstance_()

objNewLogin.SqlServerName = strSQLserver
objNewLogin.Name = "myWMILogin"
objNewLogin.Type = 2

objNewLogin.Put_()
```

The Type property is set to two in order to indicate that the instance uses an SQL Server authentication. A value of zero indicates an NT user login, and one is an NT group login. Windows group accounts are associated with `MSSQL_Login` through the `MSSQL_LoginWin32Group` association. Similarly, Windows user accounts are associated to `MSSQL_Login` through the `MSSQL_LoginWin32-UserAccount` class.

Associating a Login with an SQL Server Role

In order to assign an SQL Server role to an existing login, you must spawn an instance of the `MSSQL_MemberLogin` class. This class is used for relating an existing login to an existing SQL Server role. As with associations, the object path is defined as references in the properties:

```
' Services object
Set objWbemSvc = GetObject("winmgmts:/Root/MicrosoftSQLServer")

' Set impersonationlevel
objWbemSvc.Security_.ImpersonationLevel = 3

' Spawn a new Instance of MSSQL_MemberLogin
Set objMLogin = objWbemSvc.Get("MSSQL_MemberLogin").SpawnInstance_()

' The antededent in the association
objMLogin.Antecedent = _
"\\THEBOX\root\microsoftsqlserver:" &_
"MSSQL_SQLServerRole.Name='sysadmin',SQLServerName='THEBOX'"
```

```
' The dependent in the association
objMLogin.Dependent   = _
"\\THEBOX\root\microsoftsqlserver:" &_
MSSQL_Login.Name='myWMILogin',SQLServerName='THEBOX'"

' Put the Instance
objMLogin.Put_
```

Getting Information about a Login

When you get a login instance, you can query for its properties (as in this example):

```
' Name of login
loginname = "sa"

' Name of SQL Server
sqlserver = "MyServer"

' Locator-object
Set objWbemLoc = CreateObject("wbemscripting.swbemlocator")

' Sevices-object
Set objWbemSvc = objWbemLoc.ConnectServer(".", _
                    "root\MicrosoftSqlServer")

' Set impersonationlevel
objWbemSvc.Security_.ImpersonationLevel = 3

' Object-path
strPath = "MSSQL_Login.Name='" & loginname &_
          "',SQLServerName='" & sqlserver & "'"

' Get the object In strPath
Set objLogin = objWbemSvc.Get(strPath)

' Explicitly retrieve and echo the properties
WScript.Echo "Caption:       " & objLogin.Caption
WScript.Echo "DenyNTLogin:   " & objLogin.DenyNTLogin
WScript.Echo "Description:   " & objLogin.Description
WScript.Echo "InstallDate:   " & objLogin.InstallDate
WScript.Echo "Language:      " & objLogin.Language
WScript.Echo "LanguageAlias: " & objLogin.LanguageAlias
WScript.Echo "Name:          " & objLogin.Name
WScript.Echo "SQLServerName: " & objLogin.SQLServerName
WScript.Echo "Status:        " & objLogin.Status
WScript.Echo "SystemObject:  " & objLogin.SystemObject
WScript.Echo "Type:          " & objLogin.Type
```

You can also perform tasks such as setting a new password. This functionality is useful if, for example, you suddenly become responsible over a network that has several SQL servers where the previous administrator, student, or whomever forgot to change the sa password from its default empty string. WMI could be used to scan each server and call `SetPassword("", "new password")` on the sa login.

Starting and Stopping SQL Server

Previously, we registered for event notification when the state of our SQL Server Windows service was changed. This situation shows how WMI can be used to start the Microsoft SQL Server service after it has been stopped:

```
' Services object
Set objWbemSvc = GetObject("Winmgmts://./root/MicrosoftSqlServer")
...
' Start the MSSQLSERVER-service
objWbemSvc.Get("Win32_Service.Name='MSSQLSERVER'").StartService()
```

And, if you want to stop it, use the following code:

```
' Services Object
Set objWbemSvc = GetObject("Winmgmts://./root/MicrosoftSqlServer")
...
' Stop the MSSQLSERVER-service
objWbemSvc.Get("Win32_Service.Name='MSSQLSERVER'").StopService()
```

Dumping Properties of a Table

WQL can be used for many things. Here is a small example where a particular table is selected and the properties are accessed and echoed in a for-each loop:

```
' Full name of table
strTable = "[dbo].[Employees]"

' Locator-object
Set objWbemLoc = CreateObject("wbemscripting.swbemlocator")

' Services-object
Set objWbemSvc = objWbemLoc.ConnectServer(".", _
                      "root/MicrosoftSqlServer")

' Set impersonationlevel
objWbemSvc.Security_.ImpersonationLevel = 3
```

```
' The query to use
strQuery = "select * from MSSQL_TABLE WHERE Name" &_
           " = '" & strTable & "' AND DatabaseName='Northwind'" &_
           " AND SQLServerName='MyServer'"

' Execute query that returns the table
Set objTable = objWbemSvc.ExecQuery(strQuery)

' Get each Item In the returned set
For Each objItem In objTable
  Set objPropertySet = objItem.Properties_
    For Each objProperty In objPropertySet
          WScript.Echo objProperty.Name & "=" & objProperty.Value
    Next
  Next
Next
```

The query specifies both ways in which SQL Server instance and database get the table. It will work without those two, but there are good reasons to keep it there. First, omitting the SQL Server instance would result in every SQL Server instance being looked through for the table. Second, the dbo.employees table might exist in more than one database. It's important to be specific in queries so that you don't get some instances you never intended in case you're running multiple SQL Server instances.

Dumping All Instances of a Class

This action gets all subclasses of the MicrosoftSQLServer namespace's `MSSQL_Setting` class, prints the number of subclasses, and then gives the option of printing the instances of any subclass:

```
' Class to enumerate instances of
strClass = "MSSQL_Setting"

' Services Object
Set objWbemSvc = GetObject("Winmgmts://./root/MicrosoftSQLServer")

' Set impersonationlevel
objWbemSvc.Security_.ImpersonationLevel = 3

' SWbemObjectSet
Set objWbemSet = objWbemSvc.SubclassesOf(strClass)

' Number of Items
WScript.Echo objWbemSet.Count & " subclasses of " & strClass

' For each returned subclass of MSSQL_Setting
For Each objWbemObj In objWbemSet
    strRelPath = objWbemObj.Path_.RelPath
    strYesNo = "View the instances of " & strRelPath & "?"
```

```
        If MsgBox(strYesNo, vbYesNo) = 6 Then
            For Each objInstance In objWbemObj.Instances_
                WScript.Echo "Instance: " & objInstance.Path_.RelPath
            Next
        End If
    Next
```

Creating a Stored Procedure

A stored procedure is a block of code that is stored on the server side. Compared to ad-hoc queries, stored procedures typically perform better because they can be precompiled. Simple, compact SELECT statements are not for stored procedures, but if you look in the Northwind database, you will find that often more complex code (such as joins and computations) tends to lean towards the use of stored procedures.

A basic stored procedure in the Northwind database is "Sales by Year." We will use the text of that stored procedure in order to create a new one called "Sales by Year in WMI." Our text will look like the following:

```
CREATE PROCEDURE [dbo].[Sales by Year in WMI]
@Beginning_Date DateTime, @Ending_Date DateTime
AS
SELECT Orders.ShippedDate,
Orders.OrderID,
[Order Subtotals].Subtotal,
DATENAME(yy,ShippedDate) AS Year
FROM Orders INNER JOIN [Order Subtotals]
ON Orders.OrderID = [Order Subtotals].OrderID
WHERE Orders.ShippedDate
Between @Beginning_Date And @Ending_Date
GO
```

When a stored procedure is created through WMI, the Name property must be equivalent to the name that is declared after CREATE PROCEDURE. It must also be a name that includes the owner of the stored procedure. To ensure a good syntax and to prevent the server from rejecting the stored procedure, use plenty of newlines. A rather ugly string is the result:

```
' Procedure name
strSPname = "[dbo].[Sales by Year in WMI]"

' Procedure text
strSPtext = "CREATE PROCEDURE " & strSPname &_
    vbNewLine &_
    "@Beginning_Date DateTime, @Ending_Date DateTime" &_
    vbNewLine &_
    "AS" &_
```

```
        vbNewLine &_
      "SELECT Orders.ShippedDate,"  & vbNewLine & "Orders.OrderID," &_
        vbNewLine &_
      "[Order Subtotals].Subtotal," &_
        vbNewLine &_
      "DATENAME(yy,ShippedDate) AS Year" &_
        vbNewLine &_
      "FROM Orders INNER JOIN [Order Subtotals]" &_
        vbNewLine &_
      "ON Orders.OrderID = [Order Subtotals].OrderID" &_
        vbNewLine &_
      "WHERE Orders.ShippedDate" &_
        vbNewLine &_
      "Between @Beginning_Date And @Ending_Date" &_
        vbNewLine &_
      "GO"
```

Then, the WMI code for creating the `MSSQL_StoredProcedure` instance is as follows:

```
' Database-name
strDBname = "Northwind"

' SQL-server name
strSQLServer = "THEBOX"

' Stored procedure class
strClass = "MSSQL_StoredProcedure"

' Get the WbemServices-object
Set objWbemSvc = GetObject("Winmgmts://./root/MicrosoftSQLServer")

' Set impersonationlevel
objWbemSvc.Security_.ImpersonationLevel = 3

' Spawn a new stored procedure
Set objSProc = objWbemSvc.Get(strClass).SpawnInstance_()

' Set the key-properties and write the Instance
With objSProc
     .Name          = strSPname
     .DatabaseName  = strDBname
     .SQLServerName = strSQLServer
     .Text          = strSPtext
     .Put_()
End With
```

When `Put_()` is called, an association between the database and the stored procedure is established for you. Although you do not need to code it, here is an example to give you an idea of what happens:

```
strClass = "MSSQL_DatabaseStoredProcedure"

Set objAssoc = objWbemSvc.Get(strClass).SpawnInstance_()

objAssoc.ScopedElement = "\\THEBOX\Root\MicrosoftSQLServer:" &_
                         "MSSQL_StoredProcedure.Name='"       &_
                         strSPname                            &_
                         "',DatabaseName='"  & strDBname      &_
                         "',SQLServerName='" & strSQLServer & "'"

objAssoc.ScopingElement = "\\THEBOX\Root\MicrosoftSQLServer:" &_
                          "MSSQL_Database.Name='" &_
                          strDBname &_
                          "',SQLServerName='" &_
                          strSQLServer & "'"

objAssoc.Put_()
```

Don't type in and execute the previous code. It's merely there to show you what the provider does when it creates a stored procedure.

Assigning Permissions to a Stored Procedure

Because we have created a stored procedure, we will need to assign some permissions to it. By default, the public database role is set up with the Northwind database. Therefore, our script will give public execute permissions to the stored procedure:

```
' Variable to hold the name of the class to get
strClass = "MSSQL_DatabaseRoleStoredProcedurePermission"

' Spawn a new Instance
Set objPerms = objWbemSvc.Get(strClass).SpawnInstance_()

' The stored procedure we'll grant access to
objPerms.Element = "\\THEBOX\Root\MicrosoftSQLServer:" &_
                   "MSSQL_StoredProcedure.Name='"       &_
                   strSPname &_
                   "',DatabaseName='" &_
                   strDBname &_
                   "',SQLServerName='" &_
                   strSQLserver & "'"

' We define permission to execute a stored procedure
objPerms.PrivilegeType = 16

' The database role for which we defined the permissions
objPerms.Grantee = "\\THEBOX\Root\MicrosoftSQLServer:" &_
```

```
                    "MSSQL_DatabaseRole.DatabaseName='" &_
                    strDBname &_
                    "',Name='public'" &_
                    ",SQLServerName='" &_
                    strSQLserver & "'"

  ' We grant the access; boolean for grant/deny
  objPerms.Granted = true

  ' Put the instance
  objPerms.Put_()
```

As described in Appendix C ("Permissions"), PrivilegeType is used to define privileges on an object. The value 16 gives the database role permissions to execute the stored procedure.

Enumerating Parameters of the Stored Procedure

Well, the stored procedure has been set up and the permissions have been assigned. You might have noticed that there were parameters in the stored procedure. These parameters actually have their own class, so you can enumerate them as done in the following code fragment:

```
  ' Stored procedure to work on
  strSPname = "[dbo].[Sales by Year in WMI]"

  ' Instance of stored procedure to work on
  strClass = "MSSQL_StoredProcedureParameter"

  strQuery = "SELECT * FROM " & strClass & " WHERE " &_
             "StoredProcedureName='" & strSPname & "'"

  Set objWbemSet = objWbemSvc.ExecQuery(strQuery)

  WScript.Echo "There are " & objWbemSet.Count & " parameters.\n"

  For Each objParam In objWbemSet
       WScript.Echo objParam.DataType & " " & objParam.Name & vbNewLine Next
```

Modifying Database Settings

Part of why WMI is useful to administrators is because it makes changing settings so easy. The following script sets the AutoClose property to True in every database on every SQL server on the system. As a result of `AutoClose`, a database is closed—and all resources are freed until a user connects to the database:

```
' Services object
Set objWbemSvc = GetObject("winmgmts://./Root/MicrosoftSQLServer")

' Set impersonationlevel
objWbemSvc.Security_.ImpersonationLevel = 3

' Get name of all SQL Server Instances
Set objServers = objWbemSvc.ExecQuery("SELECT Name FROM " &_
                                      "MSSQL_SQLServer")

' Pass through each SQL Server
For Each Server In objServers
    WScript.Echo "Working instance is " & Server.Name

    strQuery = "SELECT * FROM MSSQL_DatabaseSetting " &_
               "WHERE SQLServerName='" & Server.Name & "'"

    Set objWbemSet = objWbemSvc.ExecQuery(strQuery)

    ' Pass through each database
    For Each objDBS In objWbemSet
        Select Case objDBS.SettingID
            Case "master"
                ' WScript.Echo "Skipped 'master'."
            Case "tempdb"
                ' WScript.Echo "Skipped 'tempdb'."
            Case Else
                ' If AutoClose is False, we need to set it ...
                If objDBS.AutoClose = FALSE Then
                    WScript.Echo "Done " & objDBS.SettingID & "..."
                    objDBS.AutoClose = TRUE
                    objDBS.Put_
                End If
        End Select
    Next

Next
```

Bulk-Copying a Table

To bulk-copy the contents of a table, `ExportData()` must be called on the table that is exported. `ExportData()` must also be provided with an instance of `MSSQL_BulkCopySettings` that defines how the export will operate. The code here exports a table to a tab-delimited file:

```
' Get the Services-object
Set objWbemSvc = GetObject("Winmgmts://./Root/MicrosoftSQLServer")

' Set impersonationlevel
objWbemSvc.Security_.ImpersonationLevel = 3

' Get Bulkcopy-setting instance
Set objBcp = objWbemSvc.Get("MSSQL_BulkCopySetting").SpawnInstance_()

' Table to export
Set objTable = objWbemSvc.Get("MSSQL_Table.Name='Products'," &_
              "DatabaseName='Northwind',SQLServerName='thebox'")

' File to receive the exported table
objBcp.DataFilePath="C:\\outfile.dat"

' We need this to specify "Special Delimited Char" (3)
' or else the column- and row-delimiters won't work
objBcp.DataFileType=3

' Tab delimits columns
objBcp.ColumnDelimiter = vbTab

' Newline delimits rows
objBcp.RowDelimiter = vbNewLine

' Name of the SQL Server
objBcp.SQLServerName = "THEBOX"

' Export the table to file
objTable.ExportData objBcp
```

Because the \ character is also used as an escape character, it signifies that the next character should be treated as a plain character without special meaning. Because \ has that special meaning, most languages make it necessary to escape \ by \\.

NOTE
Object paths can use either / or \. In this book, / is used because it does not have to be escaped. This feature makes statements easier to read.

WMI Context Objects

The following example demonstrates WMI context objects. The code uses standard SQL Server authentication as opposed to integrated Windows authentication. The connection settings are stored in an SWbemNamedValueSet object. The names used in the calls to Add() correspond to the properties of the MSSQL_SQL-ServerConnectionSetting class.

```
' Get Services
Set objWbemSvc = GetObject("Winmgmts://./Root/MicrosoftSQLServer")

' Create a named value set
Set objWbemNVSet = CreateObject("WbemScripting.SWbemNamedValueSet")

' Add the name-value pairs
objWbemNVSet.Add "SettingID", "THEBOX"
objWbemNVSet.Add "LoginSecure", FALSE
objWbemNVSet.Add "Login", "sa"
objWbemNVSet.Add "Password", "whatever"

Set objWbemSet = objWbemSvc.InstancesOf("MSSQL_Database",, _
objWbemNVSet)

' This shouldn't print anything unless your password is "whatever"
WScript.Echo objWbemSet.Count
```

It first connects using the default authentication method. Then, calling `Instances-Of()` with the named value set overrides the current connection settings, so even if you logged onto SQL Server with no problems, the context object's connection settings are what matters. The script will quit with an error—just like we wanted it to.

Error Checking

During operations, errors that occur within the SQL Server domain are organized and returned as properties of an `MSSQL_MethodRtnVal` object. Those properties can be examined further to get information about the error. This following example tries to change the password of the `SQL Server` sa-login. Naturally, the passwords are incorrect, so we'll get an error that we can look at.

```
Dim objWbemSvc, objRtnVal
Dim strSqlServer, strPath
    strSqlServer = "MyServer"
    strPath = "MSSQL_Login.Name='sa',SQLServerName='" &_ /
            ctrSqlServer & "'"

' Get Services
Set objWbemSvc = GetObject("Winmgmts://./root/MicrosoftSQLServer")

' Set impersonationlevel
objWbemSvc.Security_.ImpersonationLevel = 3

' Try changing the  "sa" password
Set objRtnVal = objWbemSvc.Get(strPath).SetPassword("old","blah")

' Examine the MSSQL_MethodRtnVal-instance
If Not objRtnVal.ReturnValue = 0 Then
```

```
      ' Says no changes were made due to incorrect password
      WScript.Echo objRtnVal.ReturnValue & "=" _
                & objRtnVal.Description

      ' Says where the error occured
      WScript.Echo objRtnVal.Source

      ' Stops execution
      WScript.Quit
End If
```

Registering for NT Log Events

This script registers for notification when an event is written to the NT Log. A couple of things are new:

- The namespace is `//./root/CIMv2` and not `//./root/MicrosoftSQL-Server`. The `Win32_NTLogEvent` is not part of the MicrosoftSQL Server namespace.

- The NT Event Log is a true event provider. It has a callback routine, so WMI doesn't need to poll for events in order to receive them.

- The `SeSecurityPrivilege` must be set before connecting to the server. The query registers for events from all logs, including the Security log, so the `Security` privilege must be enabled. This security feature must be *complied to* (because it is built into NT).

- `TargetInstance` is set to `Win32_NTLogEvent`, and the `SourceName` property of `Win32_NTLogEvent` must be `MSSQLSERVER` in order for it not to be ignored.

Here is the code:

```
Dim objWbemLoc, objWbemSvc, objWbemEvtSrc, objWbemObj
Dim strQuery

' Build WQL query
strQuery = "SELECT * FROM __InstanceCreationEvent " &_
           "WHERE TargetInstance ISA 'Win32_NTLogEvent' " &_
           "AND TargetInstance.SourceName='MSSQLSERVER'"

' Get Locator
Set objWbemLoc = CreateObject("WbemScripting.SWbemLocator")

' Set privileges for security-log access
objWbemLoc.Security_.Privileges.AddAsString("SeSecurityPrivilege")

' Get Services
Set objWbemSvc = objWbemLoc.ConnectServer(".", "root/CIMv2")
```

```
' Get EventSource
Set objWbemEvtSrc = objWbemSvc.ExecNotificationQuery(strQuery)

Do
    ' Get NextEvent when it arrive
    Set objWbemObj = objWbemEvtSrc.NextEvent

    ' Print the message
    WScript.Echo objWbemObj.TargetInstance.Message
Loop
```

The `__InstanceCreationEvent` is used because NT log events are created as new instances. If the Security log is not your target, you can omit the `Privilege` string by rewriting the WQL query as follows:

```
' Build WQL query
strQuery = "SELECT * FROM __InstanceCreationEvent " &_
                    "WHERE TargetInstance ISA 'Win32_NTLogEvent' " &_
                    "AND TargetInstance.SourceName='MSSQLSERVER'" &_
                    "AND TargetInstance.LogFile = 'Application'"

' Get Locator
Set objWbemLoc = CreateObject("WbemScripting.SWbemLocator")

' Get Services
Set objWbemSvc = objWbemLoc.ConnectServer(".", "root/CIMv2")
```

Finally, a detail which you may have caught: Where the security log is left out of the query, the query becomes limited to just the Application log. A better query uses the form:

```
...AND  TargetInstance.LogFile <> 'Security'...
```

The query fragment above is better because logs other than the Application log may exist. So if you want to query them, it's best to write such a query that just excludes the Security log.

Summary

This chapter covered some common SQL Server management tasks. Although the SQL Server classes are quite numerous, they should not come with any unpleasant surprises when you understand the mechanics behind these examples.

Schema Reference

Welcome to the schema reference part of this book. This section outlines the portions and classes of the Microsoft SQL Server schema. Each class is listed with a lookup table for its class features and is followed by further explanation about these features where necessary. You can use this reference section to help you navigate around the SQL Server namespace and to understand how it is structured.

Common Material

There is often common material within each class. By that, I mean that many of the class features are inherited from a superclass; thus, it makes more sense to include the feature's description in the superclass only. There is no downside really, because the inherited properties are typically common to most classes.

Each class that is not an abstract class can have instances that can be enumerated by WMI. If the class requires you to use a method other than Put_() to create the class, this method is listed in the class description field called Constructor. Likewise, an explicit destructor (when needed) can be found in the Destructor field. The class descriptions are abstract definitions; I make no attempt to thoroughly explain the subject matter relating to the SQL Server functions. For a thorough treatment, refer to a good book such as *Inside SQL Server* from Microsoft Press or the SQL Server online documentation. If the class that you are reading about is an association of the aggregation type, it is specified in the class definition. All other association types have a descriptive superclass that tells you the type of association.

A number of methods are also common. All methods and properties are listed in the tables that cover the class; however, not all methods and properties are fully described outside the table. As we mentioned, properties are inherited—so it is redundant to redefine them. That is why I have not always included property descriptions. Methods are not defined outside the table if

1. The method was inherited and not overridden.
2. The method is self-explanatory and takes zero input parameters and zero output parameters.
3. The method is the Rename() method.

The definition of Rename() is always the same, and the Rename() method is used to rename an instance because WMI itself doesn't provide that functionality:

```
MSSQL_MethodRtnVal Rename (
    [In] string Name
);
```

The `Name` parameter specifies the new name that is to be given to the instance. In other words, this method applies to instances and is not a class function.

Some abstract classes can be created, as well. These classes are abstract merely because they cannot have their instances `Put_()`. So they are not instances that can be operated on through WMI. The abstract classes like that are used to create an instance in standard fashion and then to pass the instance as a parameter to a method that requires that particular abstract class as a parameter when called. Similarly, if you look at the `Rename()` method, it returns an object of the abstract class `MSSQL_MethodRtnVal`. Thus, it is instantiated there as well.

When you create database objects that could normally be created with a CRE-ATE statement, you will find a `Name` property and a `Text` property. For the operation to succeed, the name of the database object in both properties must be in the form `[dbo].[myname]`, and they must match. The owner names identify database objects in SQL Server and are necessary for database objects like databases and stored procedures to be created.

Finally, there are some document conventions. The signature of a method is parenthesis, and possible parenthesis containing parameters. A parameter can be an output or input parameter. The in and out qualifiers are present to reflect the parameter type. Additionally, if a method is a static method, the static box will be checked. Properties can generally be read or write once created. The tables will let you know that access type. Moreover, a property that is an array has brackets following it. Some properties can have a maxlength to its value. If so, that is defined in the tables. If there are no maxlength limits other than what the data type imposes, the maxlength cell in the table is left undefined. The same goes for if the value is measured in a type of units, such as kilobytes or megabytes. Wherever properties have special values, they are listed in a table under the property description. As you know, some properties are references to instances. The references can have special max and min qualifiers. The min qualifier defines if the reference can be empty (zero) or if it has to have one reference (one). The max qualifier defines if it can have only one instance of references or an infinite (asterisk) number of references. Some methods and properties are specific to SQL Server versions. If both the 7.0 and 2000 boxes are checked, the method or property works with both SQL Server versions. If only one version is checked, the item is limited to that version.

Aggregations

T his appendix contains a list of those association classes that are aggregations.

CIM_Component

Table A.1 CIM_Component Description

Class Type	Abstract, aggregation, association class
Description	Base class for modeling part of aggregation relationships. GroupComponent is a reference to the parent element, and PartComponent is a reference to the child element
Class Path	//./Root/MicrosoftSQLServer:CIM_Component

Table A.2 CIM_Component References

Name	Reference	Read	Write	Min	Max
GroupComponent	CIM_ManagedSystemElement	✔		1	1
PartComponent	CIM_ManagedSystemElement	✔		0	*

Win32_GroupUser

Table A.3 `Win32_GroupUser` Description

Superclass	`CIM_Component`
Class Type	Aggregation, association, dynamic class
Description	Associates a group with a user or system account; the Win32 account is placed within the group
Remarks	A view class
Class Path	`//./Root/MicrosoftSQLServer:Win32_GroupUser`
Keys	GroupComponent, PartComponent

Table A.4 `Win32_GroupUser` References

Name	Reference	Read	Write	Min	Max
GroupComponent	Win32_Group	✔		1	1
PartComponent	Win32_Account	✔		0	*

MSSQL_TransactionLogDataFile

Table A.5 `MSSQL_TransactionLogDataFile` Description

Superclass	`CIM_Component`
Class Type	Aggregation, association, dynamic class
Description	Association between SQL Server transaction log and the operating system file that stores the log
Class Path	`//./Root/MicrosoftSQLServer:` `MSSQL_TransactionLogDataFile`
Keys	GroupComponent, PartComponent

Table A.6 `MSSQL_TransactionLogDataFile` References

Name	Reference	Read	Write	Min	Max
GroupComponent	MSSQL_TransactionLog	✔		1	1
PartComponent	CIM_DataFile	✔		0	*

MSSQL_TableColumn

Table A.7 MSSQL_TableColumn Description

Superclass	CIM_Component
Class Type	Aggregation, association, dynamic class
Description	Association between a table and a column that is contained in the table
Class Path	//./Root/MicrosoftSQLServer:MSSQL_TableColumn
Keys	GroupComponent, PartComponent

Table A.8 MSSQL_TableColumn References

Name	Reference	Read	Write	Min	Max
GroupComponent	MSSQL_Table	✔		1	1
PartComponent	MSSQL_Column	✔		1	*

MSSQL_SQLServerDatabase

Table A.9 MSSQL_SQLServerDatabase Description

Superclass	CIM_Component
Class Type	Aggregation, association, dynamic class
Description	Association between an SQL server installation and a database that is part of the installation
Class Path	//./Root/MicrosoftSQLServer:MSSQL_SQLServerDatabase
Keys	GroupComponent, PartComponent

Table A.10 MSSQL_SQLServerDatabase References

Name	Reference	Read	Write	Min	Max
GroupComponent	MSSQL_SQLServer	✔		1	1
PartComponent	MSSQL_Database	✔		0	*

MSSQL_KeyColumn

Table A.11 MSSQL_KeyColumn Description

Superclass	CIM_Component
Class Type	Aggregation, association, dynamic class
Description	Association between a key and a column that is part of the key
Class Path	//./Root/MicrosoftSQLServer:MSSQL_KeyColumn
Keys	GroupComponent, PartComponent

Table A.12 MSSQL_KeyColumn References

Name	Reference	Read	Write	Min	Max
GroupComponent	MSSQL_Key	✔		1	1
PartComponent	MSSQL_Column	✔		1	*

MSSQL_FileGroupDatabaseFile

Table A.13 MSSQL_FileGroupDatabaseFile Description

Superclass	CIM_Component
Class Type	Aggregation, association, dynamic class
Description	Association between a file group and a database file
Class Path	//./Root/MicrosoftSQLServer: MSSQL_FileGroupDatabaseFile
Keys	GroupComponent, PartComponent

Table A.14 MSSQL_FileGroupDatabaseFile References

Name	Reference	Read	Write	Min	Max
GroupComponent	MSSQL_FileGroup	✔		1	1
PartComponent	MSSQL_DatabaseFile	✔		0	*

MSSQL_ErrorLogErrorLogEntry

Table A.15 MSSQL_ErrorLogErrorLogEntry Description

Superclass	CIM_Component
Class Type	Aggregation, association, dynamic class
Description	Association between an error log and an error log entry
Class Path	//./Root/MicrosoftSQLServer: MSSQL_ErrorLogErrorLogEntry
Keys	GroupComponent, PartComponent

Table A.16 MSSQL_ErrorLogErrorLogEntry References

Name	Reference	Read	Write	Min	Max
GroupComponent	MSSQL_ErrorLog	✔		1	1
PartComponent	MSSQL_ErrorLogEntry	✔		0	*

MSSQL_DatabaseView

Table A.17 MSSQL_DatabaseView Description

Superclass	CIM_Component
Class Type	Aggregation, association, dynamic class
Description	Association between a database and a view
Class Path	//./Root/MicrosoftSQLServer:MSSQL_DatabaseView
Keys	GroupComponent, PartComponent

Table A.18 MSSQL_DatabaseView References

Name	Reference	Read	Write	Min	Max
GroupComponent	MSSQL_Database	✔		1	1
PartComponent	MSSQL_View	✔		0	*

MSSQL_DatabaseTable

Table A.19 MSSQL_DatabaseTable Description

Superclass	CIM_Component
Class Type	Aggregation, association, dynamic class
Description	Association between a database and a database table
Class Path	//./Root/MicrosoftSQLServer:MSSQL_DatabaseTable
Keys	GroupComponent, PartComponent

Table A.20 MSSQL_DatabaseTable References

Name	Reference	Read	Write	Min	Max
GroupComponent	MSSQL_Database	✔		1	1
PartComponent	MSSQL_Table	✔		0	*

Dependent Objects

A ppendix B contains a list of those classes that are dependent on features of another class.

CIM_Dependency

Table B.1 CIM_Dependency Description

Class Type	Abstract, association class
Description	Base class for modeling dependency relationships where the functionality of the Dependent element depends on a feature in the Antecedent element
Class Path	//./Root/MicrosoftSQLServer:CIM_Dependency

Table B.2 CIM_Dependency References

Name	Reference	Read	Write
Antecedent	CIM_ManagedSystemElement	✔	
Dependent	CIM_ManagedSystemElement	✔	

MSSQL_UserLogin

Table B.3 MSSQL_UserLogin Description

Superclass	CIM_Dependency
Class Type	Association, dynamic class
Description	Association between a database user and the login that is used to authenticate the user
Class Path	//./Root/MicrosoftSQLServer:MSSQL_UserLogin
Keys	Antecedent, Dependent

Table B.4 MSSQL_UserLogin References

Name	Reference	Read	Write	Min	Max
Antecedent	MSSQL_Login	✔		1	1
Dependent	MSSQL_User	✔		0	*

MSSQL_UserDatatypeRule

Table B.5 MSSQL_UserDatatypeRule Description

Superclass	CIM_Dependency
Class Type	Association, dynamic class
Description	Association between a user-defined data type and the rule that is bound to the column
Class Path	//./Root/MicrosoftSQLServer:MSSQL_UserDatatypeRule
Keys	Antecedent, Dependent
Constructor	Create

Table B.6 MSSQL_UserDatatypeRule References

Name	Reference	Read	Write	Max
Antecedent	MSSQL_Rule	✔		1
Dependent	MSSQL_UserDatatype	✔		*

Table B.7 MSSQL_UserDatatypeRule Methods

Name	Return Type	Static	7.0	2000
Create	MSSQL_MethodRtnVal	✔	✔	✔

Create( )

The `Create()` method is used to create a new instance.

```
MSSQL_MethodRtnVal Create (
    [In] string SQLServerName,
    [In] string DatabaseName,
    [In] string RuleName,
    [In] string UserDatatypeName,
    [In, Optional] boolean FutureOnly
);
```

Parameters

`SQLServerName`

Name of the SQL Server instance in which the instance will be created.

`DatabaseName`

Name of the database to which this object belongs.

`RuleName`

Name of the rule to which this object belongs.

`UserDatatypeName`

Name of the user-defined data type to which the object belongs.

`FutureOnly`

If `False`, this parameter applies to all columns.

MSSQL_UserDatatypeDefault

Table B.8 MSSQL_UserDatatypeDefault Description

Superclass	CIM_Dependency
Class Type	Association, dynamic class
Description	Association between a user-defined data type and the rule that is bound to the column
Class Path	//./Root/MicrosoftSQLServer: MSSQL_UserDatatypeDefault
Keys	Antecedent, Dependent

Table B.9 MSSQL_UserDatatypeDefault References

Name	Reference	Read	Write	Max
Antecedent	MSSQL_Default	✔		1
Dependent	MSSQL_UserDatatype	✔		*

Table B.10 MSSQL_UserDatatypeDefault Methods

Name	Return Type	Static	7.0	2000
Create	MSSQL_MethodRtnVal	✔	✔	✔

Create( )

The Create() method is used to create a new instance.

```
MSSQL_MethodRtnVal Create (
    [In] string SQLServerName,
    [In] string DatabaseName,
    [In] string DefaultName,
    [In] string UserDatatypeName,
    [In, Optional] boolean FutureOnly
);
```

Parameters

SQLServerName

The name of the SQL Server instance in which the instance will be created

DatabaseName

The name of the database to which this object belongs

DefaultName

Name of the default

```
UserDatatypeName
```

Name of the user data type

```
FutureOnly
```

If `False`, this parameter applies to all columns.

MSSQL_TableTrigger

Table B.11 `MSSQL_TableTrigger` Description

Superclass	`CIM_Dependency`
Class Type	Association, dynamic class
Description	Association between a table and a trigger that is defined for the table
Class Path	`//./Root/MicrosoftSQLServer:MSSQL_TableTrigger`
Keys	`Antecedent, Dependent`

Table B.12 `MSSQL_TableTrigger` References

Name	Reference	Read	Write	Min	Max
Antecedent	MSSQL_Trigger	✔		0	*
Dependent	MSSQL_Table	✔		1	1

MSSQL_TableTextFileGroup

Table B.13 `MSSQL_TableTextFileGroup` Description

Superclass	`CIM_Dependency`
Class Type	Association, dynamic class
Description	Association between a table and a file group
Class Path	`//./Root/MicrosoftSQLServer:` `MSSQL_TableTextFileGroup`
Keys	`Antecedent, Dependent`

Table B.14 `MSSQL_TableTextFileGroup` References

Name	Reference	Read	Write	Max	Min
Antecedent	MSSQL_FileGroup	✔		0	1
Dependent	MSSQL_Table	✔		1	*

MSSQL_TableKey

Table B.15 MSSQL_TableKey Description

Superclass	CIM_Dependency
Class Type	Association, dynamic class
Description	Association between a table and a key that is defined for the table
Class Path	//./Root/MicrosoftSQLServer:MSSQL_TableKey
Keys	Antecedent, Dependent

Table B.16 MSSQL_TableKey References

Name	Reference	Read	Write	Min	Max
Antecedent	MSSQL_Key	✔		1	*
Dependent	MSSQL_Table	✔		1	1

MSSQL_TableIndex

Table B.17 MSSQL_TableIndex Description

Superclass	CIM_Dependency
Class Type	Association, dynamic class
Description	Association between a table and an index that is defined for the table
Class Path	//./Root/MicrosoftSQLServer:MSSQL_TableIndex
Keys	Antecedent, Dependent

Table B.18 MSSQL_TableIndex References

Name	Reference	Read	Write	Min	Max
Antecedent	MSSQL_Index	✔		0	*
Dependent	MSSQL_Table	✔		1	1

MSSQL_TableFileGroup

Table B.19 MSSQL_TableFileGroup Description

Superclass	CIM_Dependency
Class Type	Association, dynamic class
Description	Association between a table and the file groups that are used to store the table
Class Path	//./Root/MicrosoftSQLServer:MSSQL_TableFileGroup
Keys	Antecedent, Dependent

Table B.20 MSSQL_TableFileGroup References

Name	Reference	Read	Write	Min	Max
Antecedent	MSSQL_FileGroup	✔		1	1
Dependent	MSSQL_Table	✔		1	*

MSSQL_TableCheck

Table B.21 MSSQL_TableCheck Description

Superclass	CIM_Dependency
Class Type	Association, dynamic class
Description	Association between a table and the checks that are defined for the table
Class Path	//./Root/MicrosoftSQLServer:MSSQL_TableCheck
Keys	Antecedent, Dependent

Table B.22 MSSQL_TableCheck References

Name	Reference	Read	Write	Min	Max
Antecedent	MSSQL_Check	✔		0	*
Dependent	MSSQL_Table	✔		1	1

MSSQL_SQLServerErrorLog

Table B.23 MSSQL_SQLServerErrorLog Description

Superclass	CIM_Dependency
Class Type	Association, dynamic class
Description	Association between an SQL server installation and the error log that the installation uses
Class Path	//./Root/MicrosoftSQLServer:MSSQL_SQLServerErrorLog
Keys	Antecedent, Dependent

Table B.24 MSSQL_SQLServerErrorLog References

Name	Reference	Read	Write	Min	Max
Antecedent	MSSQL_ErrorLog	✔		0	*
Dependent	MSSQL_SQLServer	✔		1	1

MSSQL_SQLServerBackupDevice

Table B.25 MSSQL_SQLServerBackupDevice Description

Superclass	CIM_Dependency
Class Type	Association, dynamic class
Description	Association between an SQL server installation and a backup device that is known to SQL Server
Class Path	//./Root/MicrosoftSQLServer: MSSQL_SQLServerBackupDevice
Keys	Antecedent, Dependent

Table B.26 MSSQL_SQLServerBackupDevice References

Name	Reference	Read	Write	Min
Antecedent	MSSQL_BackupDevice	✔		0
Dependent	MSSQL_SQLServer	✔		1

MSSQL_MemberDatabaseRole

Table B.27 MSSQL_MemberDatabaseRole Description

Superclass	CIM_Dependency
Class Type	Association, dynamic class
Description	Association between two database roles, one being a member of the other
Class Path	//./Root/MicrosoftSQLServer: MSSQL_MemberDatabaseRole
Keys	Antecedent, Dependent

Table B.28 MSSQL_MemberDatabaseRole References

Name	Reference	Read	Write	Min	Max
Antecedent	MSSQL_DatabaseRole	✔	✔	1	1
Dependent	MSSQL_DatabaseRole	✔	✔	0	*

MSSQL_LoginWin32UserAccount

Table B.29 MSSQL_LoginWin32UserAccount Description

Superclass	CIM_Dependency
Class Type	Association, dynamic class
Description	Association between a login and the Win32 user account that is used for authentication by the login
Class Path	//./Root/MicrosoftSQLServer: MSSQL_LoginWin32UserAccount
Keys	Antecedent, Dependent

Table B.30 MSSQL_LoginWin32UserAccount References

Name	Reference	Read	Write	Max
Antecedent	Win32_UserAccount	✔		1
Dependent	MSSQL_Login	✔		*

MSSQL_KeyFileGroup

Table B.31 MSSQL_KeyFileGroup Description

Superclass	CIM_Dependency
Class Type	Association, dynamic class
Description	Association between a key and the file group that is used to store the key
Class Path	//./Root/MicrosoftSQLServer:MSSQL_KeyFileGroup
Keys	Antecedent, Dependent

Table B.32 MSSQL_KeyFileGroup References

Name	Reference	Read	Write	Min	Max
Antecedent	MSSQL_FileGroup	✔		1	1
Dependent	MSSQL_CandidateKey	✔		0	*

MSSQL_ReferencedTable

Table B.33 MSSQL_ReferencedTable Description

Superclass	CIM_Dependency
Class Type	Association, dynamic class
Description	Association between a foreign key and the table that contains the primary key that is referenced by the foreign key
Class Path	//./Root/MicrosoftSQLServer:MSSQL_ReferencedTable
Keys	Antecedent, Dependent

Table B.34 MSSQL_ReferencedTable References

Name	Reference	Read	Write	Min	Max
Antecedent	MSSQL_Table	✔		1	1
Dependent	MSSQL_ForeignKey	✔		0	*

MSSQL_ReferencedKey

Table B.35 MSSQL_ReferencedKey Description

Superclass	CIM_Dependency
Class Type	Association, dynamic class
Description	Association between a foreign key and the candidate key that the foreign key references
Class Path	//./Root/MicrosoftSQLServer:MSSQL_ReferencedKey
Keys	Antecedent, Dependent

Table B.36 MSSQL_ReferencedKey References

Name	Reference	Read	Write	Min	Max
Antecedent	MSSQL_CandidateKey	✔		1	1
Dependent	MSSQL_ForeignKey	✔		0	*

MSSQL_MemberUser

Table B.37 MSSQL_MemberUser Description

Superclass	CIM_Dependency
Class Type	Association, dynamic class
Description	Association between a database role and a user who is a member of the database role
Class Path	//./Root/MicrosoftSQLServer:MSSQL_MemberUser
Keys	Antecedent, Dependent

Table B.38 MSSQL_MemberUser References

Name	Reference	Read	Write
Antecedent	MSSQL_DatabaseRole	✔	
Dependent	MSSQL_User	✔	

MSSQL_MemberLogin

Table B.39 MSSQL_MemberLogin Description

Superclass	CIM_Dependency
Class Type	Association, dynamic class
Description	Association between a login and the SQL Server role on which the login depends
Class Path	//./Root/MicrosoftSQLServer:MSSQL_MemberLogin
Keys	Antecedent, Dependent

Table B.40 MSSQL_MemberLogin References

Name	Reference	Read	Write
Antecedent	MSSQL_SQLServerRole	✔	✔
Dependent	MSSQL_Login	✔	✔

MSSQL_IndexFileGroup

Table B.41 MSSQL_IndexFileGroup Description

Superclass	CIM_Dependency
Class Type	Association, dynamic class
Description	Association between the index and the file group in which it is stored
Class Path	//./Root/MicrosoftSQLServer:MSSQL_IndexFileGroup
Keys	Antecedent, Dependent

Table B.42 MSSQL_IndexFileGroup References

Name	Reference	Read	Write	Min	Max
Antecedent	MSSQL_FileGroup	✔		1	1
Dependent	MSSQL_Index	✔		0	*

MSSQL_IndexColumn

Table B.43 MSSQL_IndexColumn Description

Superclass	CIM_Dependency
Class Type	Association, dynamic class
Description	Association between an index and an indexed column
Class Path	//./Root/MicrosoftSQLServer:MSSQL_IndexColumn
Keys	Antecedent, Dependent

Table B.44 MSSQL_IndexColumn Properties

Name	Datatype	Read	Write	7.0	2000
DescendingSortOrder	boolean			✔	✔

Table B.45 MSSQL_IndexColumn References

Name	Reference	Read	Write	Min
Antecedent	MSSQL_Column	✔		1
Dependent	MSSQL_Index	✔		0

MSSQL_ErrorLogDataFile

Table B.46 MSSQL_ErrorLogDataFile Description

Superclass	CIM_Dependency
Class Type	Association, dynamic class
Description	Association between an SQL Server error log and the file where it is stored
Class Path	//./Root/MicrosoftSQLServer:MSSQL_ErrorLogDataFile
Keys	Antecedent, Dependent

Table B.47 MSSQL_ErrorLogDataFile References

Name	Reference	Read	Write	Min	Max
Antecedent	CIM_DataFile	✔		1	1
Dependent	MSSQL_ErrorLog	✔		0	1

MSSQL_DBMSObjectOwner

Table B.48 MSSQL_DBMSObjectOwner **Description**

Superclass	CIM_Dependency
Class Type	Association, dynamic class
Description	Association between an SQL database object and the user who owns the object
Class Path	//./Root/MicrosoftSQLServer:MSSQL_DBMSObjectOwner
Keys	Antecedent, Dependent

Table B.49 MSSQL_DBMSObjectOwner **References**

Name	Reference	Read	Write	Min	Max
Antecedent	MSSQL_User	✔		1	1
Dependent	MSSQL_DBMSObject	✔			*

MSSQL_DatabaseTransactionLog

Table B.50 MSSQL_DatabaseTransactionLog **Description**

Superclass	CIM_Dependency
Class Type	Association, dynamic class
Description	Association between the database and its transaction log
Class Path	//./Root/MicrosoftSQLServer: MSSQL_DatabaseTransactionLog
Keys	Antecedent, Dependent

Table B.51 MSSQL_DatabaseTransactionLog **References**

Name	Reference	Read	Write	Min	Max
Antecedent	MSSQL_TransactionLog	✔		1	1
Dependent	MSSQL_Database	✔		1	1

MSSQL_DatabaseOwnerLogin

Table B.52 MSSQL_DatabaseOwnerLogin Description

Superclass	CIM_Dependency
Class Type	Association, dynamic class
Description	Association between a database and the SQL Server login instance that is used by the database user who owns the database
Class Path	//./Root/MicrosoftSQLServer: MSSQL_DatabaseOwnerLogin
Keys	Antecedent, Dependent

Table B.53 MSSQL_DatabaseOwnerLogin References

Name	Reference	Read	Write	Min	Max
Antecedent	MSSQL_Login	✔		1	1
Dependent	MSSQL_Database	✔			*

MSSQL_DatabaseFullTextCatalog

Table B.54 MSSQL_DatabaseFullTextCatalog Description

Superclass	CIM_Dependency
Class Type	Association, dynamic class
Description	Association between a database and a full-text catalog, enabling full-text queries against the database on which it depends
Class Path	//./Root/MicrosoftSQLServer: MSSQL_DatabaseFullTextCatalog
Keys	Antecedent, Dependent

Table B.55 MSSQL_DatabaseFullTextCatalog References

Name	Reference	Read	Write
Antecedent	MSSQL_FullTextCatalog	✔	
Dependent	MSSQL_Database	✔	

MSSQL_DatabaseFileGroup

Table B.56 MSSQL_DatabaseFileGroup Description

Superclass	CIM_Dependency
Class Type	Association, dynamic class
Description	Association between a database and the group of operating system files on which it depends for storage of the database
Class Path	//./Root/MicrosoftSQLServer:MSSQL_DatabaseFileGroup
Keys	Antecedent, Dependent

Table B.57 MSSQL_DatabaseFileGroup References

Name	Reference	Read	Write	Min	Max
Antecedent	MSSQL_FileGroup	✔		1	*
Dependent	MSSQL_Database	✔		1	1

MSSQL_ColumnRule

Table B.58 MSSQL_ColumnRule Description

Superclass	CIM_Dependency
Class Type	Association, dynamic class
Description	Association between a column and a rule on which it depends
Class Path	//./Root/MicrosoftSQLServer:MSSQL_ColumnRule
Keys	Antecedent, Dependent

Table B.59 MSSQL_ColumnRule References

Name	Reference	Read	Write	Max
Antecedent	MSSQL_Rule	✔		1
Dependent	MSSQL_Column	✔		*

MSSQL_ColumnDRIDefault

Table B.60 MSSQL_ColumnDRIDefault Description

Superclass	CIM_Dependency
Class Type	Association, dynamic class
Description	Association between a column and a DRI default on which it depends
Class Path	//./Root/MicrosoftSQLServer:MSSQL_ColumnDRIDefault
Keys	Antecedent, Dependent

Table B.61 MSSQL_ColumnDRIDefault References

Name	Reference	Read	Write	Max	Min
Antecedent	MSSQL_DRIDefault	✔		0	1
Dependent	MSSQL_Column	✔		1	1

MSSQL_ColumnDefault

Table B.62 MSSQL_ColumnDefault Description

Superclass	CIM_Dependency
Class Type	Association, dynamic class
Description	Association between a column and a default on which it depends
Class Path	//./Root/MicrosoftSQLServer:MSSQL_ColumnDefault
Keys	Antecedent, Dependent

Table B.63 MSSQL_ColumnDefault References

Name	Reference	Read	Write	Max
Antecedent	MSSQL_Default	✔		1
Dependent	MSSQL_Column	✔		*

MSSQL_ColumnDatatype

Table B.64 MSSQL_ColumnDatatype Description

Superclass	CIM_Dependency
Class Type	Association, dynamic class
Description	Association between a column and the data type on which it depends
Class Path	//./Root/MicrosoftSQLServer:MSSQL_ColumnDatatype
Keys	Antecedent, Dependent

Table B.65 MSSQL_ColumnDatatype References

Name	Reference	Read	Write	Min	Max
Antecedent	MSSQL_Datatype	✔		1	1
Dependent	MSSQL_Column	✔		0	*

MSSQL_BaseDatatype

Table B.66 MSSQL_BaseDatatype Description

Superclass	CIM_Dependency
Class Type	Association, dynamic class
Description	Association between a user-defined data type and the system data type on which it depends
Class Path	//./Root/MicrosoftSQLServer:MSSQL_BaseDatatype
Keys	Antecedent, Dependent

Table B.67 MSSQL_BaseDatatype References

Name	Reference	Read	Write	Min	Max
Antecedent	MSSQL_SystemDatatype	✔		1	1
Dependent	MSSQL_UserDatatype	✔			*

MSSQL_LoginWin32Group

Table B.68 MSSQL_LoginWin32Group Description

Superclass	CIM_Dependency
Class Type	Association, dynamic class
Description	Association between a login and the Win32 user group that is used for authentication by the login
Class Path	//./Root/MicrosoftSQLServer:MSSQL_LoginWin32Group
Keys	Antecedent, Dependent

Table B.69 MSSQL_LoginWin32Group References

Name	Reference	Read	Write	Max
Antecedent	Win32_Group	✔		1
Dependent	MSSQL_Login	✔		*

MSSQL_LoginDefaultDatabase

Table B.70 MSSQL_LoginDefaultDatabase Description

Superclass	CIM_Dependency
Class Type	Association, dynamic class
Description	Association between a login and the default database for the login
Class Path	//./Root/MicrosoftSQLServer: MSSQL_LoginDefaultDatabase
Keys	Antecedent, Dependent

Table B.71 MSSQL_LoginDefaultDatabase References

Name	Reference	Read	Write	Min	Max
Antecedent	MSSQL_Login	✔		1	1
Dependent	MSSQL_Database	✔			*

Permissions

U se the classes that are described in this appendix for defining permissions.

MSSQL_Permission

Table C.1 MSSQL_Permission Descriptions

Class Type	Abstract, association class
Description	Base class for permissions explicitly granted/denied to a user object for access to a database object. Grantee is a reference to the database user object for which the permissions are granted/denied, and the Element is a reference to the database object in the association. If the value of Granted is True, that means that the permissions are granted.
Class Path	//./Root/MicrosoftSQLServer:MSSQL_Permission

Table C.2 MSSQL_Permission Properties

Name	Datatype	Read	Write	7.0	2000
Granted	boolean	✔		✔	✔
PrivilegeType	uint32	✔		✔	✔

Table C.3 MSSQL_Permission References

Name	Reference	Read	Write
Element	MSSQL_DBMSObject	✔	
Grantee	MSSQL_DBMSUserObject	✔	

Table C.4 Possible Values for the PrivilegeType Property

Value	Privilege
0	Unknown
1	Permission to query a table
2	Permission to add rows to a table
4	Permission to update rows of a table
8	Permission to delete rows of a table
16	Permission to execute a stored procedure
32	Permission to grant declarative referential integrity (DRI) on a table
63	All privileges applicable to the database object
128	Permission to create and own a table
256	Permission to create and own a database
512	Permission to create and own a view
1024	Permission to create and own a stored procedure
2048	Permission to backup a database
4096	Permission to create a default
8192	Permission to backup a database transaction log
16384	Permission to create a rule
32768	Permission to back up to a table
65366	Permission to create a user defined function
130944	All privileges applicable to the database

MSSQL_UserStoredProcedurePermission

Table C.5 MSSQL_UserStoredProcedurePermission Description

Superclass	MSSQL_Permission
Class Type	Association, dynamic class
Description	Permissions granted to a user for a stored procedure
Class Path	//./Root/MicrosoftSQLServer: MSSQL_UserStoredProcedurePermission
Keys	Element, Grantee, PrivilegeType

Table C.6 MSSQL_UserStoredProcedurePermission Properties

Name	Datatype	Read	Write	7.0	2000
Granted	boolean	✔	✔	✔	✔
PrivilegeType	uint32	✔	✔	✔	✔

Table C.7 MSSQL_UserStoredProcedurePermission References

Name	Reference	Read	Write
Element	MSSQL_StoredProcedure	✔	
Grantee	MSSQL_User	✔	✔

MSSQL_UserDatabasePermission

Table C.8 MSSQL_UserDatabasePermission Description

Superclass	MSSQL_Permission
Class Type	Association, dynamic class
Description	Permissions granted to a user for a database
Class Path	//./Root/MicrosoftSQLServer: MSSQL_UserDatabasePermission
Keys	Element, Grantee, PrivilegeType

Table C.9 MSSQL_UserDatabasePermission Properties

Name	Datatype	Read	Write	7.0	2000
Granted	boolean	✔	✔	✔	✔
PrivilegeType	uint32	✔	✔	✔	✔

Table C.10 MSSQL_UserDatabasePermission References

Name	Reference	Read	Write
Element	MSSQL_Database	✔	✔
Grantee	MSSQL_User	✔	✔

MSSQL_UserViewPermission

Table C.11 MSSQL_UserViewPermission Description

Superclass	MSSQL_Permission
Class Type	Association, dynamic class
Description	Permissions granted to a user for a view
Class Path	//./Root/MicrosoftSQLServer: MSSQL_UserViewPermission
Keys	Element, Granted, Grantee, PrivilegeType

Table C.12 MSSQL_UserViewPermission Properties

Name	Datatype	Read	Write	7.0	2000
ColumnName	string []	✔	✔	✔	✔
Granted	Boolean	✔	✔	✔	✔
PrivilegeType	uint32	✔	✔	✔	✔

Table C.13 MSSQL_UserViewPermission References

Name	Reference	Read	Write
Element	MSSQL_View	✔	
Grantee	MSSQL_User	✔	

ColumnName [ ]

The columns on which the permissions were defined; NULL applies the permissions on all columns.

MSSQL_UserTablePermission

Table C.14 MSSQL_UserTablePermission **Description**

Superclass	MSSQL_Permission
Class Type	Association, dynamic class
Description	Permissions granted to a user for a table
Class Path	//./Root/MicrosoftSQLServer: MSSQL_UserTablePermission
Keys	Element, Granted, Grantee, PrivilegeType

Table C.15 MSSQL_UserTablePermission **Properties**

Name	Datatype	Read	Write	7.0	2000
ColumnName	string []	✔	✔	✔	✔
Granted	boolean	✔	✔	✔	✔
PrivilegeType	uint32	✔	✔	✔	✔

Table C.16 MSSQL_UserTablePermission **References**

Name	Reference	Read	Write
Element	MSSQL_Table	✔	
Grantee	MSSQL_User	✔	

ColumnName [ ]

The columns on which the permissions were defined; NULL applies the permissions to all columns.

MSSQL_UserUserDefinedFunctionPermission

Table C.17 MSSQL_UserUserDefinedFunctionPermission **Description**

Superclass	MSSQL_Permission
Class Type	Association, dynamic class
Description	Permissions explicitly granted/denied to a user for a stored procedure
Class Path	//./Root/MicrosoftSQLServer: MSSQL_UserUserDefinedFunctionPermission
Keys	Element, Grantee, PrivilegeType

Table C.18 `MSSQL_UserUserDefinedFunctionPermission` Properties

Name	Datatype	Read	Write	7.0	2000
Granted	boolean	✔	✔		✔
PrivilegeType	uint32	✔	✔		✔

Table C.19 `MSSQL_UserUserDefinedFunctionPermission` References

Name	Reference	Read	Write
Element	MSSQL_UserDefinedFunction	✔	✔
Grantee	MSSQL_User	✔	✔

MSSQL_DatabaseRoleViewPermission

Table C.20 `MSSQL_DatabaseRoleViewPermission` Description

Superclass	MSSQL_Permission
Class Type	Association, dynamic class
Description	Permissions explicitly granted/denied for a database role on a view
Class Path	//./Root/MicrosoftSQLServer: MSSQL_DatabaseRoleViewPermission
Keys	Element, Granted, Grantee, PrivilegeType

Table C.21 `MSSQL_DatabaseRoleViewPermission` Properties

Name	Datatype	Read	Write	7.0	2000
ColumnName	string [ ]	✔	✔	✔	✔
Granted	boolean	✔	✔	✔	✔
PrivilegeType	uint32	✔	✔	✔	✔

Table C.22 `MSSQL_DatabaseRoleViewPermission` References

Name	Reference	Read	Write
Element	MSSQL_View	✔	
Grantee	MSSQL_DatabaseRole	✔	

ColumnName [ ]

The columns on which the permissions were defined; NULL applies the permissions to all columns.

MSSQL_DatabaseRoleUserDefinedFunctionPermission

Table C.23 MSSQL_DatabaseRoleUserDefinedFunctionPermission Description

Superclass	MSSQL_Permission
Class Type	Association, dynamic class
Description	Permissions explicitly granted/denied to a database role on a user-defined function
Class Path	//./Root/MicrosoftSQLServer: MSSQL_DatabaseRoleUserDefinedFunctionPermission
Keys	Element, Grantee, PrivilegeType

Table C.24 MSSQL_DatabaseRoleUserDefinedFunctionPermission Properties

Name	Datatype	Read	Write	7.0	2000
Granted	boolean	✔	✔		✔
PrivilegeType	uint32	✔	✔		✔

Table C.25 MSSQL_DatabaseRoleUserDefinedFunctionPermission References

Name	Reference	Read	Write
Element	MSSQL_UserDefinedFunction	✔	✔
Grantee	MSSQL_DatabaseRole	✔	✔

MSSQL_DatabaseRoleTablePermission

Table C.26 MSSQL_DatabaseRoleTablePermission Description

Superclass	MSSQL_Permission
Class Type	Association, dynamic class
Description	Permissions explicitly granted/denied to a database role on a table
Class Path	//./Root/MicrosoftSQLServer: MSSQL_DatabaseRoleTablePermission
Keys	Element, Granted, Grantee, PrivilegeType

Table C.27 MSSQL_DatabaseRoleTablePermission Properties

Name	Datatype	Read	Write	7.0	2000
ColumnName	string [ ]	✔	✔	✔	✔
Granted	boolean	✔	✔	✔	✔
PrivilegeType	uint32	✔	✔	✔	✔

Table C.28 `MSSQL_DatabaseRoleTablePermission` References

Name	Reference	Read	Write
Element	MSSQL_Table	✔	
Grantee	MSSQL_DatabaseRole	✔	

ColumnName [ ]

The columns on which the permissions were defined; NULL applies the permissions to all columns.

MSSQL_DatabaseRoleStoredProcedurePermission

Table C.29 `MSSQL_DatabaseRoleStoredProcedurePermission` Description

Superclass	`MSSQL_Permission`
Class Type	Association, dynamic class
Description	Permissions explicitly granted/denied to a database role for a stored procedure
Class Path	`//./Root/MicrosoftSQLServer:` `MSSQL_DatabaseRoleStoredProcedurePermission`
Keys	`Element, Grantee, PrivilegeType`

Table C.30 `MSSQL_DatabaseRoleStoredProcedurePermission` Properties

Name	Datatype	Read	Write	7.0	2000
Granted	boolean	✔	✔	✔	✔
PrivilegeType	uint32	✔	✔	✔	✔

Table C.31 `MSSQL_DatabaseRoleStoredProcedurePermission` References

Name	Reference	Read	Write
Element	MSSQL_StoredProcedure	✔	✔
Grantee	MSSQL_DatabaseRole	✔	✔

MSSQL_DatabaseRoleDatabasePermission

Table C.32 MSSQL_DatabaseRoleDatabasePermission Description

Superclass	MSSQL_Permission
Class Type	Association, dynamic class
Description	Permissions explicitly granted/denied to a database role for a database
Class Path	//./Root/MicrosoftSQLServer: MSSQL_DatabaseRoleDatabasePermission
Keys	Element, Grantee, PrivilegeType

Table C.33 MSSQL_DatabaseRoleDatabasePermission **Properties**

Name	Datatype	Read	Write	7.0	2000
Granted	boolean	✔	✔	✔	✔
PrivilegeType	uint32	✔	✔	✔	✔

Table C.34 MSSQL_DatabaseRoleDatabasePermission **References**

Name	Reference	Read	Write
Element	MSSQL_Database	✔	✔
Grantee	MSSQL_DatabaseRole	✔	✔

Scoped Objects

The classes in this appendix involve scoping relationship associations.

MSSQL_Scope

Table D.1 MSSQL_Scope **Description**

Class Type	Abstract, association class
Description	Association between two logical elements in which one is scoped within the other. ScopingElement references the logical elements that define the scope for the instance that is referenced by ScopedElement. ScopedElement references the logical element that is scoped within ScopingElement. The name of this element must be unique within its scope.
Class Path	//./Root/MicrosoftSQLServer:MSSQL_Scope

Table D.2 MSSQL_Scope **References**

Name	Reference	Read	Write	Min	Max
ScopedElement	CIM_LogicalElement	✔		0	*
ScopingElement	CIM_LogicalElement	✔		1	1

MSSQL_StoredProcedureStoredProcedureParameter

Table D.3 MSSQL_StoredProcedureStoredProcedureParameter Description

Superclass	MSSQL_Scope
Class Type	Association, dynamic class
Description	Associates a stored procedure with a parameter that is used in the stored procedure
Class Path	//./Root/MicrosoftSQLServer: MSSQL_StoredProcedureStoredProcedureParameter
Keys	ScopedElement, ScopingElement

Table D.4 MSSQL_StoredProcedureStoredProcedureParameter References

Name	Reference	Read	Write	Min	Max
ScopedElement	MSSQL_StoredProcedure-Parameter	✔		0	*
ScopingElement	MSSQL_StoredProcedure	✔		1	1

MSSQL_SQLServerServerRole

Table D.5 MSSQL_SQLServerServerRole Description

Superclass	MSSQL_Scope
Class Type	Association, dynamic class
Description	Association between an SQL server and a server's role (defined within the SQL server)
Class Path	//./Root/MicrosoftSQLServer: MSSQL_SQLServerServerRole
Keys	ScopedElement, ScopingElement

Table D.6 MSSQL_SQLServerServerRole References

Name	Reference	Read	Write	Min	Max
ScopedElement	MSSQL_SQLServerRole	✔		0	*
ScopingElement	MSSQL_SQLServer	✔		1	1

MSSQL_SQLServerLogin

Table D.7 MSSQL_SQLServerLogin Description

Superclass	MSSQL_Scope
Class Type	Association, dynamic class
Description	Association between an SQL server and an SQL Server login
Class Path	//./Root/MicrosoftSQLServer:MSSQL_SQLServerLogin
Keys	ScopedElement, ScopingElement

Table D.8 MSSQL_SQLServerLogin References

Name	Reference	Read	Write	Min	Max
ScopedElement	MSSQL_Login	✔		0	*
ScopingElement	MSSQL_SQLServer	✔		1	1

MSSQL_DatabaseUser

Table D.9 MSSQL_DatabaseUser Description

Superclass	MSSQL_Scope
Class Type	Association, dynamic class
Description	Associates a database to a unique user in the scope of the database
Class Path	//./Root/MicrosoftSQLServer:MSSQL_DatabaseUser
Keys	ScopedElement, ScopingElement

Table D.10 MSSQL_DatabaseUser References

Name	Reference	Read	Write	Min	Max
ScopedElement	MSSQL_User	✔		0	*
ScopingElement	MSSQL_Database	✔		1	1

MSSQL_DatabaseUserDefinedFunction

Table D.11 MSSQL_DatabaseUserDefinedFunction Description

Superclass	MSSQL_Scope
Class Type	Association, dynamic class
Description	Associates a database with a unique, user-defined function in the scope of the database
Class Path	//./Root/MicrosoftSQLServer: MSSQL_DatabaseUserDefinedFunction
Keys	ScopedElement, ScopingElement

Table D.12 MSSQL_DatabaseUserDefinedFunction References

Name	Reference	Read	Write	Min	Max
ScopedElement	MSSQL_UserDefinedFunction	✔		0	*
ScopingElement	MSSQL_Database	✔		1	1

MSSQL_DatabaseStoredProcedure

Table D.13 MSSQL_DatabaseStoredProcedure Description

Superclass	MSSQL_Scope
Class Type	Association, dynamic class
Description	Associates a database with a unique stored procedure in the scope of the database
Class Path	//./Root/MicrosoftSQLServer: MSSQL_DatabaseStoredProcedure
Keys	ScopedElement, ScopingElement

Table D.14 MSSQL_DatabaseStoredProcedure References

Name	Reference	Read	Write	Min	Max
ScopedElement	MSSQL_StoredProcedure	✔		0	*
ScopingElement	MSSQL_Database	✔		1	1

MSSQL_DatabaseRule

Table D.15 MSSQL_DatabaseRule Description

Superclass	MSSQL_Scope
Class Type	Association, dynamic class
Description	Associates a database with a unique rule in the scope of the database
Class Path	//./Root/MicrosoftSQLServer:MSSQL_DatabaseRule
Keys	ScopedElement, ScopingElement

Table D.16 MSSQL_DatabaseRule References

Name	Reference	Read	Write	Min	Max
ScopedElement	MSSQL_Rule	✔		0	*
ScopingElement	MSSQL_Database	✔		1	1

MSSQL_DatabaseDefault

Table D.17 MSSQL_DatabaseDefault Description

Superclass	MSSQL_Scope
Class Type	Association, dynamic class
Description	Associates a database with a unique default in the scope of the database
Class Path	//./Root/MicrosoftSQLServer:MSSQL_DatabaseDefault
Keys	ScopedElement, ScopingElement

Table D.18 MSSQL_DatabaseDefault References

Name	Reference	Read	Write	Min	Max
ScopedElement	MSSQL_Default	✔		0	*
ScopingElement	MSSQL_Database	✔		1	1

MSSQL_DatabaseDatatype

Table D.19 MSSQL_DatabaseDatatype Description

Superclass	MSSQL_Scope
Class Type	Association, dynamic class
Description	Associates a database with a unique data type in the scope of the database
Class Path	//./Root/MicrosoftSQLServer:MSSQL_DatabaseDatatype
Keys	ScopedElement, ScopingElement

Table D.20 MSSQL_DatabaseDatatype References

Name	Reference	Read	Write	Min	Max
ScopedElement	MSSQL_Datatype	✔		0	*
ScopingElement	MSSQL_Database	✔		1	1

MSSQL_DatabaseDatabaseRole

Table D.21 MSSQL_DatabaseDatabaseRole Description

Superclass	MSSQL_Scope
Class Type	Association, dynamic class
Description	Associates a database with a unique database role in the scope of the database
Class Path	//./Root/MicrosoftSQLServer: MSSQL_DatabaseDatabaseRole
Keys	ScopedElement, ScopingElement

Table D.22 MSSQL_DatabaseDatabaseRole References

Name	Reference	Read	Write	Min	Max
ScopedElement	MSSQL_DatabaseRole	✔		0	*
ScopingElement	MSSQL_Database	✔		1	1

APPENDIX **E**

Containment

T his appendix contains a list of the association classes that are represented by containment relationships.

MSSQL_Containment

Table E.1 MSSQL_Containment Description

Class Type	Abstract, association class
Description	Association between a container and the contained object. Containee references a managed system element that is contained within another managed system element. Container references a managed system element that contains one or more managed system elements.
Class Path	//./Root/MicrosoftSQLServer:MSSQL_Containment

Table E.2 MSSQL_Containment References

Name	Reference	Read	Write
Containee	CIM_ManagedSystemElement	✔	
Container	CIM_ManagedSystemElement	✔	

MSSQL_DatabaseCandidateKey

Table E.3 MSSQL_DatabaseCandidateKey Description

Superclass	MSSQL_Containment
Class Type	Association, dynamic class
Description	Association between a database and a candidate key that is contained in a database table
Class Path	//./Root/MicrosoftSQLServer: MSSQL_DatabaseCandidateKey
Keys	Containee, Container

Table E.4 MSSQL_DatabaseCandidateKey References

Name	Reference	Read	Write	Min	Max
Containee	MSSQL_CandidateKey	✔		0	*
Container	MSSQL_Database	✔		1	1

MSSQL_SQLServerUser

Table E.5 MSSQL_SQLServerUser Description

Superclass	MSSQL_Containment
Class Type	Association, dynamic class
Description	Association between an SQL Server instance and a database user that is contained in a database
Class Path	//./Root/MicrosoftSQLServer:MSSQL_SQLServerUser
Keys	Containee, Container, DatabaseName, LoginName

Table E.6 MSSQL_SQLServerUser Properties

Name	Datatype	Read	Write	Maxlen	7.0	2000
DatabaseName	string	✔		128	✔	✔
LoginName	string	✔		128	✔	✔

Table E.7 MSSQL_SQLServerUser References

Name	Reference	Read	Write	Min	Max
Containee	MSSQL_User	✔		0	*
Container	MSSQL_SQLServer	✔		1	1

MSSQL_DatabaseLogin

Table E.8 MSSQL_DatabaseLogin Description

Superclass	MSSQL_Containment
Class Type	Association, dynamic class
Description	Association between a database and a login that is utilized by a user in the database. The UserName property is the database user who is mapped to Containee.
Class Path	//./Root/MicrosoftSQLServer:MSSQL_DatabaseLogin
Keys	Containee, Container, UserName

Table E.9 MSSQL_DatabaseLogin Properties

Name	Datatype	Read	Write	Maxlen	7.0	2000
UserName	string	✔		128	✔	✔

Table E.10 MSSQL_DatabaseLogin References

Name	Reference	Read	Write	Min	Max
Containee	MSSQL_Login	✔		0	*
Container	MSSQL_Database	✔		1	1

MSSQL_DatabaseCandidateKey

Table E.11 MSSQL_DatabaseCandidateKey Description

Superclass	MSSQL_Containment
Class Type	Association, dynamic class
Description	Association between a database and a candidate key that is contained in a database table
Class Path	//./Root/MicrosoftSQLServer: MSSQL_DatabaseCandidateKey
Keys	Containee, Container

Table E.12 MSSQL_DatabaseCandidateKey References

Name	Reference	Read	Write	Min	Max
Containee	MSSQL_CandidateKey	✔		0	*
Container	MSSQL_Database	✔		1	1

APPENDIX F

Static Settings

The classes listed in Appendix F contain static settings in SQL Server. All of these classes are static, so they are stored in the *Common Information Model* (CIM) Repository and are not dynamically provided by the WMI SQL Server Provider.

MSSQL_BackupSetting

Table F.1 `MSSQL_BackupSetting` Description

Superclass	`MSSQL_Setting`
Class Type	Static class
Description	`MSSQL_BackupSetting` is a static class that is used for defining settings for a backup operation that is executed through `SQLBackup()` in the `MSSQL_SQLServer` class.
Class Path	`//./Root/MicrosoftSQLServer:MSSQL_BackupSetting`
Keys	`SQLServerName, SettingID`

Table F.2 `MSSQL_BackupSetting` Properties

Name	Datatype	Read	Write	Maxlen	Units	7.0	2000
BackupSet-Description	String	✔	✔	255	n/a	✔	✔
BackupSetName	String	✔	✔	128	n/a	✔	✔
BlockSize	sint32	✔	✔	n/a	Bytes	✔	✔
Caption	String	✔		64	n/a	✔	✔
DatabaseFileGroups	string [ ]	✔	✔	n/a	n/a	✔	✔
DatabaseFiles	string [ ]	✔	✔	n/a	n/a	✔	✔
Database	String	✔	✔	n/a	n/a	✔	✔
Description	String	✔		n/a	n/a	✔	✔
Device	string [ ]	✔	✔	n/a	n/a	✔	✔
ExpirationDate	DateTime	✔	✔	n/a	n/a	✔	✔
FormatMedia	Boolean	✔	✔	n/a	n/a	✔	✔
Initialize	Boolean	✔	✔	n/a	n/a	✔	✔
MediaDescription	String	✔	✔	n/a	n/a	✔	✔
MediaName	String	✔	✔	n/a	n/a	✔	✔
Restart	Boolean	✔	✔	n/a	n/a	✔	✔
RetainDays	sint32	✔	✔	n/a	n/a	✔	✔
SQLServerName	String	✔	✔	128	n/a	✔	✔
SettingID	String	✔	✔	256	n/a	✔	✔
SkipTapeHeader	Boolean	✔	✔	n/a	n/a	✔	✔
TargetType	uint32	✔	✔	n/a	n/a	✔	✔
TruncateLog	uint32	✔	✔	n/a	n/a	✔	✔
UnloadTapeAfter	Boolean	✔	✔	n/a	n/a	✔	✔

BackupSetDescription

A textual description of the result from the backup that is executed with the settings on this object.

BackupSetName

Names a unit of backup work.

BlockSize

If the backup goes to a tape, this parameter sets the desired formatting size of the tape to use.

DatabaseFileGroups[ ]

List of named file-groups to which you limit the backup-process. An empty string, on the other hand, results in a backup of the complete database.

DatabaseFiles[ ]

A list of named database-file groups to which you limit the backup process. An empty string, on the other hand, results in a backup of the complete database.

Database

This database is the source database of the backup operations. It is not possible to perform a backup unless this property is set to a valid database.

Device[ ]

The backup device(s) targeted by the database backup.

ExpirationDate

The `ExpirationDate` property specifies the last valid date for the backup data on disk or tape. After the expiration data, it can be overwritten by other backups.

FormatMedia

If the value of this parameter is `True`, and if you are backing up to a tape, SQL Server will attempt to format the tape before any backup date is written to it.

Initialize

If the value of this parameter is `True`, this backup is written as the first backup set to the media—provided that other stored backup sets have expired and that the `BackupSetName` property matches the name on the tape. If the value is `False`, the backup set is appended after the last backup set on the media.

MediaDescription

A string that describes a backup set (used with `MediaName`).

MediaName

A string that names a backup set (used with `MediaDescription`).

Restart

If the value is `True`, a backup or restore operation that was interrupted will attempt to resume processing from the point of interruption. If the value is `False`, the complete operation is restarted.

RetainDays

The number of days before a backup set can be overwritten.

SQLServerName

The SQL Server instance to which this object applies.

SettingID

A unique identifier for this instance.

SkipTapeHeader

If the value is `True`, the backup skips the tape header and appends the backup set to the end of the media. If the value is `False`, a recorded `MediaName` on the tape is checked. Together with the Initialize property, this parameter can provide control over whether unexpired backup sets on the media are over-written or not.

TargetType

Table F.3 TargetType

Value	Meaning
0	Database
1	Differential
2	Files
3	Log

TruncateLog

Table F.4 TruncateLog

Value	Meaning
0	Truncate
1	No Truncate
2	No Log

UnloadTapeAfter

If the value is True, upon completion of the backup, the tape is physically unloaded after being rewound.

MSSQL_BulkCopySetting

Table F.5 MSSQL_BulkCopySetting Description

Superclass	MSSQL_Setting
Class Type	Static class
Description	An instance of this class is defined in order to control settings for bulk copy operations. This class is used by getting an instance of MSSQL_Table that is used as a parameter when calling ImportData() or ExportData().
Class Path	//./Root/MicrosoftSQLServer:MSSQL_BulkCopySetting
Keys	SQLServerName, SettingID

Table F.6 `MSSQL_BulkCopySetting` Properties

Name	Datatype	Read	Write	Maxlen	7.0	2000
Caption	string	✔		64	✔	✔
CodePage	sint32	✔	✔	n/a	✔	✔
ColumnDelimiter	string	✔	✔	n/a	✔	✔
DataFilePath	string	✔	✔	n/a	✔	✔
DataFileType	uint32	✔	✔	n/a	✔	✔
Description	string	✔		n/a	✔	✔
ErrorFilePath	string	✔	✔	n/a	✔	✔
ExportWideChar	boolean	✔	✔	n/a	✔	✔
FirstRow	sint32	✔	✔	n/a	✔	✔
FormatFilePath	string	✔	✔	n/a	✔	✔
ImportRowsPerBatch	sint32	✔	✔	n/a	✔	✔
IncludeIdentityValues	boolean	✔	✔	n/a	✔	✔
LastRow	sint32	✔	✔	n/a	✔	✔
LogFilePath	string	✔	✔	n/a	✔	✔
MaximumErrorsBeforeAbort	sint32	✔	✔	n/a	✔	✔
RowDelimiter	string	✔	✔	n/a	✔	✔
SQLServerName	string	✔	✔	128	✔	✔
ServerBCPDataFileType	uint32	✔	✔	n/a	✔	✔
ServerBCPKeepIdentity	boolean	✔	✔	n/a	✔	✔
ServerBCPKeepNulls	boolean	✔	✔	n/a	✔	✔
SettingID	string	✔	✔	256	✔	✔
SuspendIndexing	boolean	✔	✔	n/a	✔	✔
TableLock	boolean	✔	✔	n/a	✔	✔
TruncateLog	boolean	✔	✔	n/a	✔	✔
Use6xCompatible	boolean	✔	✔	n/a	✔	✔
UseBulkCopyOption	boolean	✔	✔	n/a	✔	✔
UseServerSideBCP	boolean	✔	✔	n/a	✔	✔

ColumnDelimiter

This property is the character(s) that is used to delimit columns in a bulk-copy data file.

DataFilePath

This property is used to define the target if the operation is `ExportData()`. It is the source if the operation is `ImportData()`, however.

DataFileType

Table F.7   `DataFileType`

Value	Meaning
1	Comma-delimited columns and carriage return/linefeed row delimiter
2	Tab-delimited character and carriage return/linefeed row delimiter
3	Defined by the `ColumnDelimiter` and `RowDelimiter` properties
4	SQL Server bulk copy native format
5	Use the format file specified in the `FormatFilePath` property

ErrorFilePath

Full path to the bulk-copy error log.

ExportWideChar

If the value is `True`, the data file that is created from `ExportData()` is a Unicode text file.

FirstRow

The starting point for bulk copy. Using `ExportData()`, this property is a row in the table. `ImportData()` is the row in the data source file.

FormatFilePath

Full path to a bulk-copy format file (only used if the `DataFileType` property is 4).

ImportRowsPerBatch

Number of rows in a single bulk-copy transaction. Typically, a bulk-copy operation only needs one transaction.

IncludeIdentityValues

If the value is True, existing identity values can be explicitly transferred. If the value is False, SQL Server does not copy identity values but instead uses the column's IdentitySeed and IdentityIncrement properties to generate values.

LastRow

End point for bulk copy; see FirstRow.

LogFilePath

Full path to bulk copy log (in general, it contains information about processing time and how much data was copied from source to destination).

MaximumErrorsBeforeAbort

Maximum errors allowed before bulk copy is aborted (default value is 10).

RowDelimiter

The character(s) used to delimit rows in a bulk-copy file.

ServerBCPDataFileType

Table F.8 ServerBCPDataFileType

Value	Meaning
1	Plain Character data
2	Bulk-Copy Native Format
4	Unicode Wide Char
8	Bulk-Copy NativeUnicode Wide Character

ServerBCPKeepIdentity

If the value is True, values for the identity column are copied to the target's identity column when using ImportData().

ServerBCPKeepNulls

If the value is `True`, missing values in the data file are replaced with NULL; if the value is `False`, the default constraint is in effect.

SettingID

The identifier by which the setting object is known.

SuspendIndexing

If the value is `True`, indices are dropped before the actual bulk copy operation and are then recreated after the bulk copy is completed as a result of `ImportData()`.

TableLock

If the value is `True`, table-level locking is in effect during bulk-copy import operation. `False` is the default.

TruncateLog

If the value is `True`, a successful `ImportData()` operation truncates the log. If the value is `False`, it is never truncated.

Use6xCompatible

If the value is `True`, a bulk-copy file is interpreted as an SQL Server 7.0 or earlier format for native bulk-copy data files.

UseBulkCopyOption

If the value is `True`, select into/bulkcopy is enabled when `ImportData()` is called.

UseServerSideBCP

If the value is `True`, the bulk-copy import operation uses `BULK  INSERT` as opposed to SQL Server *Open Database Connectivity* (ODBC) driver extensions.

MSSQL_RestoreSetting

Table F.9 MSSQL_RestoreSetting Description

Superclass	MSSQL_Setting
Class Type	Static class
Description	MSSQL_RestoreSetting is a static class that is used for defining settings for a restore operation as executed through SQLRestore() or SQLVerify() of the MSSQL_SQLServer class.
Class Path	//./Root/MicrosoftSQLServer:MSSQL_RestoreSetting
Keys	SQLServerName, SettingID

Table F.10 MSSQL_RestoreSetting Properties

Name	Datatype	Read	Write	Maxlen	7.0	2000
BackupDevice	string []	✔	✔	n/a	✔	✔
BackupSetName	string	✔	✔	128	✔	✔
Caption	string	✔		64	✔	✔
DatabaseFileGroups	string []	✔	✔	n/a	✔	✔
DatabaseFiles	string []	✔	✔	n/a	✔	✔
DatabaseName	string	✔	✔	n/a	✔	✔
Description	string	✔		n/a	✔	✔
FileNumber	uint32	✔	✔	n/a	✔	✔
LastRestore	boolean	✔	✔	n/a	✔	✔
LoadHistory	boolean	✔	✔	n/a	✔	✔
MediaName	string	✔	✔	n/a	✔	✔
RelocateFile	string []	✔	✔	n/a	✔	✔
ReplaceDatabase	boolean	✔	✔	n/a	✔	✔
Restart	boolean	✔	✔	n/a	✔	✔
RestoreTillTime	datetime	✔	✔	n/a	✔	✔
SQLServerName	string	✔	✔	128	✔	✔
SettingID	string	✔	✔	256	✔	✔
StandbyFile	string	✔	✔	n/a	✔	✔
TargetType	uint32	✔	✔	n/a	✔	✔
UnloadTapeAfter	boolean	✔	✔	n/a	✔	✔

BackupDevice[ ]

This property specifies one or more backup devices that are used as a database restore source.

BackupSetName

Names a unit of backup work.

DatabaseFileGroups[ ]

You can set this property to limit the restore operation to only those file groups that you identify by name. An empty string, on the other hand, results in a restore operation of the complete database.

DatabaseFiles[ ]

You can set this property to limit the restore operation to only those database files that you identify by name. An empty string, on the other hand, results in a restore operation of the complete database.

DatabaseName

`DatabaseName` identifies the target database for a restore operation. This property must be set before `SQLRestore()` or `MSSQL_SQLServer` are called.

FileNumber

The number that identifies a backup set on the backup medium.

LastRestore

If the value is `True`, the restore operation is performed on the last backup unit in a chain of log backups.

LoadHistory

If the value is `True`, the `msdb` backup history tables are updated when `SQLVerify()` is called.

MediaName

A string that names a backup set (used with `MediaDescription`).

RelocateFile[ ]

Logical filenames of databases and physical filenames of operating system files where database storage is redirected to when the database is restored to a new location.

ReplaceDatabase

If the value is `True`, a new image of the database is created.

Restart

If the value is `True`, the restore operation that was interrupted will attempt to resume processing from the interruption. If the value is `False`, the complete operation is restarted.

RestoreTillTime

End point for database log restoration.

SettingID

Identifier.

StandbyFile

Name of an undo file.

TargetType

Table F.11 `TargetType`

Value	Restore
0	Entire database
1	Specified files
2	Transaction log

UnloadTapeAfter

If the value is `True`, the tape is physically unloaded after being rewound upon completion of the backup operation.

MSSQL_SQLServerConnectionSetting

Table F.12 `MSSQL_SQLServerConnectionSetting` Description

Superclass	`MSSQL_Setting`
Class Type	Static class
Description	Default connection settings used by the WMI Provider to access `SQL-DMO`
Class Path	`//./Root/MicrosoftSQLServer:` `MSSQL_SQLServerConnectionSetting`
Keys	`SettingID`

Table F.13 `MSSQL_SQLServerConnectionSetting` Properties

Name	Datatype	Read	Write	Maxlen	Units	7.0	2000
AnsiNulls	boolean	✔	✔	n/a	n/a	✔	✔
ApplicationName	string	✔	✔	n/a	n/a	✔	✔
AutoReConnect	boolean	✔	✔	n/a	n/a	✔	✔
BlockingTimeout	sint32	✔	✔	n/a	n/a	✔	✔
Caption	string	✔		64	n/a	✔	✔
CommandTerminator	string	✔	✔	n/a	n/a	✔	✔
Description	string	✔		n/a	n/a	✔	✔
EnableBcp	boolean	✔	✔	n/a	n/a	✔	✔
LoginSecure	boolean	✔	✔	n/a	n/a	✔	✔
LoginTimeout	sint32	✔	✔	n/a	n/a	✔	✔
Login	string	✔	✔	n/a	n/a	✔	✔
NetPacketSize	sint32	✔	✔	n/a	Bytes	✔	✔
ODBCPrefix	boolean	✔	✔	n/a	n/a	✔	✔
Password	string	✔	✔	n/a	n/a	✔	✔
QueryTimeout	sint32	✔	✔	n/a	n/a	✔	✔
QuotedIdentifier	boolean	✔	✔	n/a	n/a	✔	✔
SettingID	string	✔	✔	256	n/a	✔	✔
TranslateChar	boolean	✔	✔	n/a	n/a	✔	✔

AnsiNulls

If the value is `True`, new columns accept NULL by default—and any comparison of NULL to any other value, including NULL, returns NULL.

ApplicationName

The `ApplicationName` property identifies the client application that is connected to Microsoft SQL Server.

AutoReConnect

If the value is `True` and the connection between the client and the server is lost, an attempt to reconnect is made.

BlockingTimeout

The timeout interval in milliseconds to wait while a request's resource is currently locked.

CommandTerminator

The `CommandTerminator` property specifies the `Transact-SQL` batch delimiter; the default is `GO`.

EnableBcp

If the value is `True`, this property enables the use of bulk copy operations.

LoginSecure

If the value is `True`, the provider uses Windows NT Authentication Mode. If the value is `False`, it uses SQL Server Authentication.

LoginTimeout

Number of seconds to wait before the connection attempt reports an error.

Login

SQL Server Authentication uses the login specified in this property to send a login to the requested server.

NetPacketSize

The `NetPacketSize` property specifies the size of a network packet that is used to transmit a block of data between a client and a server that is running Microsoft SQL Server (must be 128 through 65535; the default is 4096).

ODBCPrefix

If the value is `True`, a textual description of an error is prefixed by error-source indicators.

Password

The `Password` property indicates a password for a Microsoft SQL Server login record (used with the `Login` property for SQL Server Authentication).

QueryTimeout

Number of seconds to wait before an execution attempt reports an error.

QuotedIdentifier

If the value is `True`, identifiers can be delimited by double quotation marks—and character-literal values have to be delimited by single quotation marks.

SettingID

Object identifier.

TranslateChar

If the value is `True`, Microsoft SQL Server's ODBC driver translates data that is stored in char, varchar, and text columns from client to server (codepage by codepage).

MSSQL_TransferSetting

Table F.14 MSSQL_TransferSetting Description

Superclass	MSSQL_Setting
Class Type	Static class
Description	This class is passed as a parameter of Transfer() in MSSQL_Database. The settings define how and what objects are moved from one Microsoft SQL Server database to another.
Class Path	//./Root/MicrosoftSQLServer:MSSQL_TransferSetting
Keys	DatabaseName, SQLServerName, SettingID

Table F.15 MSSQL_TransferSetting Properties

Name	Datatype	Read	Write	Maxlen	7.0	2000
Caption	string	✔		64	✔	✔
CopyAllDefaults	boolean	✔	✔	n/a	✔	✔
CopyAllFunctions	boolean	✔	✔	n/a	✔	✔
CopyAllObjects	boolean	✔	✔	n/a	✔	✔
CopyAllRules	boolean	✔	✔	n/a	✔	✔
CopyAllStoredProcedures	boolean	✔	✔	n/a	✔	✔
CopyAllTables	boolean	✔	✔	n/a	✔	✔
CopyAllTriggers	boolean	✔	✔	n/a	✔	✔
CopyAllUserDefinedDatatypes	boolean	✔	✔	n/a	✔	✔
CopyAllViews	boolean	✔	✔	n/a	✔	✔
CopyData	uint32	✔	✔	n/a	✔	✔
CopySchema	boolean	✔	✔	n/a	✔	✔
DatabaseName	string	✔	✔	128	✔	✔
DatatypeName	string [ ]	✔	✔	n/a	✔	✔
DefaultName	string [ ]	✔	✔	n/a	✔	✔
Description	string	✔		n/a	✔	✔
DestDatabase	string	✔	✔	n/a	✔	✔
DestLogin	string	✔	✔	n/a	✔	✔
DestPassword	string	✔	✔	n/a	✔	✔
DestServer	string	✔	✔	n/a	✔	✔
DestTranslateChar	boolean	✔	✔	n/a	✔	✔
DestUseTrustedConnection	boolean	✔	✔	n/a	✔	✔

Table F.15 (Continued)

Name	Datatype	Read	Write	Maxlen	7.0	2000
DropDestObjectsFirst	boolean	✔	✔	n/a	✔	✔
IncludeDB	boolean	✔	✔	n/a	✔	✔
IncludeDependencies	boolean	✔	✔	n/a	✔	✔
IncludeLogins	boolean	✔	✔	n/a	✔	✔
IncludeUsers	boolean	✔	✔	n/a	✔	✔
RuleName	string []	✔	✔	n/a	✔	✔
SQLServerName	string	✔	✔	128	✔	✔
Script2Type	uint32	✔	✔	n/a	✔	✔
ScriptType	uint32	✔	✔	n/a	✔	✔
SettingID	string	✔	✔	256	✔	✔
SourceTranslateChar	boolean	✔	✔	n/a	✔	✔
StoredProcedureName	string []	✔	✔	n/a	✔	✔
TableName	string []	✔	✔	n/a	✔	✔
TriggerName	string []	✔	✔	n/a	✔	✔
UseCollation	boolean	✔	✔	n/a	✔	✔
UseDestTransaction	boolean	✔	✔	n/a	✔	✔
ViewName	string []	✔	✔	n/a	✔	✔

CopyAllDefaults

If the value is True, all defaults in the source database are copied to the target.

CopyAllFunctions

If the value is True, all user-defined functions in the source database are copied to the target.

CopyAllObjects

If the value is True, all objects in the source database are copied to the target.

CopyAllRules

If the value is True, all rules in the source database are copied to the target.

CopyAllStoredProcedures

If the value is True, all stored procedures in the source database are copied to the target.

CopyAllTables

If the value is True, all tables in the source database are copied to the target.

CopyAllTriggers

If the value is True, all triggers in the source database are copied to the target.

CopyAllUserDefinedDatatypes

If the value is True, all user-defined data types in the source database are copied to the target.

CopyAllViews

If the value is True, all views in the source database are copied to the target.

CopyData

Table F.16 CopyData

Value	Description
0	Copy schema only
1	Copy data and replace existing data
2	Copy data and append to existing tables

CopySchema

If the value is True, tables are created before being copied to the target.

DatabaseName

Name of the database for which the transfer setting has been defined.

DatatypeName[ ]

List of names of data types to transfer.

DefaultName[ ]

List of names of data types to transfer.

DestDatabase

The target database for the transfer.

DestLogin

The login that is used on the target server.

DestPassword

The password used on the target server.

DestServer

The target server.

DestTranslateChar

If the value is True, character translation occurs on the target server.

DestUseTrustedConnection

If the value is True, Windows NT Authentication will be requested on the target server.

DropDestObjectsFirst

If the value is True, a database object on the target server will be attempted to be dropped by SQL Server before a database object is copied from the source.

IncludeDB

If the value is True, a target database is created at the target server if it is not already there.

IncludeDependencies

If the value is `True`, database objects that are dependent on the user-defined objects are transferred.

IncludeLogins

If the value is `True`, system administrator-created logins are transferred.

IncludeUsers

If the value is `True`, users are transferred.

RuleName[ ]

List of rules to transfer.

SQLServerName

The SQL server for which the transfer setting has been defined.

Script2Type

Options for the script that are generated for transferring source data to the destination.

Table F.17 Script2Type

Value	Abstract Description
0	Ansi Padding
1	Ansi File
2	Unicode File
4	No FG
7	Encrypt PWD
9	No What If Indexes
10	Agent Notify
11	Agent Alert Job
19	Full Text Index
20	Login SID
21	Full Text Cat
22	Extended Property
23	No Collation

ScriptType

Options for the script that are generated for transferring source data to the destination.

Table F.18 ScriptType

Value	Abstract Description
0	Drops
1	Object Permissions
2	Primary Object
3	Clustered Indexes
4	Triggers
5	Database Permissions
7	Bindings
10	UDDTs To Base Type
12	Include If Not Exists
13	Non Clustered Indexes
17	Include Headers
18	Owner Qualify
19	Timestamp To Binary
22	DRI Non Clustered
23	DRI Clustered
24	DRI Checks
25	DRI Defaults
26	DRI Unique Keys
27	DRI Foreign Keys
28	DRI Primary Key
29	DRI With No Check
30	No Identity
31	Use Quoted Identifiers

SettingID

Object identifier.

SourceTranslateChar

If the value is True, character translation occurs on the source server.

StoredProcedureName[ ]

A list of stored procedures to transfer.

TableName[ ]

A list of tables to transfer.

TriggerName[ ]

A list of triggers to transfer.

UseCollation

If the value is True, the source-instance, column-level collation settings are set to fit the destination's collation settings for codepages.

UseDestTransaction

If the value is True, the transfer is done within a transaction that rolls back if a command fails.

ViewName[ ]

The names of the views to be transferred.

Dynamic Settings

A ppendix G contains a list of the settings classes that are dynamic. These classes derive from `MSSQL_Setting` and `CIM_ElementSetting`.

CIM_ElementSetting

Table G.1 `CIM_ElementSetting` Description

Class Type	Abstract, association class
Description	Association between a `ManagedSystemElement` and the setting applied to it. The `Setting` property references the settings, and the `Element` property is a reference to the instance to which this setting applies.
Class Path	`//./Root/MicrosoftSQLServer:CIM_ElementSetting`

Table G.2 `CIM_ElementSetting` References

Name	Reference	Read	Write
Element	CIM_ManagedSystemElement	✔	
Setting	CIM_Setting	✔	

MSSQL_RegistrySetting

Table G.3 `MSSQL_RegistrySetting` Description

Superclass	`MSSQL_Setting`
Class Type	Dynamic class
Description	Installation and run-time parameters of SQL Server stored in the registry
Class Path	`//./Root/MicrosoftSQLServer:MSSQL_RegistrySetting`
Keys	`SettingID`

Table G.4 `MSSQL_RegistrySetting` Properties

Name	Datatype	Read	Write	Maxlen	7.0	2000
ADSP	string	✔		n/a	✔	✔
AgentLogFile	string	✔	✔	n/a	✔	✔
AutoStartMail	boolean	✔	✔	n/a	✔	✔
AutostartDTC	boolean	✔	✔	n/a	✔	✔
AutostartLicensing	boolean	✔	✔	n/a	✔	✔
BackupDirectory	string	✔	✔	n/a	✔	✔
Caption	string	✔		64	✔	✔
CaseSensitive	boolean	✔		n/a	✔	✔
CharacterSet	string	✔		n/a	✔	✔
Description	string	✔		n/a	✔	✔
ErrorLogPath	string	✔	✔	n/a	✔	✔
MailAccountName	string	✔	✔	n/a	✔	✔
MailPassword	string	✔	✔	n/a	✔	✔
MasterDBPath	string	✔	✔	n/a	✔	✔
NP	string	✔		n/a	✔	✔
NTEventLogging	boolean	✔		n/a	✔	✔
NumberOfProcessors	sint32	✔		n/a	✔	✔
PerfMonMode	uint32	✔	✔	n/a	✔	✔
RegisteredOrganization	string	✔		n/a	✔	✔
RegisteredOwner	string	✔		n/a	✔	✔
ReplicationInstalled	boolean	✔		n/a	✔	✔

Table G.4 (Continued)

Name	Datatype	Read	Write	Maxlen	7.0	2000
RpcEncrypt	boolean	✔		n/a	✔	✔
RpcList	string	✔		n/a	✔	✔
RpcMaxCalls	uint32	✔		n/a	✔	✔
RpcMinCalls	uint32	✔		n/a	✔	✔
SNMPCurrentVersion	string	✔		n/a	✔	✔
SNMPExtensionAgentsData	string	✔		n/a	✔	✔
SNMP	boolean	✔		n/a	✔	✔
SQLDataRoot	string	✔	✔	n/a	✔	✔
SQLRootPath	string	✔	✔	n/a	✔	✔
SettingID	string	✔		256	✔	✔
SortOrder	string	✔		n/a	✔	✔
SpxFlag	boolean	✔		n/a	✔	✔
SpxPort	uint32	✔		n/a	✔	✔
SpxServiceName	string	✔		n/a	✔	✔
SuperSocketEncrypt	boolean	✔		n/a	✔	✔
SuperSocketList	string []	✔		n/a	✔	✔
TapeLoadWaitTime	sint32	✔	✔	n/a	✔	✔
TcpFlag	boolean	✔		n/a	✔	✔
TcpPort	string	✔	✔	n/a	✔	✔
VinesGroupName	string	✔		n/a	✔	✔
VinesItemName	string	✔		n/a	✔	✔
VinesOrgName	string	✔		n/a	✔	✔
WSProxyAddress	string	✔		n/a	✔	✔
WSProxyPort	uint32	✔		n/a	✔	✔

Table G.5 Possible Values for the PerfMonMode Property

Value	Meaning
0	Continuous
1	On Demand

MSSQL_LanguageSetting

Table G.6 MSSQL_LanguageSetting Description

Superclass	MSSQL_Setting
Class Type	Dynamic class
Description	Properties of an installed SQL Server language record
Class Path	//./Root/MicrosoftSQLServer:MSSQL_LanguageSetting
Keys	SQLServerName, SettingID

Table G.7 MSSQL_LanguageSetting Properties

Name	Datatype	Read	Write	Maxlen	7.0	2000
Alias	string	✔		n/a	✔	✔
Caption	string	✔		64	✔	✔
Days	string []	✔		n/a	✔	✔
Description	String	✔		n/a	✔	✔
FirstDayOfWeek	uint32	✔		n/a	✔	✔
LangDateFormat	String	✔		n/a	✔	✔
Months	string []	✔		n/a	✔	✔
SQLServerName	String	✔		128	✔	✔
SettingID	String	✔		256	✔	✔
ShortMonths	string []	✔		n/a	✔	✔

MSSQL_IntegratedSecuritySetting

Table G.8 MSSQL_IntegratedSecuritySetting Description

Superclass	MSSQL_Setting
Class Type	Dynamic class
Description	Security settings of an SQL Server installation. This setting affects all login connections to SQL Server regardless of the login authentication type.
Class Path	//./Root/MicrosoftSQLServer: MSSQL_IntegratedSecuritySetting
Keys	SettingID

Table G.9 MSSQL_IntegratedSecuritySetting Properties

Name	Datatype	Read	Write	Maxlen	7.0	2000
AuditLevel	uint32	✔	✔	n/a	✔	✔
Caption	string	✔		64	✔	✔
Description	string	✔		n/a	✔	✔
ImpersonateClient	boolean	✔	✔	n/a	✔	✔
SecurityMode	uint32	✔	✔	n/a	✔	✔
SettingID	string	✔		256	✔	✔

Table G.10 Possible Values for the AuditLevel Property

Value	Meaning
0	None
1	Success
2	Failure
3	All

Table G.11 Possible Values for the SecurityMode Property

Value	Authentication Mode
0	Normal
1	Integrated
2	Mixed

MSSQL_DatabaseSetting

Table G.12 MSSQL_DatabaseSetting Description

Superclass	MSSQL_Setting
Class Type	Dynamic class
Description	A database setting
Class Path	//./Root/MicrosoftSQLServer:MSSQL_DatabaseSetting
Keys	SQLServerName, SettingID

Table G.13 MSSQL_DatabaseSetting **Properties**

Name	Datatype	Read	Write	Maxlen	Unit	7.0	2000
AssignmentDiag	boolean	✔	✔	n/a	n/a	✔	✔
AutoClose	boolean	✔	✔	n/a	n/a	✔	✔
AutoCreateStat	boolean	✔	✔	n/a	n/a	✔	✔
AutoShrink	boolean	✔	✔	n/a	n/a	✔	✔
AutoUpdateStat	boolean	✔	✔	n/a	n/a	✔	✔
Caption	string	✔		64	n/a	✔	✔
ColumnsNullBy-Default	boolean	✔	✔	n/a	n/a	✔	✔
CompareNull	boolean	✔	✔	n/a	n/a	✔	✔
ContactNull	boolean	✔	✔	n/a	n/a	✔	✔
CursorCloseOn-Commit	boolean	✔	✔	n/a	n/a	✔	✔
DBOUseOnly	boolean	✔	✔	n/a	n/a	✔	✔
DataSpaceUsage	real32	✔		n/a	MB	✔	✔
DefaultCursor	boolean	✔	✔	n/a	n/a	✔	✔
Description	string	✔		n/a	n/a	✔	✔
IndexSpaceUsage	real32	✔		n/a	KiB	✔	✔
Offline	boolean	✔	✔	n/a	n/a	✔	✔
QuoteDelimiter	boolean	✔	✔	n/a	n/a	✔	✔
ReadOnly	boolean	✔	✔	n/a	n/a	✔	✔
RecoveryType	uint32	✔	✔	n/a	n/a	✔	✔
RecursiveTriggers	boolean	✔	✔	n/a	n/a	✔	✔
SQLServerName	string	✔		128	n/a	✔	✔
SelectIntoBulkCopy	boolean	✔	✔	n/a	n/a	✔	✔
SettingID	string	✔		256	n/a	✔	✔
SingleUser	boolean	✔	✔	n/a	n/a	✔	✔
TornPageDetection	boolean	✔	✔	n/a	n/a	✔	✔
TruncateLogOn-Checkpoint	boolean	✔	✔	n/a	n/a	✔	✔

MSSQL_ConfigValue

Table G.14 MSSQL_ConfigValue Description

Superclass	MSSQL_Setting
Class Type	Dynamic class
Description	SQL Server configuration values. You can change the values by changing the CurrentValue property, but if the DynamicReconfigure property is False, SQL Server has to be restarted before any changes will be visible.
Class Path	//./Root/MicrosoftSQLServer:MSSQL_ConfigValue
Keys	SQLServerName, SettingID

Table G.15 MSSQL_ConfigValue Properties

Name	Datatype	Read	Write	Maxlen	7.0	2000
Caption	string	✔		64	✔	✔
CurrentValue	sint32	✔	✔	n/a	✔	✔
Description	string	✔		n/a	✔	✔
DynamicReconfigure	boolean	✔		n/a	✔	✔
ID	uint32	✔		n/a	✔	✔
MaximumValue	sint32	✔		n/a	✔	✔
MinimumValue	sint32	✔		n/a	✔	✔
RunningValue	sint32	✔		n/a	✔	✔
SQLServerName	string	✔		128	✔	✔
SettingID	string	✔		256	✔	✔

CurrentValue

The current configuration value.

DynamicReconfigure

If the value is True, the configuration value can be modified and the changes can take effect without SQL Server being stopped and started.

ID

Table G.16 MSSQL_ConfigValue IDs

Configuration ID Value	Meaning
101	Recovery interval
102	Allow updates
103	User connections
106	Locks
107	Open objects
109	Fill factor
115	Nested triggers
117	Remote access
124	Default language
125	Language in cache
502	Max Async IO
503	Max Worker Threads
505	Network packet size
518	Show advanced option
542	Remote Proc Trans
543	Remote Conn Timeout
1110	Time slice
1123	Default Sortorder ID
1514	Spin counter
1517	Priority boost
1519	Remote login timeout
1520	Remote query timeout
1531	Cursor threshold
1532	Set working set size
1533	Resource timeout
1534	User options
1535	Processor affinity mask
1536	Max Text Repl Size
1124	Unicode local ID
1125	Unicode comparison style
1126	Language neutral

Table G.16 (Continued)

Configuration ID Value	Meaning
1127	Two-digit year cutoff
1505	Index Create Mem
1537	Media retention
1538	Cost threshold for parallelism
1539	MaxDegree of parallelism
1540	Min Memory Per Query
1541	Query wait
1542	VLM size
1543	Min Memory
1544	Max Memory
1545	Query Max Time
1546	Lightweight pooling

MaximumValue

The maximum value that can be held by the configuration value.

MinimumValue

The minimum value that can be held by the configuration value.

RunningValue

The SQL Server setting that is currently used for the instance of this class. If you change `CurrentValue`, the `RunningValue` will not change if the server must be restarted before it takes effect.

SettingID

String that identifies the setting.

MSSQL_SQLServerSQLServerConnectionSetting

Table G.17 `MSSQL_SQLServerSQLServerConnectionSetting` Description

Superclass	`CIM_ElementSetting`
Class Type	Association, dynamic class
Description	Association between an SQL Server installation and the settings that are used by the SQL Server provider to connect to SQL Server
Class Path	`//./Root/MicrosoftSQLServer:` `MSSQL_SQLServerSQLServerConnectionSetting`
Keys	`Element, Setting`

Table G.18 `MSSQL_SQLServerSQLServerConnectionSetting` References

Name	Reference	Read	Write
`Element`	`MSSQL_SQLServer`	✔	
`Setting`	`MSSQL_SQLServerConnectionSetting`	✔	

MSSQL_SQLServerRegistry

Table G.19 `MSSQL_SQLServerRegistry` Description

Superclass	`CIM_ElementSetting`
Class Type	Association, dynamic class
Description	Association between an SQL Server installation and its registry setting
Class Path	`//./Root/MicrosoftSQLServer:MSSQL_SQLServerRegistry`
Keys	`Element, Setting`

Table G.20 `MSSQL_SQLServerRegistry` References

Name	Reference	Read	Write	Min	Max
`Element`	`MSSQL_SQLServer`	✔		1	1
`Setting`	`MSSQL_RegistrySetting`	✔		1	1

MSSQL_SQLServerLanguageSetting

Table G.21 MSSQL_SQLServerLanguageSetting Description

Superclass	CIM_ElementSetting
Class Type	Association, dynamic class
Description	Association between an SQL Server installation and its language settings
Class Path	//./Root/MicrosoftSQLServer: MSSQL_SQLServerLanguageSetting
Keys	Element, Setting

Table G.22 MSSQL_SQLServerLanguageSetting References

Name	Reference	Read	Write	Min	Max
Element	MSSQL_SQLServer	✔		1	1
Setting	MSSQL_LanguageSetting	✔		0	*

MSSQL_SQLServerIntegratedSecuritySetting

Table G.23 MSSQL_SQLServerIntegratedSecuritySetting Description

Superclass	CIM_ElementSetting
Class Type	Association, dynamic class
Description	Association between an SQL Server installation and its security settings
Class Path	//./Root/MicrosoftSQLServer: MSSQL_SQLServerIntegratedSecuritySetting
Keys	Element, Setting

Table G.24 MSSQL_SQLServerIntegratedSecuritySetting References

Name	Reference	Read	Write	Min	Max
Element	MSSQL_SQLServer	✔		1	1
Setting	MSSQL_IntegratedSecuritySetting	✔		1	1

MSSQL_SQLServerConfigValue

Table G.25 MSSQL_SQLServerConfigValue Description

Superclass	CIM_ElementSetting
Class Type	Association, dynamic class
Description	Association between an SQL Server installation and the configured value settings for the installation
Class Path	//./Root/MicrosoftSQLServer: MSSQL_SQLServerConfigValue
Keys	Element, Setting

Table G.26 MSSQL_SQLServerConfigValue References

Name	Reference	Read	Write	Min	Max
Element	MSSQL_SQLServer	✔		1	1
Setting	MSSQL_ConfigValue	✔		0	*

MSSQL_DatabaseDatabaseSetting

Table G.27 MSSQL_DatabaseDatabaseSetting Description

Superclass	CIM_ElementSetting
Class Type	Association, dynamic class
Description	The DatabaseDatabaseSetting association associates an SQL Server database with its appropriate configuration settings.
Class Path	//./Root/MicrosoftSQLServer: MSSQL_DatabaseDatabaseSetting
Keys	Element, Setting

Table G.28 MSSQL_DatabaseDatabaseSetting References

Name	Reference	Read	Write	Min	Max
Element	MSSQL_Database	✔		1	1
Setting	MSSQL_DatabaseSetting	✔		1	1

Extensions

H ere is a list of the classes that are extensions through the extension class.

MSSQL_Extension

Table H.1 MSSQL_Extension Description

Class Type	Abstract class
Description	A base class for extensions that are made to a managed system element
Class Path	\\.\Root\MicrosoftSQLServer:MSSQL_Extension

MSSQL_Extends

Table H.2 MSSQL_Extends Description

Class Type	Abstract, association class
Description	Associates a single class with a class that serves as an extension. Extension references an extension that is applied to the ExtendedElement.
Class Path	\\.\Root\MicrosoftSQLServer:MSSQL_Extends

Table H.3 MSSQL_Extends References

Name	Reference	Read	Write	Min	Max
ExtendedElement	CIM_ManagedSystemElement	✔		1	1
Extension	MSSQL_Extension	✔		0	1

MSSQL_DatabaseFile

Table H.4 MSSQL_DatabaseFile Description

Superclass	MSSQL_Extension
Class Type	Dynamic class
Description	This class represents an SQL Server database operating-system file.
Class Path	\\.\Root\MicrosoftSQLServer:MSSQL_DatabaseFile
Keys	DatabaseName, FileGroupName, Name, SQLServerName

Table H.5 MSSQL_DatabaseFile Properties

Name	Datatype	Read	Write	Maxlen	Unit	7.0	2000
DatabaseName	string	✔		128	n/a	✔	✔
FileGroupName	string	✔		128	n/a	✔	✔
FileGrowthInKB	real32	✔		n/a	n/a	✔	✔
FileGrowthType	uint32	✔	✔	n/a	n/a	✔	✔
FileGrowth	sint32	✔	✔	n/a	n/a	✔	✔
MaximumSize	sint32	✔	✔	n/a	n/a	✔	✔
Name	string	✔		128	n/a	✔	✔
PhysicalName	string	✔		n/a	n/a	✔	✔
PrimaryFile	boolean	✔		n/a	n/a	✔	✔
SQLServerName	string	✔		128	n/a	✔	✔
SpaceAvailableInMB	sint32	✔		n/a	MB	✔	✔

Table H.6 MSSQL_DatabaseFile Methods

Name	Return Type	Static	7.0	2000
Shrink	MSSQL_MethodRtnVal		✔	✔

FileGrowthType

Table H.7 FileGrowthType

Value	Unit
0	Megabyte
1	Percent
99	Invalid

Shrink( )

Use this method to reduce the size of operating-system files that are associated with maintaining the database.

```
MSSQL_MethodRtnVal Shrink (
    [In] sint32 NewSizeInMB,
    [In] uint32 Truncate
);
```

Parameters

`NewSizeInMB`

If this parameter is a negative number, files will be shrunk to their smallest size. If it is a positive number, it becomes the attempted size in *megabytes* (MB).

`Truncate`

`Truncate` can be set as follows.

Table H.8 `Truncate`

Value	Description
0	Move data in pages at the end of the file to the beginning of the file and truncate the file
1	Move data in pages at the end of the file to the beginning of the file, but do not truncate
2	Truncate file and try to recover free space at the end of the file
3	Move data from file to other files in the same file group

MSSQL_DatabaseFileDataFile

Table H.9 `MSSQL_DatabaseFileDataFile` Description

Superclass	`MSSQL_Extends`
Class Type	Association, dynamic class
Description	Associated `CIM_DataFile` with the `MSSQL_DatabaseFile` extension
Class Path	`\\.\Root\MicrosoftSQLServer:` `MSSQL_DatabaseFileDataFile`
Keys	`ExtendedElement, Extension`

Table H.10 `MSSQL_DatabaseFileDataFile` References

Name	Reference	Read	Write	Min	Max
`ExtendedElement`	`CIM_DataFile`	✔		1	1
`Extension`	`MSSQL_DatabaseFile`	✔		0	1

Statistics

You will find statistics-related classes in this appendix.

CIM_Statistics

Table I.1 CIM_Statistics Description

Class Type	Abstract, association class
Description	Association between a managed system element that is referenced by Element and an object that has statistical information and is referenced by Stats
Class Path	\\.\Root\MicrosoftSQLServer:CIM_Statistics

Table I.2 CIM_Statistics References

Name	Reference	Read	Write
Element	CIM_ManagedSystemElement	✔	
Stats	CIM_StatisticalInformation	✔	

CIM_StatisticalInformation

Table I.3 CIM_StatisticalInformation Description

Class Type	Abstract class
Description	The base class for a collection of statistical data that are related to one or more managed system elements. Caption is a short description of the statistic or metric (the description is more elaborate), and Name labels the instance.
Class Path	\\.\Root\MicrosoftSQLServer: CIM_StatisticalInformation

Table I.4 CIM_StatisticalInformation Properties

Name	Datatype	Read	Write	Maxlen	7.0	2000
Caption	string	✔		64	✔	✔
Description	string	✔		n/a	✔	✔
Name	string	✔		256	✔	✔

MSSQL_IndexStatistics

Table I.5 MSSQL_IndexStatistics Description

Superclass	CIM_Statistics
Class Type	Association, dynamic class
Description	This class associates an index with an instance that represents statistical information on the index.
Class Path	\\.\Root\MicrosoftSQLServer:MSSQL_IndexStatistics
Keys	Element, Stats

Table I.6 MSSQL_IndexStatistics References

Name	Reference	Read	Write	Min	Max
Element	MSSQL_Index	✔		1	1
Stats	MSSQL_IndexTableInformation	✔		1	1

MSSQL_IndexTableInformation

Table I.7 MSSQL_IndexTableInformation Description

Superclass	CIM_StatisticalInformation
Class Type	Dynamic class
Description	Statistical information about an index
Class Path	\\.\Root\MicrosoftSQLServer: MSSQL_IndexTableInformation
Keys	DatabaseName, Name, SQLServerName, TableName

Table I.8 MSSQL_IndexTableInformation Properties

Name	Datatype	Read	Write	Maxlen	7.0	2000
AverageKeyLength	real32	✔		n/a	✔	✔
Caption	String	✔		64	✔	✔
DatabaseName	String	✔		128	✔	✔
Density	real32	✔		n/a	✔	✔
Description	String	✔		n/a	✔	✔
LastUpdate	datetime	✔		n/a	✔	✔
Name	String	✔		256	✔	✔
RowsSampled	uint64	✔		n/a	✔	✔
Rows	uint64	✔		n/a	✔	✔
SQLServerName	String	✔		128	✔	✔
Steps	uint32	✔		n/a	✔	✔
TableName	String	✔		128	✔	✔

Logical Elements

Appendix J lists the logical elements in the Microsoft SQL Server namespace.

CIM_LogicalElement

Table J.1 `CIM_LogicalElement` Description

Superclass	`CIM_ManagedSystemElement`
Class Type	Abstract class
Description	The base class for all of the components of the system that represent abstract system components
Class Path	`//./Root/MicrosoftSQLServer:CIM_LogicalElement`

Table J.2 `CIM_LogicalElement` Properties

Name	Datatype	Read	Write	Maxlen	7.0	2000
Caption	string	✔		64	✔	✔
Description	string	✔		n/a	✔	✔
InstallDate	datetime	✔		n/a	✔	✔
Name	string	✔		n/a	✔	✔
Status	string	✔		10	✔	✔

MSSQL_ErrorLogEntry

Table J.3 MSSQL_ErrorLogEntry Description

Superclass	CIM_LogicalElement
Class Type	Dynamic class
Description	Entry in an SQL Service error log
Class Path	//./Root/MicrosoftSQLServer:MSSQL_ErrorLogEntry
Keys	ArchiveID, EntryID, SQLServerName

Table J.4 MSSQL_ErrorLogEntry Properties

Name	Datatype	Read	Write	Maxlen	7.0	2000
ArchiveID	string	✔		128	✔	✔
Caption	string	✔		64	✔	✔
Description	string	✔		n/a	✔	✔
EntryID	string	✔		128	✔	✔
InstallDate	datetime	✔		n/a	✔	✔
Name	string	✔		n/a	✔	✔
SQLServerName	string	✔		128	✔	✔
Status	string	✔		10	✔	✔
Text	string	✔		n/a	✔	✔

MSSQL_FileGroup

Table J.5 MSSQL_FileGroup Description

Superclass	CIM_LogicalElement
Class Type	Dynamic class
Description	The groups of operating system files that are used to store a single SQL Server database
Class Path	//./Root/MicrosoftSQLServer:MSSQL_FileGroup
Keys	DatabaseName, Name, SQLServerName

Table J.6 MSSQL_FileGroup Properties

Name	Datatype	Read	Write	Maxlen	Unit	7.0	2000
Caption	string	✔		64	n/a	✔	✔
DatabaseName	string	✔		128	n/a	✔	✔
Default	boolean	✔	✔	n/a	n/a	✔	✔
Description	string	✔		n/a	n/a	✔	✔
InstallDate	datetime	✔		n/a	n/a	✔	✔
Name	string	✔		n/a	n/a	✔	✔
ReadOnly	boolean	✔	✔	n/a	n/a	✔	✔
SQLServerName	string	✔		128	n/a	✔	✔
Size	sint32	✔		n/a	MB	✔	✔
Status	string	✔		10	n/a	✔	✔
Type	uint32	✔		n/a	n/a	✔	✔

Table J.7 MSSQL_FileGroup Methods

Name	Return Type	Static	7.0	2000
CheckFilegroupDataOnly	String		✔	✔
CheckFilegroup	String		✔	✔
EnumStoredObjects	MSSQL_MethodRtnVal		✔	✔

Type

Table J.8 Type

Value	Description
0	User defined
8	On read-only media
16	Primary

CheckFilegroupDataOnly( )

Use this method to check the allocation and structure of database pages that store table data in this file group:

```
string CheckFilegroupDataOnly (
    [Out] MSSQL_MethodRtnVal NativeMethodRtnVal
);
```

CheckFilegroup( )

Use this method to check the integrity of database pages in this file group:

```
string CheckFilegroup (
    [Out] MSSQL_MethodRtnVal NativeMethodRtnVal
);
```

EnumStoredObjects( )

Use this method to enumerate the names of index, table, and statistical mechanisms in the file group:

```
MSSQL_MethodRtnVal EnumStoredObjects (
    [Out] string ObjectName []
);
```

MSSQL_TransactionLog

Table J.9 MSSQL_TransactionLog Description

Superclass	CIM_LogicalElement
Class Type	Dynamic class
Description	Transaction log of a database
Class Path	//./Root/MicrosoftSQLServer:MSSQL_TransactionLog
Keys	Name, SQLServerName

Table J.10 MSSQL_TransactionLog Properties

Name	Datatype	Read	Write	Maxlen	Unit	7.0	2000
Caption	string	✔		64	n/a	✔	✔
CreateDate	datetime	✔		n/a	n/a	✔	✔
Description	string	✔		n/a	n/a	✔	✔
InitialSize	uint32	✔		n/a	n/a	✔	✔
InstallDate	datetime	✔		n/a	n/a	✔	✔
LastBackup	datetime	✔		n/a	n/a	✔	✔
Name	string	✔		n/a	n/a	✔	✔
SQLServerName	string	✔		128	n/a	✔	✔
SpaceAvailable	real32	✔		n/a	MB	✔	✔
Status	string	✔		10	n/a	✔	✔

Table J.11 MSSQL_TransactionLog Methods

Name	Return Type	Static	7.0	2000
Truncate	MSSQL_MethodRtnVal		✔	✔

Truncate( )

Use this method to archive log records.

Users and Accounts

Appendix K lists the classes that contain users, roles, accounts, and so forth.

MSSQL_Role

Table K.1 `MSSQL_Role` Description

Superclass	`MSSQL_DBMSUserObject`
Class Type	Abstract class
Description	A base class for database roles and SQL Server roles
Class Path	`//./Root/MicrosoftSQLServer:MSSQL_Role`

Table K.2 `MSSQL_Role` Properties

Name	Datatype	Read	Write	Maxlen	7.0	2000
Caption	string	✔		64	✔	✔
Description	string	✔		n/a	✔	✔
InstallDate	datetime	✔		n/a	✔	✔
Name	string	✔		n/a	✔	✔
Status	string	✔		10	✔	✔

Win32_Account

Table K.3 Win32_Account Description

Superclass	CIM_LogicalElement
Class Type	Abstract class
Description	The information that is needed to represent a Windows account. Name is the name of the Windows account, and Domain is the Windows domain to which the account belongs. SID is the security identifier for the account, and SIDType defines the type of SID.
Class Path	//./Root/MicrosoftSQLServer:Win32_Account
Keys	Domain, Name

Table K.4 Win32_Account Properties

Name	Datatype	Read	Write	Maxlen	7.0	2000
Caption	string	✔		64	✔	✔
Description	string	✔		n/a	✔	✔
Domain	string	✔		n/a	✔	✔
InstallDate	datetime	✔		n/a	✔	✔
Name	string	✔		n/a	✔	✔
SIDType	uint8	✔		n/a	✔	✔
SID	string	✔		n/a	✔	✔
Status	string	✔		10	✔	✔

Table K.5 Possible Values for the SIDType Property

Value	Meaning
1	SidTypeUser
2	SidTypeGroup
3	SidTypeDomain
4	SidTypeAlias
5	SidTypeWellKnownGroup
6	SidTypeDeletedAccount
7	SidTypeInvalid
8	SidTypeUnknown
9	SidTypeComputer

MSSQL_DBMSUserObject

Table K.6 MSSQL_DBMSUserObject Description

Superclass	CIM_LogicalElement
Class Type	Abstract class
Description	A base class for all user objects (such as users, logins, and roles)
Class Path	//./Root/MicrosoftSQLServer:MSSQL_DBMSUserObject

Table K.7 MSSQL_DBMSUserObject Properties

Name	Datatype	Read	Write	Maxlen	7.0	2000
Caption	string	✔		64	✔	✔
Description	string	✔		n/a	✔	✔
InstallDate	datetime	✔		n/a	✔	✔
Name	string	✔		n/a	✔	✔
Status	string	✔		10	✔	✔

MSSQL_User

Table K.8 MSSQL_User Description

Superclass	MSSQL_DBMSUserObject
Class Type	Dynamic class
Description	Data about a database user
Class Path	//./Root/MicrosoftSQLServer:MSSQL_User
Keys	DatabaseName, Name, SQLServerName
Constructor	Create

Table K.9 MSSQL_User **Properties**

Name	Datatype	Read	Write	Maxlen	7.0	2000
Caption	string	✔		64	✔	✔
DatabaseName	string	✔		128	✔	✔
Description	string	✔		n/a	✔	✔
InstallDate	datetime	✔		n/a	✔	✔
Name	string	✔		n/a	✔	✔
SQLServerName	string	✔		128	✔	✔
Status	string	✔		10	✔	✔
SystemObject	boolean	✔		n/a	✔	✔

Table K.10 MSSQL_User **Methods**

Name	Return Type	Static	7.0	2000
Create	MSSQL_MethodRtnVal	✔	✔	✔

Create( )

The Create() method is used to create a new instance:

```
MSSQL_MethodRtnVal Create (
    [In, Optional] string Name,
    [In] string SQLServerName,
    [In] string DatabaseName,
    [In] string Login
);
```

Parameters

Name

Name to give to the user object.

SQLServerName

Name of the SQL Server instance to which it will belong.

DatabaseName

Name of the database where it will reside.

Login

Name of an existing login that is used to authenticate the user.

MSSQL_Login

Table K.11 MSSQL_Login Description

Superclass	MSSQL_DBMSUserObject
Class Type	Dynamic class
Description	A Microsoft SQL Server login
Class Path	//./Root/MicrosoftSQLServer:MSSQL_Login
Keys	Name, SQLServerName

Table K.12 MSSQL_Login Properties

Name	Datatype	Read	Write	Maxlen	7.0	2000
Caption	string	✔		64	✔	✔
DenyNTLogin	boolean	✔	✔	n/a	✔	✔
Description	string	✔		n/a	✔	✔
InstallDate	datetime	✔		n/a	✔	✔
Language	string	✔	✔	n/a	✔	✔
Name	string	✔		n/a	✔	✔
SQLServerName	string	✔		128	✔	✔
Status	string	✔		10	✔	✔
SystemObject	boolean	✔		n/a	✔	✔
Type	uint32	✔	✔	n/a	✔	✔

Table K.13 MSSQL_Login Methods

Name	Return Type	Static	7.0	2000
GetUserName	string		✔	✔
SetPassword	MSSQL_MethodRtnVal		✔	✔

DenyNTLogin

If the value is True, Windows NT users and groups cannot login.

Type

Table K.14 Type

Value	Authentication Type
0	NT User Authentication
1	NT Group Authentication
2	SQL Server Authentication

GetUserName( )

Gets the database user from this login when accessing the database named in the method call:

```
string GetUserName (
    [In] string DatabaseName,
    [Out] MSSQL_MethodRtnVal NativeMethodRtnVal
);
```

SetPassword( )

Use this method to define a password that will be used in SQL Server authentication:

```
MSSQL_MethodRtnVal SetPassword (
    [In] string OldPassword,
    [In] string NewPassword
);
```

MSSQL_SQLServerRole

Table K.15 MSSQL_SQLServerRole Description

Superclass	MSSQL_Role
Class Type	Dynamic class
Description	An SQL Server security role
Class Path	//./Root/MicrosoftSQLServer:MSSQL_SQLServerRole
Keys	Name, SQLServerName

Table K.16 MSSQL_SQLServerRole Properties

Name	Datatype	Read	Write	Maxlen	7.0	2000
Caption	string	✔		64	✔	✔
Description	string	✔		n/a	✔	✔
FullName	string	✔		n/a	✔	✔
InstallDate	datetime	✔		n/a	✔	✔
Name	string	✔		n/a	✔	✔
SQLServerName	string	✔		128	✔	✔
Status	string	✔		10	✔	✔

Win32_UserAccount

Table K.17 Win32_UserAccount Description

Superclass	Win32_Account
Class Type	Dynamic class
Description	A Windows user account
Remarks	A union view class
Class Path	//./Root/MicrosoftSQLServer:Win32_UserAccount
Keys	Domain, Name

Table K.18 `Win32_UserAccount` Properties

Name	Datatype	Read	Write	Maxlen	7.0	2000
AccountType	uint32	✔		n/a	✔	✔
Caption	string	✔		64	✔	✔
Description	string	✔		n/a	✔	✔
Disabled	boolean	✔		n/a	✔	✔
Domain	string	✔		n/a	✔	✔
FullName	string	✔		n/a	✔	✔
InstallDate	datetime	✔		n/a	✔	✔
Lockout	boolean	✔		n/a	✔	✔
Name	string	✔		n/a	✔	✔
PasswordChangeable	boolean	✔		n/a	✔	✔
PasswordExpires	boolean	✔		n/a	✔	✔
PasswordRequired	boolean	✔		n/a	✔	✔
SIDType	Uint8	✔		n/a	✔	✔
SID	string	✔		n/a	✔	✔
Status	string	✔		10	✔	✔

AccountType

Table K.19 `AccountType`

Value	Meaning
8	Temporary duplicate account
9	Normal account
11	Inter-domain trust account
12	Workstation trust account
13	Server trust account

Disabled

If the value is `True`, the user account is disabled.

Domain

The domain in which the user account resides.

FullName

The full name of the local user.

Lockout

If the value is `True`, the user account is locked out of the system.

Name

Name of the user account.

PasswordChangeable

If the value is `True`, the user account's password can be changed.

PasswordExpires

If the value is `True`, the user account's password can expire.

PasswordRequired

If the value is `True`, the password is required for the user account.

Win32_Group

Table K.20 `Win32_Group` Description

Superclass	`Win32_Account`
Class Type	Dynamic class
Description	A Windows group account
Remarks	A union view class
Class Path	`//./Root/MicrosoftSQLServer:Win32_Group`
Keys	`Domain, Name`

Table K.21 `Win32_Group` Properties

Name	Datatype	Read	Write	Maxlen	7.0	2000
Caption	string	✔		64	✔	✔
Description	string	✔		n/a	✔	✔
Domain	string	✔		n/a	✔	✔
InstallDate	datetime	✔		n/a	✔	✔
Name	string	✔		n/a	✔	✔
SIDType	uint8	✔		n/a	✔	✔
SID	string	✔		n/a	✔	✔
Status	string	✔		10	✔	✔

Domain

Domain of the group account.

Name

Name of the group account.

Service and Process Classes

A ppendix L contains a list of classes that are related to services and processes.

CIM_Process

Table L.1 CIM_Process Description

Superclass	CIM_LogicalElement
Class Type	Abstract class
Description	A process that is running under an operating system
Class Path	//./Root/MicrosoftSQLServer:CIM_Process

Table L.2 CIM_Process Properties

Name	Datatype	Read	Write	Maxlen	Unit	7.0	2000
CSCreationClass-Name	string	✔		256	n/a	✔	✔
CSName	string	✔		256	n/a	✔	✔
Caption	string	✔		64	n/a	✔	✔
CreationClassName	string	✔		256	n/a	✔	✔
CreationDate	datetime	✔		n/a	n/a	✔	✔
Description	string	✔		n/a	n/a	✔	✔
ExecutionState	uint16	✔		n/a	n/a	✔	✔
Handle	string	✔		n/a	n/a	✔	✔
InstallDate	datetime	✔		n/a	n/a	✔	✔
KernelModeTime	uint64	✔		n/a	MS	✔	✔
Name	string	✔		n/a	n/a	✔	✔
OSCreationClass-Name	string	✔		256	n/a	✔	✔
OSName	string	✔		256	n/a	✔	✔
Priority	uint32	✔		n/a	n/a	✔	✔
Status	string	✔		10	n/a	✔	✔
TerminationDate	datetime	✔		n/a	n/a	✔	✔
UserModeTime	uint64	✔		n/a	MS	✔	✔
WorkingSetSize	uint64	✔		n/a	Bytes	✔	✔

CIM_Service

Table L.3 CIM_Service Description

Superclass	CIM_LogicalElement
Class Type	Abstract class
Description	A base class for service-related classes
Remarks	A union view class
Class Path	//./Root/MicrosoftSQLServer:CIM_Service

Table L.4 CIM_Service Properties

Name	Datatype	Read	Write	Maxlen	7.0	2000
Caption	string	✔		64	✔	✔
CreationClassName	string	✔		n/a	✔	✔
Description	string	✔		n/a	✔	✔
InstallDate	datetime	✔		n/a	✔	✔
Name	string	✔		n/a	✔	✔
StartMode	string	✔		n/a	✔	✔
Started	boolean	✔		n/a	✔	✔
Status	string	✔		10	✔	✔
SystemCreationClassName	string	✔		n/a	✔	✔
SystemName	string	✔		n/a	✔	✔

Table L.5 CIM_Service Methods

Name	Return Type	Static	7.0	2000
StartService	uint32		✔	✔
StopService	uint32		✔	✔

Win32_BaseService

Table L.6 Win32_BaseService Description

Superclass	CIM_Service
Class Type	Abstract class
Description	The information that is needed to represent and manage a service on the Windows operating system. AcceptX properties return a boolean value, indicating whether Operation X can be performed on the object.
Remarks	A union view class
Class Path	//./Root/MicrosoftSQLServer:Win32_BaseService
Keys	Name

Table L.7 `Win32_BaseService` Properties

Name	Datatype	Read	Write	Maxlen	7.0	2000
AcceptPause	boolean	✔		n/a	✔	✔
AcceptStop	boolean	✔		n/a	✔	✔
Caption	string	✔		64	✔	✔
CreationClassName	string	✔		n/a	✔	✔
Description	string	✔		n/a	✔	✔
DesktopInteract	boolean	✔		n/a	✔	✔
DisplayName	string	✔		n/a	✔	✔
ErrorControl	string	✔		n/a	✔	✔
ExitCode	uint32	✔		n/a	✔	✔
InstallDate	datetime	✔		n/a	✔	✔
Name	string	✔		256	✔	✔
PathName	string	✔		n/a	✔	✔
ServiceSpecificExitCode	uint32	✔		n/a	✔	✔
ServiceType	string	✔		n/a	✔	✔
StartMode	string	✔		n/a	✔	✔
StartName	string	✔		n/a	✔	✔
Started	boolean	✔		n/a	✔	✔
State	string	✔		n/a	✔	✔
Status	string	✔		10	✔	✔
SystemCreationClassName	string	✔		n/a	✔	✔
SystemName	string	✔		n/a	✔	✔
TagId	uint32	✔		n/a	✔	✔

Table L.8 `Win32_BaseService` Methods

Name	Return Type	Static	7.0	2000
ChangeStartMode	uint32		✔	✔
Change	uint32		✔	✔
Create	uint32	✔	✔	✔
Delete	uint32		✔	✔
InterrogateService	uint32		✔	✔
PauseService	uint32		✔	✔

Table L.8 (Continued)

Name	Return Type	Static	7.0	2000
ResumeService	uint32		✔	✔
StartService	uint32		✔	✔
StopService	uint32		✔	✔
UserControlService	uint32		✔	✔

Table L.9 Common Return Values for the Methods of This Class

Return Value	Description
0	Success
1	Not Supported
2	Access Denied
3	Dependent Services Running
4	Invalid Service Control
5	Service Cannot Accept Control
6	Service Not Active
7	Service Request Timeout
8	Unknown Failure
9	Path Not Found
10	Service Already Running
11	Service Database Locked
12	Service Dependency Deleted
13	Service Dependency Failure
14	Service Disabled
15	Service Logon Failed
16	Service Marked For Deletion
17	Service No Thread
18	Status Circular Dependency
19	Status Duplicate Name
20	Status Invalid Name
21	Status Invalid Parameter
22	Status Invalid Service Account
23	Status Service Exists
24	Service Already Paused

DisplayName

The display name of the service (not the same as the service name that is used to locate a service).

Table L.10 Possible Values for the `ErrorControl` Property

Value	Description
Ignore	System does not notify the user and continues with starting the service
Normal	System notifies user and continues starting the service
Severe	System restarts with last-known good configuration
Critical	System restarts with a good configuration
Unknown	Unknown

ExitCode

A code for any error during the start and stop operations of the service.

Name

Name of the service.

PathName

Full path to the file that provides the service.

ServiceSpecificExitCode

Service-specific error code for errors during start and stop operations.

Table L.11 Possible Values for the `ServiceType` Property

Value	Service Type
0	Kernel Driver
1	File System Driver
2	Adapter
3	Recognizer Driver
4	Own Process
5	Share Process
8	Interactive Process

Table L.12 Possible Values for the `StartMode` Property

Mode	Meaning
Automatic	Service is started automatically by the Service Control Managers at system startup
Manual	Service by the service manager through a call to `StartService()`
Disabled	Service has been disabled and cannot be started
Boot	Service is a device driver that is started by the system loader
System	Service is a device driver started by the system

StartName

The name of the account that the service is logged on and run as.

Remarks

If the type of service is Own Process, the account will be `DomainName\User-Name`. Kernel drivers and file-system drivers use the object name that is used by the system when loading the device driver. If it is an Interactive Process or a Share Process, the `LocalSystem` account is used.

Table L.13 Possible Values for the `State` Property

Value	State
Stopped	Stopped
Start Pending	Start Pending
Stop Pending	Stop Pending
Running	Running
Continue Pending	Continue Pending
Pause Pending	Pause Pending
Paused	Paused
Unknown	Unknown

TagID

If service has been assigned a `TagID`, it is available in this property.

Return Value

`0` means no tag. Anything else is a `TagID`.

ChangeStartMode( )

Use this method to change the start mode of the service:

```
uint32 ChangeStartMode (
    [In] string StartMode
);
```

Parameters

StartMode

Refer to the StartMode property for the possible values of this parameter.

Change( )

Use this method to change the settings of a service:

```
uint32 Change (
    [In] string DisplayName,
    [In] string PathName,
    [In] uint8 ServiceType,
    [In] uint8 ErrorControl,
    [In] string StartMode,
    [In] boolean DesktopInteract,
    [In] string StartName,
    [In] string StartPassword,
    [In] string LoadOrderGroup,
    [In] string LoadOrderGroupDependencies [],
    [In] string ServiceDependencies []
);
```

Parameters

DisplayName

Refer to the DisplayName property.

PathName

Refer to the PathName property.

ServiceType

Refer to the ServiceType property.

ErrorControl

Refer to the ErrorControl property.

StartMode

Refer to the `StartMode` property.

```
DesktopInteract
```

Refer to the `DesktopInteract` property.

```
StartName
```

Refer to the `StartName` property.

```
StartPassword
```

The password for the account name that is used in `StartName`. An empty string sets no password; however, NULL means that you are not changing the password.

```
LoadOrderGroup
```

The name of the group to which the service belongs. An empty string or NULL is equivalent to no group.

```
LoadOrderGroupDependencies
```

List of load-ordering groups that must be started before this service can start. An empty string or NULL is equivalent to no dependencies.

```
ServiceDependencies
```

List of names of services that must be started before this service can start. An empty string or NULL is equivalent to no group.

Create( )

The `Create()` method creates a new service:

```
uint32 Create (
    [In] string Name,
    [In] string DisplayName,
    [In] string PathName,
    [In] uint8 ServiceType,
    [In] uint0 ErrorControl,
    [In] string StartMode,
    [In] boolean DesktopInteract,
    [In] string StartName,
    [In] string StartPassword,
    [In] string LoadOrderGroup,
    [In] string LoadOrderGroupDependencies [],
    [In] string ServiceDependencies []
);
```

Parameters

`Name`

Refer to the `Name` property.

`DisplayName`

The `DisplayName` parameter passes the display name of the service.

`PathName`

Refer to the `PathName` property.

`ServiceType`

Refer to the `ServiceType` property.

`ErrorControl`

Refer to the `ErrorControl` property.

`StartMode`

Refer to the `StartMode` property.

`DesktopInteract`

Refer to the `DessktopInteract` property.

`StartName`

Refer to the `StartName` property.

`StartPassword`

The password for the account name that is used in `StartName`. An empty string sets no password; however, NULL means that you are not changing the password.

`LoadOrderGroup`

The name of the group to which the service belongs. An empty string or NULL is equivalent to no group.

`LoadOrderGroupDependencies`

A list of load-ordering groups that must be started before this service can start. An empty string or NULL is equivalent to no dependencies.

```
ServiceDependencies
```

A list of names of services that must be started before this service can start. An empty string or NULL is equivalent to no group.

Delete( )

Use this method to delete service:

```
uint32 Delete ();
```

InterrogateService( )

Use this method to request the service to update its state to the service manager:

```
uint32 InterrogateService ();
```

PauseService( )

Use this method to pause service:

```
uint32 PauseService ();
```

ResumeService( )

Use this method to resume service:

```
uint32 ResumeService ();
```

StartService( )

Use this method to start service:

```
uint32 StartService ();
```

StopService( )

Use this method to stop service:

```
uint32 StopService ();
```

UserControlService( )

Use this method to send your user-defined control code to the service:

```
uint32 UserControlService (
    [In] uint8 ControlCode
);
```

Parameters

ControlCode

This parameter is a value from 128 to 255 that provides control commands.

Win32_Process

Table L.14 Win32_Process Description

Superclass	CIM_Process
Class Type	Dynamic class
Description	A Windows process
Remarks	The WMI View Provider provides this class for Microsoft SQL Server. The one remark is that the ParentProcessID property can return return the ID of a terminated process (process IDs are reused). As a result, returned information might not be what you expect.
Class Path	//./Root/MicrosoftSQLServer:Win32_Process
Keys	Handle
Constructor	Create
Destructor	Terminate

Table L.15 Win32_Process Properties

Name	Datatype	Read	Write	Maxlen	Unit	7.0	2000
CSCreationClass-Name	string	✔		256	n/a	✔	✔
CSName	string	✔		256	n/a	✔	✔
Caption	string	✔		64	n/a	✔	✔
CreationClassName	string	✔		256	n/a	✔	✔
CreationDate	datetime	✔		n/a	n/a	✔	✔
Description	string	✔		n/a	n/a	✔	✔
ExecutablePath	string	✔		n/a	n/a	✔	✔
ExecutionState	uint16	✔		n/a	n/a	✔	✔
HandleCount	uint32	✔		n/a	n/a	✔	✔

Table L.15 (Continued)

Name	Datatype	Read	Write	Maxlen	Unit	7.0	2000
Handle	string	✔		n/a	n/a	✔	✔
InstallDate	datetime	✔		n/a	n/a	✔	✔
KernelModeTime	uint64	✔		n/a	MS	✔	✔
MaximumWorking-SetSize	uint32	✔		n/a	KB	✔	✔
MinimumWorking-SetSize	uint32	✔		n/a	KB	✔	✔
Name	string	✔		n/a	n/a	✔	✔
OSCreationClass-Name	string	✔		256	n/a	✔	✔
OSName	string	✔		256	n/a	✔	✔
OtherOperation-Count	uint64	✔		n/a	n/a	✔	✔
OtherTransferCount	uint64	✔		n/a	Bytes	✔	✔
PageFaults	uint32	✔		n/a	n/a	✔	✔
PageFileUsage	uint32	✔		n/a	KB	✔	✔
ParentProcessId	uint32	✔		n/a	n/a	✔	✔
PeakPageFileUsage	uint32	✔		n/a	KB	✔	✔
PeakVirtualSize	uint64	✔		n/a	Bytes	✔	✔
PeakWorkingSetSize	uint32	✔		n/a	KB	✔	✔
Priority	uint32	✔		n/a	n/a	✔	✔
PrivatePageCount	uint64	✔		n/a	n/a	✔	✔
ProcessId	uint32	✔		n/a	n/a	✔	✔
QuotaNonPaged-PoolUsage	uint32	✔		n/a	n/a	✔	✔
QuotaPagedPool-Usage	uint32	✔		n/a	n/a	✔	✔
QuotaPeakNonPaged-PoolUsage	uint32	✔		n/a	n/a	✔	✔
QuotaPeakPaged-Pool-Usage	uint32	✔		n/a	n/a	✔	✔
ReadOperationCount	uint64	✔		n/a	n/a	✔	✔
ReadTransferCount	uint64	✔		n/a	Bytes	✔	✔
SessionId	uint32	✔		n/a	n/a	✔	✔
Status	string	✔		10	n/a	✔	✔

(continues)

Table L.15 Win32_Process Properties (Continued)

Name	Datatype	Read	Write	Maxlen	Unit	7.0	2000
TerminationDate	datetime	✔		n/a	n/a	✔	✔
ThreadCount	uint32	✔		n/a	n/a	✔	✔
UserModeTime	uint64	✔		n/a	MS	✔	✔
VirtualSize	uint64	✔		n/a	Bytes	✔	✔
WindowsVersion	string	✔		n/a	n/a	✔	✔
WorkingSetSize	uint64	✔		n/a	Bytes	✔	✔
WriteOperation-Count	uint64	✔		n/a	n/a	✔	✔
WriteTransfer-Count	uint64	✔		n/a	Bytes	✔	✔

Table L.16 Win32_Process Methods

Name	Return Type	Static	7.0	2000
Create	uint32	✔	✔	✔
GetOwnerSid	uint32		✔	✔
GetOwner	uint32		✔	✔
Terminate	uint32		✔	✔

ExecutablePath

The full path to the executable file.

HandleCount

The total number of handles opened by all threads in the process.

Handle

A string used to identify the process.

MaximumWorkingSetSize

Maximum working set size for the process.

MinimumWorkingSetSize

Minimum working set size for the process.

OtherOperationCount

The total number of run *input/output* (I/O) operations that were not read or write operations.

OtherTransferCount

The total amount of transferred data during operations that were not read or write operations.

PageFaults

Total number of occurred page faults.

PageFileUsage

Page file space that is in use by the process.

ParentProcessId

The Process ID of the process that launched this current instance.

PeakPageFileUsage

The largest amount of page file space ever used by the process.

PeakVirtualSize

The largest amount of virtual address space ever used at once by the process.

PeakWorkingSetSize

The largest working set size of the process.

Priority

The scheduling priority (0–31) of the process.

PrivatePageCount

The number of pages allocated especially for this process.

ProcessId

The ID of the running process.

QuotaNonPagedPoolUsage

The quota of non-paged pool usage for the process.

QuotaPagedPoolUsage

The quota amount of paged pool usage for the process.

QuotaPeakNonPagedPoolUsage

The peak quota amount of non-paged pool usage for the process.

QuotaPeakPagedPoolUsage

The peak quota amount of paged pool usage for the process.

ReadOperationCount

The number of read operations performed by the process.

ReadTransferCount

The amount of data transferred in read operations.

SessionId

The unique ID assigned by the operating system.

ThreadCount

The total number of active threads in the process (Windows NT/2000 only).

VirtualSize

The virtual address space in use by the process.

WindowsVersion

The version of Windows in which the process runs.

WriteOperationCount

The number of write operations performed by the process.

WriteTransferCount

The amount of data transferred in write operations.

Create( )

Use this method to create a new process from the executable file that is specified in the CommandLine parameter:

```
uint32 Create (
    [In]  string CommandLine,
    [In]  string CurrentDirectory,
    [In]  Win32_ProcessStartup ProcessStartupInformation,
    [Out] uint32 ProcessId
);
```

Return Value

The return value for success is 0. Any other number is an error.

Parameters

CommandLine

The command line to execute.

CurrentDirectory

The path for the child process (if set to NULL, the path of the calling process is used).

ProcessStartupInformation

Startup configuration information about items such as windows and errors.

ProcessId

The process ID of the new process.

GetOwnerSid( )

Use this method to get the *security identifier* (SID) for the owner of this process:

```
uint32 GetOwnerSid (
    [Out] string Sid
);
```

Parameters

Sid

The SID property returns the security identifier descriptor for this process.

GetOwner( )

Use this method to get the username and domain name under which the process is running:

```
uint32 GetOwner (
    [Out] string User,
    [Out] string Domain
);
```

Return Value

The return value for success is 0; anything else is an error.

Parameters

User

Username of the process's owner.

Domain

Domain in which the process is running.

Terminate( )

Use this method to terminate a process and its threads:

```
uint32 Terminate (
    [In] uint32 Reason
);
```

Return Value

The return value for success is 0; anything else is an error.

Parameters

Reason

The exit code for the process and all threads terminated.

Win32_Service

Table L.17 Win32_Service Description

Superclass	Win32_BaseService
Class Type	Dynamic class
Description	A Windows service management and operational data. CheckPoint is a value that is progressively incremented by the service in order to show signs of progress during a start, stop, pause, or continue operation. WaitHint is (in milliseconds) the time to wait during a start, stop, pause, or continue operation. CheckPoint is incremented, and CurrentState is changed—or if those fail to occur, it is considered an error.
Remarks	Union view class
Class Path	//./Root/MicrosoftSQLServer:Win32_Service
Keys	Name
Constructor	Create
Destructor	Delete

Table L.18 Win32_Service Properties

Name	Datatype	Read	Write	Maxlen	7.0	2000
AcceptPause	boolean	✔		n/a	✔	✔
AcceptStop	boolean	✔		n/a	✔	✔
Caption	string	✔		64	✔	✔
CheckPoint	uint32	✔		n/a	✔	✔
CreationClassName	string	✔		n/a	✔	✔
Description	string	✔		n/a	✔	✔
DesktopInteract	boolean	✔		n/a	✔	✔
DisplayName	string	✔		n/a	✔	✔
ErrorControl	string	✔		n/a	✔	✔
ExitCode	uint32	✔		n/a	✔	✔
InstallDate	datetime	✔		n/a	✔	✔
Name	string	✔		n/a	✔	✔
PathName	string	✔		n/a	✔	✔
ProcessId	uint32	✔		n/a	✔	✔
ServiceSpecificExitCode	uint32	✔		n/a	✔	✔

(continues)

Table L.18 `Win32_Service` Properties (Continued)

Name	Datatype	Read	Write	Maxlen	7.0	2000
ServiceType	string	✔		n/a	✔	✔
StartMode	string	✔		n/a	✔	✔
StartName	string	✔		n/a	✔	✔
Started	boolean	✔		n/a	✔	✔
State	string	✔		n/a	✔	✔
Status	string	✔		10	✔	✔
SystemCreationClassName	string	✔		n/a	✔	✔
SystemName	string	✔		n/a	✔	✔
TagId	uint32	✔		n/a	✔	✔
WaitHint	uint32	✔		n/a	✔	✔

Table L.19 `Win32_Service` Methods

Name	Return Type	Static	7.0	2000
ChangeStartMode	uint32		✔	✔
Change	uint32		✔	✔
Create	uint32	✔	✔	✔
Delete	uint32		✔	✔
InterrogateService	uint32		✔	✔
PauseService	uint32		✔	✔
ResumeService	uint32		✔	✔
StartService	uint32		✔	✔
StopService	uint32		✔	✔

MSSQL_Process

Table L.20 `MSSQL_Process` Description

Superclass	CIM_Process
Class Type	Dynamic class
Description	An SQL Server process
Class Path	//./Root/MicrosoftSQLServer:MSSQL_Process
Keys	Handle, SQLServerName

Table L.21 MSSQL_Process Properties

Name	Datatype	Read	Write	Maxlen	Unit	7.0	2000
BlockedProcessID	uint32	✔		n/a	n/a	✔	✔
CPUTime	uint32	✔		n/a	n/a	✔	✔
CSCreationClass-Name	string	✔		256	n/a	✔	✔
CSName	string	✔		256	n/a	✔	✔
Caption	string	✔		64	n/a	✔	✔
ClientName	string	✔		n/a	n/a	✔	✔
Command	string	✔		n/a	n/a	✔	✔
CreationClassName	string	✔		256	n/a	✔	✔
CreationDate	datetime	✔		n/a	n/a	✔	✔
DatabaseName	string	✔		n/a	n/a	✔	✔
Description	string	✔		n/a	n/a	✔	✔
ExecutionState	uint16	✔		n/a	n/a	✔	✔
Handle	string	✔		n/a	n/a	✔	✔
HostName	string	✔		n/a	n/a	✔	✔
InstallDate	datetime	✔		n/a	n/a	✔	✔
KernelModeTime	uint64	✔		n/a	MS	✔	✔
Login	string	✔		n/a	n/a	✔	✔
MemoryUsage	uint32	✔		n/a	n/a	✔	✔
Name	string	✔		n/a	n/a	✔	✔
OSCreationClass-Name	string	✔		256	n/a	✔	✔
OSName	string	✔		256	n/a	✔	✔
Priority	uint32	✔		n/a	n/a	✔	✔
SQLServerName	string	✔		128	n/a	✔	✔
State	string	✔		n/a	n/a	✔	✔
Status	string	✔		10	n/a	✔	✔
TerminationDate	datetime	✔		n/a	n/a	✔	✔
UserModeTime	uint64	✔		n/a	MS	✔	✔
WorkingSetSize	uint64	✔		n/a	Bytes	✔	✔

Table L.22 MSSQL_Process **Methods**

Name	Return Type	Static	7.0	2000
ProcessInputBuffer	string		✔	✔
ProcessOutputBuffer	string		✔	✔

ProcessInputBuffer( )

Use this method to return the buffer that is used by an SQL Server process for input:

```
string ProcessInputBuffer (
    [Out] MSSQL_MethodRtnVal NativeMethodRtnVal
);
```

ProcessOutputBuffer( )

Use this method to return the buffer that is used by an SQL Server process for output:

```
string ProcessOutputBuffer (
    [Out] MSSQL_MethodRtnVal NativeMethodRtnVal
);
```

MSSQL_FullTextWin32Service

Table L.23 MSSQL_FullTextWin32Service **Description**

Superclass	CIM_LogicalIdentity
Class Type	Association, dynamic class
Description	Association between two aspects of Microsoft Search full-text service
Class Path	//./Root/MicrosoftSQLServer: MSSQL_FullTextWin32Service
Keys	SameElement, SystemElement

Table L.24 MSSQL_FullTextWin32Service **References**

Name	References	Read	Write	Max	Min
SameElement	MSSQL_FullTextCatalog-Service	✔		0	1
SystemElement	Win32_Service	✔		1	1

MSSQL_FullTextCatalogService

Table L.25 MSSQL_FullTextCatalogService Description

Superclass	CIM_Service
Class Type	Dynamic class
Description	Microsoft Search full-text indexing service
Class Path	//./Root/MicrosoftSQLServer: MSSQL_FullTextCatalogService
Keys	Name

Table L.26 MSSQL_FullTextCatalogService Properties

Name	Datatype	Read	Write	Maxlen	7.0	2000
Caption	String	✔		64	✔	✔
ConnectTimeout	sint32	✔	✔	n/a	✔	✔
CreationClassName	String	✔		n/a	✔	✔
DefaultPath	String	✔		n/a	✔	✔
Description	String	✔		n/a	✔	✔
InstallDate	Datetime	✔		n/a	✔	✔
IsFullTextInstalled	Boolean	✔		n/a	✔	✔
Name	String	✔		n/a	✔	✔
ResourceUsage	sint32	✔	✔	n/a	✔	✔
ServiceStatus	uint32	✔		n/a	✔	✔
StartMode	String	✔		n/a	✔	✔
Started	Boolean	✔		n/a	✔	✔
Status	String	✔		10	✔	✔
SystemCreationClassName	String	✔		n/a	✔	✔
SystemName	String	✔		n/a	✔	✔

Table L.27 MSSQL_FullTextCatalogService Methods

Name	Return Type	Static	7.0	2000
CleanUp	MSSQL_MethodRtnVal		✔	✔
StartService	uint32		✔	✔
StopService	uint32		✔	✔

ServiceStatus

Table L.28 ServiceStatus

Value	Meaning
0	Unknown
1	Running
2	Paused
3	Stopped
4	Starting
5	Stopping
6	Pausing

CleanUp( )

Use this method to remove full-text catalog mappings without entries in the system table sysfulltextcatalogs:

```
MSSQL_MethodRtnVal CleanUp ();
```

Storage

The storage-related classes in Appendix M provide information that is related to media that are available for storage and for data retrieval. Refer to the following tables.

CIM_StorageExtent

Table M.1 `CIM_StorageExtent` Descriptions

Superclass	`CIM_LogicalDevice`
Class Type	Abstract class
Description	This base class describes a media for storing and retrieving data. The `Purpose` property describes the media and what it is used for; the `Access` property contains the access type; and the `ErrorMethodology` property describes the supported type of error detection and correction. `BlockSize` and `NumberOfBlocks` can be used to calculate the storage capabilities of this media.
Class Path	`//./Root/MicrosoftSQLServer:CIM_StorageExtent`

Table M.2 CIM_StorageExtent Properties

Name	Datatype	Read	Write	Maxlen	Unit	7.0	2000
Access	uint16	✔		n/a	n/a	✔	✔
Availability	uint16	✔		n/a	n/a	✔	✔
BlockSize	uint64	✔		n/a	Bytes	✔	✔
Caption	string	✔		64	n/a	✔	✔
ConfigManager-ErrorCode	uint32	✔		n/a	n/a	✔	✔
ConfigManager-UserConfig	boolean	✔		n/a	n/a	✔	✔
CreationClassName	string	✔		n/a	n/a	✔	✔
Description	string	✔		n/a	n/a	✔	✔
DeviceID	string	✔		n/a	n/a	✔	✔
ErrorCleared	boolean	✔		n/a	n/a	✔	✔
ErrorDescription	string	✔		n/a	n/a	✔	✔
ErrorMethodology	string	✔		n/a	n/a	✔	✔
InstallDate	datetime	✔		n/a	n/a	✔	✔
LastErrorCode	uint32	✔		n/a	n/a	✔	✔
Name	string	✔		n/a	n/a	✔	✔
NumberOfBlocks	uint64	✔		n/a	n/a	✔	✔
PNPDeviceID	string	✔		n/a	n/a	✔	✔
PowerManagement-Capabilities	uint16 [ ]	✔		n/a	n/a	✔	✔
PowerManagement-Supported	boolean	✔		n/a	n/a	✔	✔
Purpose	string	✔		n/a	n/a	✔	✔
StatusInfo	uint16	✔		n/a	n/a	✔	✔
Status	string	✔		10	n/a	✔	✔
SystemCreation-ClassName	string	✔		n/a	n/a	✔	✔
SystemName	string	✔		n/a	n/a	✔	✔

Table M.3 CIM_StorageExtent Methods

Name	Return Type	Static	7.0	2000
Reset	uint32		✔	✔
SetPowerState	uint32		✔	✔

Table M.4 Possible Values for the `Access` Property

Value	Access Type
0	Unknown
1	Read-Only
2	Write-Only
3	Read/Write

MSSQL_BackupDevice

Table M.5 `MSSQL_BackupDevice` Description

Superclass	`CIM_StorageExtent`
Class Type	Dynamic class
Description	This class represents an SQL server backup device.
Class Path	`//./Root/MicrosoftSQLServer:MSSQL_BackupDevice`
Keys	`Name, SQLServerName`

Table M.6 `MSSQL_BackupDevice` Properties

Name	Datatype	Read	Write	Maxlen	Unit	7.0	2000
Access	uint16	✔		n/a	n/a	✔	✔
Availability	uint16	✔		n/a	n/a	✔	✔
BlockSize	uint64	✔		n/a	bytes	✔	✔
Caption	string	✔		64	n/a	✔	✔
ConfigManager-ErrorCode	uint32	✔		n/a	n/a	✔	✔
ConfigManager-UserConfig	boolean	✔		n/a	n/a	✔	✔
CreationClassName	string	✔		n/a	n/a	✔	✔
Description	string	✔		n/a	n/a	✔	✔
DeviceID	string	✔		n/a	n/a	✔	✔
ErrorCleared	boolean	✔		n/a	n/a	✔	✔
ErrorDescription	string	✔		n/a	n/a	✔	✔
ErrorMethodology	string	✔		n/a	n/a	✔	✔
InstallDate	datetime	✔		n/a	n/a	✔	✔

(continues)

Table M.6 MSSQL_BackupDevice Properties (Continued)

Name	Datatype	Read	Write	Maxlen	Unit	7.0	2000
LastErrorCode	uint32	✔		n/a	n/a	✔	✔
Name	string	✔		n/a	n/a	✔	✔
NumberOfBlocks	uint64	✔		n/a	n/a	✔	✔
PNPDeviceID	string	✔		n/a	n/a	✔	✔
PhysicalLocation	string	✔	✔	n/a	n/a	✔	✔
PowerManagement-Capabilities	uint16 []	✔		n/a	n/a	✔	✔
PowerManagement-Supported	boolean	✔		n/a	n/a	✔	✔
Purpose	string	✔		n/a	n/a	✔	✔
SQLServerName	string	✔		128	n/a	✔	✔
SkipTapeLabel	Boolean	✔	✔	n/a	n/a	✔	✔
StatusInfo	uint16	✔		n/a	n/a	✔	✔
Status	string	✔		10	n/a	✔	✔
SystemCreation-ClassName	string	✔		n/a	n/a	✔	✔
SystemName	string	✔		n/a	n/a	✔	✔
SystemObject	boolean	✔		n/a	n/a	✔	✔
Type	uint32	✔		n/a	n/a	✔	✔

Table M.7 MSSQL_BackupDevice Methods

Name	Return Type	Static	7.0	2000
ReadBackupHeader	MSSQL_MethodRtnVal		✔	✔
ReadMediaHeader	MSSQL_MethodRtnVal		✔	✔
Reset	uint32		✔	✔
SetPowerState	uint32		✔	✔

PhysicalLocation

This name is what the operating system uses to locate the backup device. Examples of backup devices are tape machines and .bak files.

SkipTapeLabel

If the value is True, no verification that the device media is loaded is performed.

Type

This parameter describes the type of backup media with one of the following values shown in Table M.8.

Table M.8   Values for Backup Media Type

Value	Media Type
100	Unknown
2	Disk File
3	File On Removable Media In A:
4	File On Removable Media In B:
5	Tape
6	Named Pipe
7	CD-ROM

ReadBackupHeader( )

This method returns information about the header of the backed-up data:

```
aMSSQL_MethodRtnVal ReadBackupHeader (
    [Out] MSSQL_BackupHeader BackupHeader []
);
```

Parameters

```
BackupHeader
```

An output parameter that is initialized with the information returned by the method call.

ReadMediaHeader( )

Returns information about a backup media header record:

```
MSSQL_MethodRtnVal ReadMediaHeader (

    [Out] MSSQL_MediaHeader MediaHeader
);
```

Parameters

```
MediaHeader
```

An output parameter that is initialized with the information returned by the method.

Database Management System (DBMS) Objects

T he classes in Appendix N are *Database Management System* (DBMS) objects or objects that are directly related to some part of the DBMS.

MSSQL_Constraint

Table N.1 MSSQL_Constraint Descriptions

Superclass	MSSQL_DBMSObject
Class Type	Abstract class
Description	A base class for the constraints that can be used in an SQL server database
Class Path	//./Root/MicrosoftSQLServer:MSSQL_Constraint

Table N.2 MSSQL_Constraint Properties

Name	Datatype	Read	Write	Maxlen	7.0	2000
Caption	string	✔		64	✔	✔
Description	string	✔		n/a	✔	✔
InstallDate	datetime	✔		n/a	✔	✔
Name	string	✔		n/a	✔	✔
Status	string	✔		10	✔	✔

MSSQL_CandidateKey

Table N.3 MSSQL_CandidateKey Description

Superclass	MSSQL_Key
Class Type	Abstract class
Description	A base class for a candidate key in a SQL server table
Class Path	//./Root/MicrosoftSQLServer:MSSQL_CandidateKey
Keys	DatabaseName, Name, SQLServerName, TableName

Table N.4 MSSQL_CandidateKey Properties

Name	Datatype	Read	Write	Maxlen	7.0	2000
Caption	string	✔		64	✔	✔
DatabaseName	string	✔		n/a	✔	✔
Description	string	✔		n/a	✔	✔
InstallDate	datetime	✔		n/a	✔	✔
Name	string	✔		n/a	✔	✔
SQLServerName	string	✔		n/a	✔	✔
Status	string	✔		10	✔	✔
TableName	string	✔		128	✔	✔

MSSQL_Key

Table N.5 MSSQL_Key Description

Superclass	MSSQL_Constraint
Class Type	Abstract class
Description	A base class for keys in a table
Class Path	//./Root/MicrosoftSQLServer:MSSQL_Key
Keys	DatabaseName, Name, SQLServerName, TableName

Table N.6 MSSQL_Key Properties

Name	Datatype	Read	Write	Maxlen	7.0	2000
Caption	string	✔		64	✔	✔
DatabaseName	string	✔		n/a	✔	✔
Description	string	✔		n/a	✔	✔

Table N.6   (Continued)

Name	Datatype	Read	Write	Maxlen	7.0	2000
InstallDate	datetime	✔		n/a	✔	✔
Name	string	✔		n/a	✔	✔
SQLServerName	string	✔		n/a	✔	✔
Status	string	✔		10	✔	✔
TableName	string	✔		128	✔	✔

MSSQL_ForeignKey

Table N.7 MSSQL_ForeignKey Description

Superclass	MSSQL_Key
Class Type	Dynamic class
Description	A foreign key
Class Path	//./Root/MicrosoftSQLServer:MSSQL_ForeignKey
Keys	DatabaseName, Name, SQLServerName, TableName
Constructor	Create

Table N.8 MSSQL_ForeignKey Properties

Name	Datatype	Read	Write	Maxlen	7.0	2000
Caption	string	✔		64	✔	✔
Checked	boolean	✔	✔	n/a	✔	✔
DatabaseName	string	✔		n/a	✔	✔
Description	string	✔		n/a	✔	✔
ExcludeReplication	boolean	✔		n/a	✔	✔
InstallDate	datetime	✔		n/a	✔	✔
Name	string	✔		n/a	✔	✔
SQLServerName	string	✔		n/a	✔	✔
Status	string	✔		10	✔	✔
TableName	string	✔		128	✔	✔

Table N.9 MSSQL_ForeignKey Methods

Name	Return Type	Static	7.0	2000
Create	MSSQL_MethodRtnVal	✔	✔	✔
Rename	MSSQL_MethodRtnVal		✔	✔

Create( )

Use this method to create a new foreign key:

```
MSSQL_MethodRtnVal Create (
    [In] string Name,
    [In] string SQLServerName,
    [In] string DatabaseName,
    [In] string TableName,
    [In] string ColumnName [],
    [In] string ReferencedTable,
    [In] string ReferencedColumn []
);
```

MSSQL_PrimaryKey

Table N.10 MSSQL_PrimaryKey Description

Superclass	MSSQL_CandidateKey
Class Type	Dynamic class
Description	A primary key
Class Path	//./Root/MicrosoftSQLServer:MSSQL_PrimaryKey
Keys	DatabaseName, Name, SQLServerName, TableName
Constructor	Create

Table N.11 MSSQL_PrimaryKey Properties

Name	Datatype	Read	Write	Maxlen	7.0	2000
Caption	string	✔		64	✔	✔
Clustered	boolean	✔		n/a	✔	✔
DatabaseName	string	✔		n/a	✔	✔
Description	string	✔		n/a	✔	✔
InstallDate	datetime	✔		n/a	✔	✔
FillFactor	sint32	✔		n/a	✔	✔
Name	string	✔		n/a	✔	✔
SQLServerName	string	✔		n/a	✔	✔
Status	string	✔		10	✔	✔
TableName	string	✔		128	✔	✔

Table N.12 MSSQL_PrimaryKey Methods

Name	Return Type	Static	7.0	2000
Create	MSSQL_MethodRtnVal	✔	✔	✔
RebuildIndex	MSSQL_MethodRtnVal		✔	✔
Rename	MSSQL_MethodRtnVal		✔	✔

Create( )

Use this method to create a new primary key instance:

```
MSSQL_MethodRtnVal Create (
    [In] string Name,
    [In] string SQLServerName,
    [In] string DatabaseName,
    [In] string TableName,
    [In] string ColumnName [],
    [In, Optional] boolean Clustered
);
```

MSSQL_Check

Table N.13 MSSQL_Check Description

Superclass	MSSQL_Constraint
Class Type	Dynamic class
Description	SQL Server integrity constraint. The Checked property, if True, ensures that integrity constraints are enforced when rows are added to the table with the constraint.
Class Path	//./Root/MicrosoftSQLServer:MSSQL_Check
Keys	DatabaseName, Name, SQLServerName, TableName

Table N.14 MSSQL_Check Properties

Name	Datatype	Read	Write	Maxlen	7.0	2000
Caption	string	✔		64	✔	✔
Checked	boolean	✔		n/a	✔	✔
DatabaseName	string	✔		128	✔	✔
Description	string	✔		n/a	✔	✔
InstallDate	datetime	✔		n/a	✔	✔

(continues)

Table N.14 MSSQL_Check Properties (Continued)

Name	Datatype	Read	Write	Maxlen	7.0	2000
Name	string	✔		n/a	✔	✔
SQLServerName	string	✔		128	✔	✔
Status	string	✔		10	✔	✔
TableName	string	✔		128	✔	✔
Text	string	✔	✔	n/a	✔	✔

Table N.15 MSSQL_Check Methods

Name	Return Type	Static	7.0	2000
Rename	MSSQL_MethodRtnVal		✔	✔

MSSQL_DBMSObject

Table N.16 MSSQL_DBMSObject Description

Superclass	CIM_LogicalElement
Class Type	Abstract class
Description	A base class for DBMS objects
Class Path	//./Root/MicrosoftSQLServer:MSSQL_DBMSObject

Table N.17 MSSQL_DBMSObject Properties

Name	Datatype	Read	Write	Maxlen	7.0	2000
Caption	string	✔		64	✔	✔
Description	string	✔		n/a	✔	✔
InstallDate	datetime	✔		n/a	✔	✔
Name	string	✔		n/a	✔	✔
Status	string	✔		10	✔	✔

MSSQL_Datatype

Table N.18   MSSQL_Datatype Description

Superclass	MSSQL_DBMSObject
Class Type	Abstract class
Description	A base class for SQL Server data types
Class Path	//./Root/MicrosoftSQLServer:MSSQL_Datatype
Keys	DatabaseName, Name, SQLServerName

Table N.19   MSSQL_Datatype Properties

Name	Datatype	Read	Write	Maxlen	7.0	2000
AllowIdentity	boolean	✔		n/a	✔	✔
AllowNulls	boolean	✔		n/a	✔	✔
Caption	string	✔		64	✔	✔
DatabaseName	string	✔		128	✔	✔
Description	string	✔		n/a	✔	✔
InstallDate	datetime	✔		n/a	✔	✔
Name	string	✔		n/a	✔	✔
SQLServerName	string	✔		128	✔	✔
Status	string	✔		10	✔	✔

MSSQL_SystemDatatype

Table N.20   MSSQL_SystemDatatype Description

Superclass	MSSQL_Datatype
Class Type	Dynamic class
Description	A base data type defined in Microsoft SQL Server
Class Path	//./Root/MicrosoftSQLServer:MSSQL_SystemDatatype
Keys	DatabaseName, Name, SQLServerName

Table N.21 MSSQL_SystemDatatype Properties

Name	Datatype	Read	Write	Maxlen	7.0	2000
AllowIdentity	boolean	✔		n/a	✔	✔
AllowLength	boolean	✔		n/a	✔	✔
AllowNulls	boolean	✔		n/a	✔	✔
Caption	string	✔		64	✔	✔
Collation	string	✔		n/a	✔	✔
DatabaseName	string	✔		128	✔	✔
Description	string	✔		n/a	✔	✔
InstallDate	datetime	✔		n/a	✔	✔
MaximumChar	sint32	✔		n/a	✔	✔
MaximumLength	sint32	✔		n/a	✔	✔
Name	string	✔		n/a	✔	✔
Numeric	boolean	✔		n/a	✔	✔
SQLServerName	string	✔		128	✔	✔
Status	string	✔		10	✔	✔
VariableLength	boolean	✔		n/a	✔	✔

MSSQL_Column

Table N.22 MSSQL_Column Description

Superclass	MSSQL_DBMSObject
Class Type	Dynamic class
Description	This class represents a column in an SQL Server table. Use the properties to define the attributes of the columns (such as whether it is a computed column, an identity column, and so forth). Although these properties are marked as read only, they are writeable upon creation—so you can set their values before a new instance calls Put_() in order to store its data.
Class Path	//./Root/MicrosoftSQLServer:MSSQL_Column
Keys	DatabaseName, Name, SQLServerName, TableName

Table N.23 MSSQL_Column Properties

Name	Datatype	Read	Write	Maxlen	7.0	2000
AllowNulls	boolean	✔	✔	n/a	✔	✔
AnsiPaddingStatus	boolean	✔		n/a	✔	✔

Table N.23 (Continued)

Name	Datatype	Read	Write	Maxlen	7.0	2000
Caption	string	✔		64	✔	✔
Collation	string	✔	✔	n/a	✔	✔
ComputedText	string	✔	✔	n/a	✔	✔
Computed	boolean	✔		n/a	✔	✔
DatabaseName	string	✔		128	✔	✔
Datatype	string	✔	✔	n/a	✔	✔
Description	string	✔		n/a	✔	✔
FullTextIndex	boolean	✔	✔	n/a	✔	✔
IdentityIncrement	sint32	✔		n/a	✔	✔
IdentitySeed	sint32	✔		n/a	✔	✔
Identity	boolean	✔		n/a	✔	✔
InstallDate	datetime	✔		n/a	✔	✔
Length	sint32	✔	✔	n/a	✔	✔
Name	string	✔		n/a	✔	✔
NotForRepl	boolean	✔		n/a	✔	✔
NumericPrecision	sint32	✔	✔	n/a	✔	✔
NumericScale	sint32	✔	✔	n/a	✔	✔
RowGuidCol	boolean	✔	✔	n/a	✔	✔
SQLServerName	string	✔		128	✔	✔
Status	string	✔		10	✔	✔
TableName	string	✔		128	✔	✔

Table N.24 MSSQL_Column Methods

Name	Return Type	Static	7.0	2000
Rename	MSSQL_MethodRtnVal		✔	✔
UpdateStatisticsWith	MSSQL_MethodRtnVal		✔	✔

UpdateStatisticsWith( )

Use this method to force a data distribution statistics update:

```
MSSQL_MethodRtnVal UpdateStatisticsWith (
    [In] uint32 ScanType,
    [In, Optional] uint32 ScanNumber,
```

```
    [In, Optional] boolean ReCompute
);
```

Parameters

ScanType

ScanType is the data sampling method that is used to scan the column or index.

Table N.25 UpdateStatisticsWith() ScanType

Value	Description
3	Full scan to calculate statistics
2	Scan a percentage; set ScanNumber to a percentage
1	Scan a number of rows; set ScanNumber to an integer value
0	Percentage sampled scan; the system defines the percentage

ScanNumber

The sample size.

ReCompute

If the value is False, the automatic update of data distribution statistics is disabled. If the value is True (True by default), the setting remains as configured.

MSSQL_Database

Table N.26 MSSQL_Database Description

Superclass	MSSQL_DBMSObject
Class Type	Dynamic class
Description	An SQL Server database (use the Create() method to create a new database). EnableFullTextCatalog() and DisableFullTextCatalog() are used to define whether Microsoft Search full-text indexing is in effect on the database. If it is currently enabled, the FullTextEnables property will return True.
Class Path	//./Root/MicrosoftSQLServer:MSSQL_Database
Keys	Name, SQLServerName
Constructor	Create

Table N.27 MSSQL_Database Properties

Name	Datatype	Read	Write	Maxlen	Unit	7.0	2000
Caption	string	✔		64	n/a	✔	✔
Collation	string	✔	✔	n/a	n/a	✔	✔
CompatibilityLevel	uint32	✔	✔	n/a	n/a	✔	✔
CreateDate	datetime	✔		n/a	n/a	✔	✔
CreateForAttach	boolean	✔		n/a	n/a	✔	✔
DatabaseStatus	uint32	✔		n/a	n/a	✔	✔
Description	string	✔		n/a	n/a	✔	✔
FullTextEnabled	boolean	✔		n/a	n/a	✔	✔
InstallDate	datetime	✔		n/a	n/a	✔	✔
Name	string	✔		n/a	n/a	✔	✔
PrimaryFilePath	string	✔		n/a	n/a	✔	✔
SQLServerName	string	✔		128	n/a	✔	✔
Size	sint32	✔		n/a	MB	✔	✔
SpaceAvailable	sint32	✔		n/a	KB	✔	✔
Status	string	✔		10	n/a	✔	✔
SystemObject	boolean	✔		n/a	n/a	✔	✔
Version	sint32	✔		n/a	n/a	✔	✔

Table N.28 MSSQL_Database Methods

Name	Return Type	Static	7.0	2000
CheckAllocations	string		✔	✔
CheckCatalog	string		✔	✔
CheckIdentityValues	MSSQL_MethodRtnVal		✔	✔
CheckTablesDataOnly	string		✔	✔
CheckTables	string		✔	✔
Checkpoint	MSSQL_MethodRtnVal		✔	✔
Create	MSSQL_MethodRtnVal	✔	✔	✔
DisableFullText-Catalogs	MSSQL_MethodRtnVal		✔	✔
EnableFullText-Catalogs	MSSQL_MethodRtnVal		✔	✔
EnumerateStored-Procedures	MSSQL_MethodRtnVal		✔	✔

(continues)

Table N.28 `MSSQL_Database` Methods (Continued)

Name	Return Type	Static	7.0	2000
ExecuteImmediate	MSSQL_MethodRtnVal		✔	✔
FullTextIndexScript	string		✔	✔
IsValidKeyDatatype	boolean		✔	✔
RecalcSpaceUsage	MSSQL_MethodRtnVal		✔	✔
RemoveFullText-Catalogs	MSSQL_MethodRtnVal		✔	✔
Rename	MSSQL_MethodRtnVal		✔	✔
Shrink	MSSQL_MethodRtnVal		✔	✔
Transfer	MSSQL_MethodRtnVal		✔	✔
UpdateIndex-Statistics	MSSQL_MethodRtnVal		✔	✔

Table N.29 Possible Values for the `CompatibilityLevel` Property

Value	SQL Server Version
0	Unknown
60	6.0
65	6.5
70	7.0
80	2000

Table N.30 Possible Values for the `Status` Property

Status	Meaning
0	Normal
32	Loading
192	Recovering
256	Suspect
512	Offline
1024	Standby
32768	Emergency Mode

CheckAllocations( )

Use this method to test the integrity of the database pages and to possibly repair them:

```
string CheckAllocations (
    [In, Optional] uint32 RepairType,
    [Out] MSSQL_MethodRtnVal NativeMethodRtnVal
);
```

Parameters

RepairType

To actually repair a database, you must set the SingleUser property of MSSQL_DatabaseSetting so that single-user mode is enabled. Each repair type does what its predecessor did. For example, Allow Data Loss does everything that Rebuild does.

Table N.31 CheckAllocations() RepairTypes

RepairType	Description
None	Do not repair.
Fast	Minor operations without risk for data loss
Rebuild	Rebuilds indices without risk for data loss
Allow Data Loss	Corrects allocation errors, structural errors, and more

CheckCatalog( )

Use this method to check the integrity of the system tables in the database. The syscolumns table's data types are checked for matches in the systypes table. The tables and views in the sysobjects table must match one or more columns in the syscolumns table:

```
string CheckCatalog (
    [Out] MSSQL_MethodRtnVal NativeMethodRtnVal
);
```

CheckTablesDataOnly( )

Use this method to check the integrity of data, index, text, ntext, and image pages for all tables in the database:

```
string CheckTablesDataOnly (
    [Out] MSSQL_MethodRtnVal NativeMethodRtnVal
);
```

CheckTables( )

Use this method to check integrity in allocation and structure for all database tables and indices:

```
string CheckTables (
    [In, Optional] uint32 RepairType,
    [Out] MSSQL_MethodRtnVal NativeMethodRtnVal
);
```

Parameters

RepairType

To actually repair a database, you must set the SingleUser property of MSSQL_DatabaseSetting so that single-user mode is enabled. Each repair type includes the tasks of the repair type below it. For example, Allow Data Loss does everything that Rebuild does.

Table N.32 CheckTables() RepairTypes

RepairType	Description
None	Do not repair
Fast	Minor operations without risk for data loss
Rebuild	Rebuilds indices without risk for data loss
Allow Data Loss	Corrects allocation errors, structural errors, and more

Create( )

Use this method to create a new database:

```
MSSQL_MethodRtnVal Create (
    [In] string Name,
    [In] string SQLServerName,
    [In] MSSQL_DatabaseFile DatabaseFile,
    [In, Optional] uint32 InitialSize
);
```

Parameters

Name

Name of the database to create.

SQLServerName

The SQL Server instance of which the database will be part.

```
DatabaseFile
```

Name of the primary operating system file.

```
InitialSize
```

The initial size in *megabytes* (MB) for the database file.

EnumerateStoredProcedures( )

Enumerates the stored procedures and `Text` property contents that match the sequence of characters in the `Str` parameter:

```
MSSQL_MethodRtnVal EnumerateStoredProcedures (
    [In] string Str,
    [In, Optional] boolean IncludeSystemDefined,
    [Out] string SP []
);
```

Parameters

```
Str
```

The string that must match the stored procedure's `Text` property.

```
IncludeSystemDefined
```

If the value is `True`, system stored procedures are searched.

```
SP
```

The output parameter that receives the variant array that contains the names of the stored procedures that match the search criteria.

ExecuteImmediate( )

Use this method to run a non-rowset that returns the `T-SQL` command:

```
MSSQL_MethodRtnVal ExecuteImmediate (
    [In] string Command,
    [In, Optional] uint32 ExecutionType,
    [In, Optional] sint32 Length
);
```

Parameters

Command

The Command parameter specifies a Transact-SQL command batch.

ExecutionType

The ExecutionType parameter sets execution options as defined in the values in Table N.33.

Table N.33 ExecuteImmediate() ExecutionTypes

Type	Meaning
0	Default
1	Ignore Command Terminator
2	Continue On Error
4	No Execute
8	Parse Only
16	Quoted Identifiers On

Length

The Length parameter specifies the statement batch length.

FullTextIndexScript( )

Use this method to return a T-SQL command batch enabling Microsoft Search full-text indexing on the database:

```
string FullTextIndexScript (
    [Out] MSSQL_MethodRtnVal NativeMethodRtnVal
);
```

IsValidKeyDatatype( )

If True is returned, the data type can participate in primary- or foreign-key constraints:

```
boolean IsValidKeyDatatype (
    [In] string KeyColType,
    [In, Optional] string ReferencingColType,
    [Out] MSSQL_MethodRtnVal NativeMethodRtnVal
);
```

Parameters

```
KeyColType
```

Name of the single base or user-defined data type.

```
ReferencingColType
```

Name of the second base or user-defined data type.

Shrink( )

Use this method to reduce the size of operating system files that are associated with maintaining the database:

```
MSSQL_MethodRtnVal Shrink (
    [In] sint32 FreeSpaceInPercent,
    [In] uint32 Truncate
);
```

Parameters

```
FreeSpaceInPercent
```

If this parameter is a negative number, files will be shrunk to their smallest size.

```
Truncate
```

`Truncate` can be set as follows in Table N.34.

Table N.34 Truncate

Value	Description
0	Move data in pages at the end of the file to the beginning of the file, and truncate the file
1	Move data in pages at the end of the file to the beginning of the file, but do not truncate
2	Truncate the file, and try to recover free space at the end of the file
3	Move data from the file to other files in the same file group

Transfer( )

This method copies what is defined in the `MSSQL_TransferSetting` instance from one database to the other:

```
MSSQL_MethodRtnVal Transfer (
    [In] MSSQL_TransferSetting TransferSetting
);
```

Parameters

TransferSettingx

Defines the transfer.

MSSQL_Default

Table N.35 MSSQL_Default **Description**

Superclass	MSSQL_DBMSObject
Class Type	Dynamic class
Description	An SQL Server default
Class Path	//./Root/MicrosoftSQLServer:MSSQL_Default
Keys	DatabaseName, Name, SQLServerName

Table N.36 MSSQL_Default **Properties**

Name	Datatype	Read	Write	Maxlen	7.0	2000
Caption	string	✔		64	✔	✔
CreateDate	datetime	✔		n/a	✔	✔
DatabaseName	string	✔		128	✔	✔
Description	string	✔		n/a	✔	✔
InstallDate	datetime	✔		n/a	✔	✔
Name	string	✔		n/a	✔	✔
SQLServerName	string	✔		128	✔	✔
Status	string	✔		10	✔	✔
Text	string	✔	✔	n/a	✔	✔

Table N.37 MSSQL_Default **Methods**

Name	Return Type	Static	7.0	2000
Rename	MSSQL_MethodRtnVal		✔	✔

MSSQL_DRIDefault

Table N.38 MSSQL_DRIDefault Description

Superclass	MSSQL_DBMSObject
Class Type	Dynamic class
Description	A declarative, referential integrity column default
Class Path	//./Root/MicrosoftSQLServer:MSSQL_DRIDefault
Keys	ColumnName, DatabaseName, Name, SQLServerName, TableName

Table N.39 MSSQL_DRIDefault Properties

Name	Datatype	Read	Write	Maxlen	7.0	2000
Caption	string	✔		64	✔	✔
ColumnName	string	✔		128	✔	✔
DatabaseName	string	✔		128	✔	✔
Description	string	✔		n/a	✔	✔
InstallDate	datetime	✔		n/a	✔	✔
Name	string	✔		n/a	✔	✔
SQLServerName	string	✔		128	✔	✔
Status	string	✔		10	✔	✔
TableName	string	✔		128	✔	✔
Text	string	✔	✔	n/a	✔	✔

MSSQL_Index

Table N.40 MSSQL_Index Description

Superclass	MSSQL_DBMSObject
Class Type	Dynamic class
Description	An SQL Server index
Class Path	//./Root/MicrosoftSQLServer:MSSQL_Index
Keys	DatabaseName, Name, SQLServerName, TableName
Constructor	Create

Table N.41 MSSQL_Index Properties

Name	Datatype	Read	Write	Maxlen	Unit	7.0	2000
Caption	string	✔		64	n/a	✔	✔
DatabaseName	string	✔		128	n/a	✔	✔
Description	string	✔		n/a	n/a	✔	✔
FillFactor	sint32	✔		n/a	n/a	✔	✔
InstallDate	datetime	✔		n/a	n/a	✔	✔
IsFullTextKey	boolean	✔		n/a	n/a	✔	✔
Name	string	✔		n/a	n/a	✔	✔
NoRecompute	boolean	✔		n/a	n/a	✔	✔
SQLServerName	string	✔		128	n/a	✔	✔
SpaceUsed	sint32	✔		n/a	KB	✔	✔
StatisticsIndex	boolean	✔		n/a	n/a	✔	✔
Status	string	✔		10	n/a	✔	✔
TableName	string	✔		128	n/a	✔	✔
Type	uint32	✔		n/a	n/a	✔	✔

Table N.42 MSSQL_Index Methods

Name	Return Type	Static	7.0	2000
CheckIndex	string		✔	✔
Create	MSSQL_MethodRtnVal	✔	✔	✔
GetIndexedColumnDESC	boolean		✔	✔
Rebuild	MSSQL_MethodRtnVal		✔	✔
RecalcSpaceUsage	MSSQL_MethodRtnVal		✔	✔
Rename	MSSQL_MethodRtnVal		✔	✔
SetIndexedColumnDESC	MSSQL_MethodRtnVal		✔	✔
UpdateStatisticsWith	MSSQL_MethodRtnVal		✔	✔
UpdateStatistics	MSSQL_MethodRtnVal		✔	✔

Table N.43 Possible Values for the Type Property

Value	Meaning
0	Ignore Duplicate Key
1	Unique
4	Clustered
8	Pad Index

Table N.43   (Continued)

Value	Meaning
15	Drop Exist
5	Hypothetical
11	DRI Primary Key
12	DRI Unique Key
24	No Recompute

CheckIndex( )

Use this method to run a physical consistency check on the index:

```
string CheckIndex (
    [Out] MSSQL_MethodRtnVal NativeMethodRtnVal
);
```

Create( )

Use this method to create a new index:

```
MSSQL_MethodRtnVal Create (
    [In] string Name,
    [In] string SQLServerName,
    [In] string DatabaseName,
    [In] string TableName,
    [In] string ColumnName [],
    [In, Optional] uint32 Type,
    [In, Optional] string FileGroup
);
```

Parameters

```
Type
```

Refer to the `Type` property.

GetIndexedColumnDESC( )

If this method returns `True`, the sort order of the column is in the descending index:

```
boolean GetIndexedColumnDESC (
    [In] string ColumnName,
    [Out] MSSQL_MethodRtnVal NativeMethodRtnVal
);
```

SetIndexedColumnDESC( )

Use this method to set a column's sort order to descending before creating the index:

```
MSSQL_MethodRtnVal SetIndexedColumnDESC (
    [In] string ColumnName,
    [In] boolean Descending
);
```

UpdateStatisticsWith( )

Use this method to force a data-distribution update:

```
MSSQL_MethodRtnVal UpdateStatisticsWith (
    [In] uint32 ScanType,
    [In, Optional] uint32 ScanNumber,
    [In, Optional] boolean ReCompute
);
```

Parameters

ScanType

The `ScanType` is the data sampling method that is used to scan the column or index.

Table N.44 UpdateStatisticsWith() ScanType

Value	Description
3	Full scan to calculate statistics
2	Scan a percentage; set ScanNumber to a percentage
1	Scan a number of rows; set ScanNumber to an integer value
0	Percentage-sampled scan; the system defines the percentage

ScanNumber

The sample size.

ReCompute

If the value is `False`, the automatic update of data distribution statistics is disabled. If the value is `True`, the setting remains as configured. `True` is the default.

MSSQL_Rule

Table N.45 MSSQL_Rule Description

Superclass	MSSQL_Constraint
Class Type	Dynamic class
Description	An SQL Server rule that can be bound to a column or to a user-defined data type
Class Path	//./Root/MicrosoftSQLServer:MSSQL_Rule
Keys	DatabaseName, Name, SQLServerName

Table N.46 MSSQL_Rule Properties

Name	Datatype	Read	Write	Maxlen	7.0	2000
Caption	string	✔		64	✔	✔
CreateDate	datetime	✔		n/a	✔	✔
DatabaseName	string	✔		128	✔	✔
Description	string	✔		n/a	✔	✔
InstallDate	datetime	✔		n/a	✔	✔
Name	string	✔		n/a	✔	✔
SQLServerName	string	✔		128	✔	✔
Status	string	✔		10	✔	✔
Text	string	✔	✔	n/a	✔	✔

Table N.47 MSSQL_Rule Methods

Name	Return Type	Static	7.0	2000
Rename	MSSQL_MethodRtnVal		✔	✔

MSSQL_StoredProcedure

Table N.48 MSSQL_StoredProcedure **Description**

Superclass	MSSQL_DBMSObject
Class Type	Dynamic class
Description	A stored procedure in a database (a Startup property returns True and indicates that the stored procedure is executed upon startup)
Class Path	//./Root/MicrosoftSQLServer:MSSQL_StoredProcedure
Keys	DatabaseName, Name, SQLServerName

Table N.49 MSSQL_StoredProcedure **Properties**

Name	Datatype	Read	Write	Maxlen	7.0	2000
AnsiNullsStatus	boolean	✔		n/a	✔	✔
Caption	string	✔		64	✔	✔
CreateDate	datetime	✔		n/a	✔	✔
DatabaseName	string	✔		128	✔	✔
Description	string	✔		n/a	✔	✔
InstallDate	datetime	✔		n/a	✔	✔
Name	string	✔	✔	n/a	✔	✔
QuotedIdentifierStatus	boolean	✔		n/a	✔	✔
SQLServerName	string	✔		128	✔	✔
Startup	boolean	✔	✔	n/a	✔	✔
Status	string	✔		10	✔	✔
SystemObject	boolean	✔		n/a	✔	✔
Text	string	✔	✔	n/a	✔	✔
Type	uint32	✔	✔	n/a	✔	✔

Table N.50 MSSQL_StoredProcedure **Methods**

Name	Return Type	Static	7.0	2000
Rename	MSSQL_MethodRtnVal		✔	✔

Table N.51 Possible Values for the `Type` Property

Value	Type of Stored Procedure
0	Unknown
1	Standard
2	Extended
3	Macro
4	Replication Filter

MSSQL_Table

Table N.52 `MSSQL_Table` Description

Superclass	`MSSQL_DBMSObject`
Class Type	Dynamic class
Description	A table in a database. Aside from the ordinary values that you can find in a table, if the `FullTextIndexActive` property is `True`, the table is configured for participation in Microsoft Search. Also, if the `FullTextCatalogName` property is `True`, full-text queries can be run on the table for the table.
Class Path	`//./Root/MicrosoftSQLServer:MSSQL_Table`
Keys	`DatabaseName`, `Name`, `SQLServerName`
Constructor	`Create`

Table N.53 `MSSQL_Table` Properties

Name	Datatype	Read	Write	Maxlen	Unit	7.0	2000
AnsiNullsStatus	boolean	✔		n/a	n/a	✔	✔
Attributes	uint32	✔		n/a	n/a	✔	✔
Caption	string	✔		64	n/a	✔	✔
CreateDate	datetime	✔		n/a	n/a	✔	✔
DataSpaceUsed	sint32	✔		n/a	KB	✔	✔
DatabaseName	string	✔		128	n/a	✔	✔
Description	string	✔		n/a	n/a	✔	✔
FakeSystemTable	boolean	✔		n/a	n/a	✔	✔
FullTextCatalog-Name	string	✔	✔	n/a	n/a	✔	✔

(continues)

Table N.53 `MSSQL_Table` Properties (Continued)

Name	Datatype	Read	Write	Maxlen	Unit	7.0	2000
FullTextIndex-Active	boolean	✔	✔	n/a	n/a	✔	✔
FullTextKeyColumn	sint32	✔		n/a	n/a	✔	✔
FullTextPopulate-Status	uint32	✔		n/a	n/a	✔	✔
IndexSpaceUsed	sint32	✔		n/a	KB	✔	✔
InstallDate	datetime	✔		n/a	n/a	✔	✔
Name	string	✔		n/a	n/a	✔	✔
QuotedIdentifier-Status	boolean	✔		n/a	n/a	✔	✔
Rows	sint32	✔		n/a	n/a	✔	✔
SQLServerName	string	✔		128	n/a	✔	✔
Status	string	✔		10	n/a	✔	✔
SystemObject	boolean	✔		n/a	n/a	✔	✔
TableFullText-hangeTrackingOn	boolean	✔	✔	n/a	n/a	✔	✔
TableFullText-UpdateIndexOn	boolean	✔	✔	n/a	n/a	✔	✔
UniqueIndexFor-FullText	string	✔	✔	n/a	n/a	✔	✔
UsesFullTextIndex	boolean	✔	✔	n/a	n/a	✔	✔

Table N.54 `MSSQL_Table` Methods

Name	Return Type	Static	7.0	2000
CheckIdentityValue	MSSQL_MethodRtnVal		✔	✔
CheckTableDataOnly	string		✔	✔
CheckTable	string		✔	✔
Create	MSSQL_MethodRtnVal	✔	✔	✔
ExportData	sint32		✔	✔
FullTextIndexScript	string		✔	✔
FullTextUpdateIndex	MSSQL_MethodRtnVal		✔	✔
ImportData	sint32		✔	✔
ReCompileReferences	MSSQL_MethodRtnVal		✔	✔
RebuildIndexes	MSSQL_MethodRtnVal		✔	✔

Table N.54 (Continued)

Name	Return Type	Static	7.0	2000
RecalcSpaceUsage	MSSQL_MethodRtnVal		✔	✔
Rename	MSSQL_MethodRtnVal		✔	✔
StartFullTextPopulation	MSSQL_MethodRtnVal		✔	✔
StopFullTextPopulation	MSSQL_MethodRtnVal		✔	✔
TruncateData	MSSQL_MethodRtnVal		✔	✔
UpdateStatisticsWith	MSSQL_MethodRtnVal		✔	✔
UpdateStatistics	MSSQL_MethodRtnVal		✔	✔

Table N.55 Possible Values for the `Attributes` Property

Value	Meaning
0	Identity
1	System Object
2	Foreign Key
3	Referenced
5	Published
6	Replicated
7	Check
8	Replica
9	Primary Key
10	Unique
11	Default
12	Replication Check

Table N.56 Possible Values for the `FullTextPopulateStatus` Property

Value	Meaning
0	No population
1	Full population
2	Incremental population

CheckTableDataOnly( )

Use this method to check the integrity of data, index, text, ntext, and image pages for all tables in the database:

```
string CheckTableDataOnly (
    [Out] MSSQL_MethodRtnVal NativeMethodRtnVal
);
```

CheckTable( )

Use this method to check integrity in allocation and structure for all database tables and indices:

```
string CheckTable (
    [Out] MSSQL_MethodRtnVal NativeMethodRtnVal
);
```

Create( )

Use this method to create a new instance:

```
MSSQL_MethodRtnVal Create (
    [In] string Name,
    [In] string SQLServerName,
    [In] string DatabaseName,
    [In] MSSQL_Column ColumnName [],
    [In, Optional] String FileGroupName,
    [In, Optional] string TextFileGroupName
);
```

Parameters

Name

Name of the new table.

SQLServerName

Name of the SQL server with which to associate the table.

DatabaseName

Name of the database with which to associate the table.

ColumnName

List of the columns that are contained in the database.

FileGroupName

The file group that is used to store the table data.

TextFileGroupName

The file group that is used to store the text data in the table.

ExportData( )

The ExportData method is used to copy data to a data file:

```
sint32 ExportData (
    [In] MSSQL_BulkcopySetting BulkcopyObject,
    [Out] MSSQL_MethodRtnVal NativeMethodRtnVal
);
```

The method returns the number of rows that are written to the data file.

Parameters

```
BulkcopyObject
```

Settings for the export data operation.

FullTextIndexScript( )

Use this method to return a T-SQL command batch, enabling Microsoft Search full-text indexing on the database:

```
string FullTextIndexScript (
    [Out] MSSQL_MethodRtnVal NativeMethodRtnVal
);
```

ImportData( )

Use this method to bulk copy data:

```
sint32 ImportData (
    [In] MSSQL_BulkcopySetting BulkcopyObject,
    [Out] MSSQL_MethodRtnVal NativeMethodRtnVal
);
```

This method returns the number of rows that are copied from the data file.

Parameters

```
BulkcopyObject
```

Settings for the import data operation.

RebuildIndexes( )

The RebuildIndexes method recreates all indices that are defined in the table:

```
MSSQL_MethodRtnVal RebuildIndexes (
    [In, Optional] uint32 SortedDatatype,
    [In, Optional] uint32 FillFactor
);
```

Parameters

```
SortedDatatype
```

Ignored (do not use).

```
FillFactor
```

Index fill factor from 1–100.

StartFullTextPopulation( )

Use this method to populate the Microsoft Search full-text table with data:

```
MSSQL_MethodRtnVal StartFullTextPopulation (
    [In] uint32 Type
);
```

Parameters

```
Type
```

Either full population or incremental.

UpdateStatisticsWith( )

Use this method to force a data distribution statistics update:

```
MSSQL_MethodRtnVal UpdateStatisticsWith (
    [In] uint32 AffectType,
    [In] uint32 ScanType,
    [In, Optional] uint32 ScanNumber,
    [In, Optional] boolean ReCompute
);
```

Parameters

```
AffectType
```

Table N.57 UpdateStatisticsWith() AffectType

Value	Abstract
0	Affect Index
1	Affect Column
2	Affect All

ScanType

ScanType is the data-sampling method that is used to scan the column or index.

Table N.58 UpdateStatisticsWith() ScanType

Value	Description
3	Full scan to calculate statistics
2	Scan a percentage; set ScanNumber to a percentage
1	Scan a number of rows; set ScanNumber to an integer value
0	Percentage sampled scan; the system defines the percentage

ScanNumber

The sample size.

ReCompute

If the value is False, the automatic update of data distribution statistics is disabled. If the value is True, the setting remains as configured. True is the default.

MSSQL_Trigger

Table N.59 MSSQL_Trigger Description

Superclass	MSSQL_DBMSObject
Class Type	Dynamic class
Description	Represents a trigger. The Enabled property specifies whether the trigger is enabled. You can then find out what type of trigger is being used by using the AfterTrigger and InsteadOfTrigger properties. If the trigger is an *after* trigger, AfterTrigger returns True.
Class Path	//./Root/MicrosoftSQLServer:MSSQL_Trigger
Keys	DatabaseName, Name, SQLServerName, TableName

Table N.60 MSSQL_Trigger Properties

Name	Datatype	Read	Write	Maxlen	7.0	2000
AfterTrigger	boolean	✔		n/a	✔	✔
AnsiNullsStatus	boolean	✔		n/a	✔	✔
Caption	string	✔		64	✔	✔

(continues)

Table N.60 MSSQL_Trigger Properties (Continued)

Name	Datatype	Read	Write	Maxlen	7.0	2000
CreateDate	datetime	✔		n/a	✔	✔
DatabaseName	string	✔		128	✔	✔
Description	string	✔		n/a	✔	✔
Enabled	boolean	✔	✔	n/a	✔	✔
InstallDate	datetime	✔		n/a	✔	✔
InsteadOfTrigger	boolean	✔		n/a	✔	✔
Name	string	✔		n/a	✔	✔
QuotedIdentifierStatus	boolean	✔		n/a	✔	✔
SQLServerName	string	✔		128	✔	✔
Status	string	✔		10	✔	✔
SystemObject	boolean	✔		n/a	✔	✔
TableName	string	✔		128	✔	✔
Text	string	✔	✔	n/a	✔	✔
Type	uint32	✔		n/a	✔	✔

Table N.61 MSSQL_Trigger Methods

Name	Return Type	Static	7.0	2000
Rename	MSSQL_MethodRtnVal		✔	✔

Type

The Type property indicates the type of trigger.

Return Value

Table N.62 Type Return Value

Value	Meaning
0	Unknown
1	Insert
2	Update
4	Delete
7	All

MSSQL_UniqueKey

Table N.63 MSSQL_UniqueKey Description

Superclass	MSSQL_CandidateKey
Class Type	Dynamic class
Description	A unique key in a database
Class Path	//./Root/MicrosoftSQLServer:MSSQL_UniqueKey
Keys	DatabaseName, Name, SQLServerName, TableName
Constructor	Create

Table N.64 MSSQL_UniqueKey Properties

Name	Datatype	Read	Write	Maxlen	7.0	2000
Caption	string	✔		64	✔	✔
Description	string	✔		n/a	✔	✔
InstallDate	datetime	✔		n/a	✔	✔
DatabaseName	string	✔		n/a	✔	✔
Status	string	✔		10	✔	✔
Name	string	✔		n/a		✔
SQLServerName	string	✔		n/a	✔	✔
TableName	string	✔		128	✔	✔

Table N.65 MSSQL_UniqueKey Methods

Name	Return Type	Static	7.0	2000
Create	MSSQL_MethodRtnVal	✔	✔	✔
RebuildIndex	MSSQL_MethodRtnVal		✔	✔
Rename	MSSQL_MethodRtnVal		✔	✔

Create( )

Use this method to create a new, unique key:

```
MSSQL_MethodRtnVal Create (
    [In] string Name,
    [In] string SQLServerName,
    [In] string DatabaseName,
```

```
        [In] string TableName,
        [In] string ColumnName []
);
```

Parameters

Name

Name of the object to create.

SQLServerName

Name of the SQL Server object that will be created.

DatabaseName

Name of the database of which the object is part.

TableName

Name of the table in which the key is created.

ColumnName

List of columns that are part of the object; the order of column names defines the order of participation in the index that maintains the object constraints.

MSSQL_UserDatatype

Table N.66 MSSQL_UserDatatype **Description**

Superclass	MSSQL_Datatype
Class Type	Dynamic class
Description	The MSSQL_UserDatatype class represents a data type that is defined by a user. The BaseDatatype property indicates the system data type from which the user data type was derived. If IsVariableLength is true, the data type supports variable data-length handling for a data type. The Length property specifies the maximum number of characters or bytes that are accepted for the user-defined data type. Furthermore, the MaxSize property returns the greatest length of a data type in bytes (or the precision of the type).
Class Path	//./Root/MicrosoftSQLServer:MSSQL_UserDatatype
Keys	DatabaseName, Name, SQLServerName

Table N.67 MSSQL_UserDatatype Properties

Name	Datatype	Read	Write	Maxlen	7.0	2000
AllowIdentity	boolean	✔		n/a	✔	✔
AllowNulls	boolean	✔		n/a	✔	✔
BaseDatatype	string	✔		n/a	✔	✔
Caption	string	✔		64	✔	✔
Collation	string	✔		n/a	✔	✔
DatabaseName	string	✔		128	✔	✔
Description	string	✔		n/a	✔	✔
InstallDate	datetime	✔		n/a	✔	✔
IsVariableLength	boolean	✔		n/a	✔	✔
Length	sint32	✔		n/a	✔	✔
MaxSize	sint32	✔		n/a	✔	✔
Name	string	✔		n/a	✔	✔
NumericPrecision	sint32	✔		n/a	✔	✔
NumericScale	sint32	✔		n/a	✔	✔
SQLServerName	string	✔		128	✔	✔
Status	string	✔		10	✔	✔

Table N.68 MSSQL_UserDatatype Methods

Name	Return Type	Static	7.0	2000
Rename	MSSQL_MethodRtnVal		✔	✔

MSSQL_UserDefinedFunction

Table N.69 MSSQL_UserDefinedFunction Description

Superclass	MSSQL_DBMSObject
Class Type	Dynamic class
Description	A user-defined function in a database. If Deterministic is true, the user-defined function is a deterministic function. The Name property defines the label by which the object is known. Remember that Name must include the owner, such as [dbo].[name], and it must be identical to the name that is used in the CREATE statement in the Text property that contains the Transact-SQL script that defines the object.

(continues)

Table N.69 MSSQL_UserDefinedFunction Description (Continued)

Class Path	//./Root/MicrosoftSQLServer: MSSQL_UserDefinedFunction
Keys	DatabaseName, Name, SQLServerName

Table N.70 MSSQL_UserDefinedFunction Properties

Name	Datatype	Read	Write	Maxlen	7.0	2000
AnsiNullsStatus	boolean	✔	✔	n/a		✔
Caption	string	✔		64		✔
CreateDate	datetime	✔		n/a		✔
DatabaseName	string	✔		128		✔
Description	string	✔		n/a		✔
Deterministic	boolean	✔		n/a		✔
InstallDate	datetime	✔		n/a		✔
Name	string	✔		n/a		✔
QuotedIdentifierStatus	boolean	✔		n/a		✔
SQLServerName	string	✔		128		✔
Status	string	✔		10		✔
SystemObject	boolean	✔		n/a		✔
Text	string	✔	✔	n/a		✔

MSSQL_View

Table N.71 MSSQL_View Description

Superclass	MSSQL_DBMSObject
Class Type	Dynamic class
Description	A view table in the database
Class Path	//./Root/MicrosoftSQLServer:MSSQL_View
Keys	DatabaseName, Name, SQLServerName

Table N.72 MSSQL_View Properties

Name	Datatype	Read	Write	Maxlen	7.0	2000
AnsiNullsStatus	boolean	✔		n/a	✔	✔
Caption	string	✔		64	✔	✔
CreateDate	datetime	✔		n/a	✔	✔
DatabaseName	string	✔		128	✔	✔
Description	string	✔		n/a	✔	✔
InstallDate	datetime	✔		n/a	✔	✔
Name	string	✔	✔	n/a	✔	✔
QuotedIdentifierStatus	boolean	✔		n/a	✔	✔
SQLServerName	string	✔		128	✔	✔
Status	string	✔		10	✔	✔
SystemObject	boolean	✔		n/a	✔	✔
Text	string	✔	✔	n/a	✔	✔

Table N.73 MSSQL_View Methods

Name	Return Type	Static	7.0	2000
ExportData	sint32		✔	✔
Rename	MSSQL_MethodRtnVal		✔	✔

ExportData( )

Use this method to copy data from a database to a data file that is defined by an instance of MSSQL_BulkCopySetting:

```
sint32 ExportData (
    [In] MSSQL_BulkCopySetting BulkcopyObject,
    [Out] MSSQL_MethodRtnVal NativeMethodRtnVal
);
```

Return Value

The number of rows that are written to the data file.

Parameters

BulkcopyObject

Instance that has the required settings for the bulk-copy operation.

Top-Level Classes, Parameters, and More

A ppendix O is a collection of important classes presented together here in a loose grouping.

CIM_ManagedSystemElement

Table O.1 CIM_ManagedSystemElement Descriptions

Class Type	Abstract class
Description	A base class for the system element hierarchy. Caption is a one-line description. The description is more of an elaborate text about the meaning of the managed system element. Name labels the object, and Status returns the current state of the element.
Class Path	//./Root/MicrosoftSQLServer: CIM_ManagedSystemElement

Table O.2 CIM_ManagedSystemElement Properties

Name	Datatype	Read	Write	Maxlen	7.0	2000
Caption	string	✔		64	✔	✔
Description	string	✔		n/a	✔	✔
InstallDate	datetime	✔		n/a	✔	✔
Name	string	✔		n/a	✔	✔
Status	string	✔		10	✔	✔

Table O.3 Possible Values for the `Status` Property

Value
OK
Error
Degraded
Unknown
Pred Fail
Starting
Stopping
Service

MSSQL_StoredProcedureParameter

Table O.4 `MSSQL_StoredProcedureParameter` Description

Class Type	Dynamic class
Description	The input and output parameters of an SQL Server stored procedure
Class Path	`//./Root/MicrosoftSQLServer:` `MSSQL_StoredProcedureParameter`
Keys	`DatabaseName, Name, SQLServerName, StoredProcedureName`

Table O.5 `MSSQL_StoredProcedureParameter` Properties

Name	Datatype	Read	Write	Maxlen	Unit	7.0	2000
ColId	uint32	✔		n/a	n/a	✔	✔
DatabaseName	string	✔		128	n/a	✔	✔
Datatype	string	✔		n/a	n/a	✔	✔
Length	uint32	✔		n/a	bytes	✔	✔
Name	string	✔		128	n/a	✔	✔
Output	boolean	✔		n/a	n/a	✔	✔
SQLServerName	string	✔		128	n/a	✔	✔
StoredProcedureName	string	✔		128	n/a	✔	✔

MSSQL_MethodRtnVal

Table O.6 MSSQL_MethodRtnVal Description

Class Type	Abstract class
Description	An abstract class is used as a return type. Methods can return an instance of MSSQL_MethodRtnVal, whose properties contain SQL Server-specific information about the success or failure of the underlying method call made by WMI. Source is the location in SQL Server where the error occurred; ReturnValue is the error code; and Description is a textual representation of the error. If ReturnValue is zero, there was no error.
Class Path	//./Root/MicrosoftSQLServer:MSSQL_MethodRtnVal

Table O.7 MSSQL_MethodRtnVal Properties

Name	Datatype	Read	Write	7.0	2000
Description	string	✔		✔	✔
ReturnValue	uint32	✔		✔	✔
Source	string	✔		✔	✔

MSSQL_ProviderStatus

Table O.8 MSSQL_ProviderStatus Description

Superclass	__ExtendedStatus
Class Type	Abstract class
Description	Error status information returned by the WMI provider. Examine the Object and Property properties for information about what the object was working on when it failed. ParameterInfo names parameters that are associated with the occurred error, and ProviderName specifies a provider if one caused the error. Source is the COM error, and if StatusCode is a value other than zero, you generally have an error.
Class Path	//./Root/MicrosoftSQLServer:MSSQL_ProvideStatus

Table O.9 MSSQL_ProviderStatus Properties

Name	Datatype	Read	Write	7.0	2000
Description	string	✔		✔	✔
Object	uint32	✔		✔	✔
Operation	string	✔		✔	✔
ParameterInfo	string	✔		✔	✔
Property	uint32	✔		✔	✔
ProviderName	string	✔		✔	✔
Routine	string	✔		✔	✔
Source	uint32	✔		✔	✔
StatusCode	string	✔		✔	✔

What Is on the CD-ROM?

On the CD-ROM, you can find the sample scripts in the book. These scripts are available both in VBScript and Perl. Additional scripts demonstrating WMI and XML are also included on the CD-ROM.

Index

A

absolute locations, XPath, 26–27
abstract classes, 128, 129, 222, 223
access type selection, 52–54
Active Directory, network
    information, 148
Active Server Pages (ASPs),
    xvi–xvii
    MDAC and, 114–115
    XML-to-HTML-to-ASP
      translation in, 114–115
ActiveX Data Objects (ADO),
    MDAC and, 109–112
Add( ) method, 216
    SWbemNamedValueSet
      Object, 179
    SWbemPrivilegeSet Object,
      175–176
    SWbemProperty Object,
      174–174
AddAsString ( ) method, SWbem-
    PrivilegeSet Object, 175–177
administration, xv. *See also*
    Windows Management
    Instrumentation
Administration Provider, WMI,
    125, 132–134
after elements, updategrams,
    97–99
aggregations, 136–137, 225–230
Analysis Services, SQL Server
    2000, 4, 15
annotations, xvi, 79–86

antecedent classes, 138–139
Application Programming
    Interfaces (APIs), xvii
    COM API in WMI, 123–124
    Distributed COM (DCOM)
      for, 125
    Scripting API in WMI, 124–125,
      147–190
assign permission to stored
    procedure, 213–214
associate login with SQL Server
    role, 207–208
associations, 158–159, 167–168
    Common Information Model
      (CIM), 130, 136–141,
      142–144
    configuration and settings for,
      139–140
ASSOCIATOR OF statements in
    WQL, 194–195
at sign, expression building and, 26
attribute-based documents, 57
attribute-centric mapping, 90–91
attributes, 25–26, 41–43, 90–91, 126
    attribute-centric mapping in,
      90–91
    Common Information Model
      (CIM), 128
    Extensible Markup Language
      (XML), 57
    foreign key, 83
    metaproperties and, 92
    nested, 43–44

primary key, 83
    updategram, 100–101
    XPath, 27
authentication, 50–51, 130–132
authentication mode, SQL Server
    2000, 14
AuthenticationLevel DCOM
    setting, 130, 132
Auto mode, 73–75
auto-starting services in SQL
    Server 2000, 16–17
AutoClose, 214–215
axes, XPath, 27, 30

B

backups, 11, 238, 271–275, 355–357
before elements, updategrams,
    97–99
Binary Large Objects (BLOBs), 81
books online, SQL Server 2000, 13
Boolean functions, XPath, 28, 30
bulk copy
    MSSQL_BulkCopySetting,
      275–279
    table, 215–216
BY argument, WQL, 198

C

capacity of SQL Server 2000, 3–4
catalog, MSSQL_FullTextCatalog-
    Service, 350–352
CD-ROM companion disc,
    xviii, 401

CDATA, MDAC and, 110
CIM_Component, 225
CIM_Dependency, 231
CIM_ElementSetting, 293
CIM_LogicalElement, 313
CIM_ManagedSystemElement, 397–398
CIM_Process, 329–330
CIM_Service, 330–331
CIM_StatisticalInformation, 310
CIM_Statistics, 309
CIM_StorageExtent, 353–355
classes, xvi, xvii, 122, 126–129, 134–141
  abstract, 222, 223
  aggregations in, 136–137, 225–230
  antecedent, 138–139
  associations as, 130, 136–142, 143–144
  associator return in, Associator_( ), 167
  associator return in, AssociatorOf( ), 158
  ASSOCIATOR OF statements in WQL, 194–195
  asynchronously get class or instance in, GetAsync( ), 155
  asynchronously receive subclasses, SubclassesOfAsync( ), 157
  Common Information Model (CIM), 126–127, 128–129
  configuration and settings for associations in, 139–140
  constructors, 222
  containment in, 139, 267–269
  create derived class, SpawnDerivedClass_( ), 170
  create instance, SpawnInstance_( ), 170
  delete, Delete( ), 155
  delete, DeleteAsync( ), 155–156, 166
  dependencies in, 138–139, 231–249
  destructors, 222
  dumping all instances of, 210–211
  dynamic, 293–304
  enumerate instances, Instances_( ), 166
  extension associations in, 141, 305
  get instance or class in, 152–153, 154–155
  identity relationships in, 140
  instances of. *See* instances

MSSQL, 134–141
  overriding, 129
  parent-child relationships in, 137
  permissions in, 141, 251–259
  put classes and instances in, Put( ), 164–165
  put classes and instances in, PutAsync( ), 164–165
  qualifiers for, 129
  receive instances, InstancesAsync_( ), 166
  REFERENCES OF statements in WQL, 195–196
  Rename( ), 222–223
  scope associations in, 137–138, 261–266
  services and processes, 329–352
  statistics associations in, 140, 309–311
  storage, 353–357
  subclass enumeration in, SubclassesOf( ), 156–157
  subclasses, Subclasses_( ), 166–167
  subclasses, SubclassesAsync_( ), 167
  superclasses in, 222
  SWbemObject, 161–170
  SWbemServices Object in, 151–161
  top-level, 397–400
  user, user accounts, 319–328
client connectivity, SQL Server 2000, 13
Client Tools Only installation, SQL Server 2000, 9–10
clustering in SQL Server 2000, 4
code samples, SQL Server 2000, 13
collation settings for SQL Server 2000, 14–15
collection object (SQLVDirs), virtual directory management, 104, 105
columns, 206, 243–248, 366–368
COM API, Windows Management Instrumentation (WMI), 123–124
command dialects, MDAC, 108–109
Command object, ADO, MDAC and, 108–109, 110
comment ( ) node test in XPath, 28–31
Common Information Models (CIMs), 23–24, 127–130, 225, 231, 293, 309–310, 313, 329–331, 353–355, 397–398
  abstract classes in, 128, 129

  associations in, 130, 136–141, 142–144
  attributes in, 126, 128
  classes in, 126–129
  Common Model schema for, 127–128
  concrete classes in, 128
  Core Model schema for, 127–128
  data types in, 128
  extensions to, 127
  functions in, 128
  inheritance in, 128, 129
  instances, class instances in, 126, 128–130
  keys in, 129–130
  Managed Object Format (MOF) in, 126, 169
  methods in, 126, 128
  namespaces and, 126, 129–130
  non-abstract classes in, 129–130
  object manager in WMI for, 125–127
  operations in, 128
  overriding a class in, 129
  parameters in, 128–129
  properties in, 126, 128
  qualifiers in, 126, 129
  repository in WMI for, 125–127
  schema in, 126
  side-effects of operations in, 128
  static classes in, 271–292
  static vs. dynamic classes in, 127
  subclasses in, 129
  superclasses in, 129
common management tasks, 203–219
  add new column, 206
  assign permission to stored procedure, 213–214
  associate login with SQL server role, 207–208
  bulk-copy a table, 215–216
  context objects and, 216–217
  create new database, 203–204
  create new login, 207
  create new table, 205–206
  create stored procedure, 211–213
  dumping all instances of class, 210–211
  dumping properties of table, 209–210
  enumerate parameters of stored procedure, 214

error checking in, 217–218
get login information, 208–209
modify database settings, 214–215
register NT log events, 218–219
start/stop SQL Server, 209
Common Model schema for CIM, 127–128
compare objects, CompareTo_( ), 170
COMPUTE expressions, 78
concrete classes, Common Information Model (CIM), 128
conditional processing, XSLT, 34–36
configurations, 299–304
Connect( ) method, virtual directory management, 103–104
Connection object, ADO, MDAC and, 110–112
ConnectServer( ) method, Windows Management Instrumentation (WMI), 151
console, 19
constants, enumerated constants in WMI, 184–189, 185–189
constraints, MSSQL_Constraint, 359
constructors, 222
containment, 139, 267–269
content types, 58–59
context objects, WMI, 216–217
conventions, 223
copying data
    bulk-copy a table, 215–216
    MSSQL_BulkCopySetting, 275–279
core functions, XPath, 28
Core Model schema for CIM, 127–128
Count( ) method, SWbem-PropertyObject, 174
create new database, 203–204
create new login, 207
create new table, 205–206
CREATE statement, 223
create stored procedure, 211–213
Create( ), 203–204

D

data mining with SQL Server 2000, 4
data queries, WMI Query Language (WQL), 191, 192–195
Data Source, Internet Information Services (IIS), 51–52

data types, 80–81, 223, 232–235, 248, 266, 365–366, 392–393
    annotations for, 84
    Common Information Model (CIM), 128
    Scripting API in WMI, 183–184
Database Management System (DBMS) objects, 359–395
database objects, 59–60
databases, xv, 239, 244–246, 249, 253–254, 256–259, 263–269, 297–298, 304, 308, 321, 359, 368–376. See also Database Management System (DBMS) objects
    add new column, 206
    AutoClose, 214–215
    create new, 203–204
    Database Management System (DBMS) objects in, 359–395
    modify settings in, 214–215
decision trees in SQL Server 2000, 4
Delegate setting, Windows Management Instrumentation (WMI), 133–134
DELETE statement in, 95–96
Delete( ), 155, 165
DeleteAsync( ), 155–156, 166
deleting data in XML, 95
    OpenXML function, 95–96
    updategrams for, 98–99
dependencies, 138–139, 231–249
destructors, 222
development tools for SQL Server 2000, 13
directory object (SQLVDir), virtual directory management, 104–106
Disconnect( ) method, virtual directory management, 104
Distributed COM (DCOM) for WMI, 125
Distributed Management Task Force (DMTF), 121–122, 125–126
Document Object Model (DOM), 24, 37
document-level elements, 25
domain user accounts, SQL Server 2000, 13–14
DOMDocument object, MDAC, 112
dumping all instances of class, 210–211
dumping properties of table, 209–210
dynamic classes, 293–304
    CIM, 127

E

edge-table mapping, 91–92
electronic commerce (e-commerce), 3
element-based documents, 57–58
elements, 24–26, 41–44, 57–61, 88–90
    document-level, 25
    element-centric mapping, 88–90
    logical, 313–317
    metaproperties and, 92
    nested in, 43–44
    root-level, 25
    top-level, 25, 57–61
    updategram, 100–101
English Query, SQL Server 2000, 15
Enterprise Edition, SQL Server 2000, 3–4
Enterprise Evaluation Edition of SQL Server 2000, 4, 5
Enterprise Manager (EM), 3
    Properties configuration in, 17–18
    SQL Server 2000, 17–19
    Tree pane in, 17
    Wizards for, 18–19
enumerated constants in WMI, 184–189, 185–189
error checking, 184, 186–189, 217–218, 238, 243, 314–317
event programming, 200–201
event queries, WMI Query Language (WQL), 191, 196–198, 196, 197
events, 170–173, 180, 316–317
    event programming and, 200–201
    event queries in WQL and, 191, 196–198
    register NT log events, 218–219
ExecMethod( ), 160
ExecMethod_( ), 169
ExecMethodAsync( ), 161
ExecMethodAsync_( ), 169
ExecNotificationQuery( ), 160
ExecNotificationQuery-Async( ), 160
ExecQuery( ), 154, 157
ExecQueryAsync( ), 157
Explicit mode, 75–78
ExportData( ), 215–216
expressions, XPath, 26, 27–28
Extensible Stylesheet Language Transformations (XSLT), 23, 33–38, 60–61
    conditional processing in, 34–36
    Document Object Model (DOM) and, 37

for-each processing in, 33–34
free-threaded objects in, 37
instructions in, table of, 38, 39
sorting in, 34–36
SQL Server 2000, 4
template files in, 33, 37, 63
transformation process in, 37–38
tree structures in, 33
extensions, 141, 305–308
extensions to CIM, 127
extensions to XML, 79

F
failover support in SQL Server 2000, 4
file management, 314–316
filtering, XPath, 32–33
firewalls and SQL Server 2000, 4
FOR XML clause, 55–56, 71–78
for-each processing, XSLT, 33–34
foreign key attributes, 83, 361–362
free-threaded objects, XSLT, 37
functions, Common Information Model (CIM), 128

G
Generalized Markup Language (GML), 21
Get( ) method, 152–153, 154–155
GetAsync( ), 155
GetObjectText_( ), 169
GROUP clause, WQL, 198

H
HAVING clause, WQL, 198
hiding fields, 82
HTTP listener for SQL Server 2000, 4
Hypertext Markup Language (HTML), 22–23
Extensible Markup Language (XML) and, 47, 59, 61
SQL Server 2000 and, 4
streaming binary data in, 59
template files in, 63–65
XML-to-HTML-to-ASP translation in, 114–115
Hypertext Transfer Protocol (HTTP), 45–46
Extensible Markup Language (XML) and, 47
POST method and MDACs in, 113

I
IBM, WBEM and, 121–122
identity relationships, 140
image display, 59–60

Impersonate setting, WMI, 133–134
ImpersonationLevel DCOM setting, WMI, 130, 131, 133–134
indexes, 236, 242–243, 310–311, 377–380
indexed views in SQL Server 2000, 4
inheritance, Common Information Model (CIM), 128, 129
INSERT statements, 78
inserting data in XML, 92–94
OpenXML function, 92–94
updategrams for, 98–99
installation of SQL Server, xvi
instance name for SQL Server 2000, 10–11
InstanceOf( ), 153, 156
instances, class instances, 222, 223
asynchronously get class or instance in, GetAsync( ), 155
Common Information Model (CIM), 126, 128–130
create instance, SpawnInstance_( ), 170
delete, Delete( ), 155
delete, DeleteAsync( ), 155–156, 166
dumping all instances of class, 210–211
enumerate instances, Instances_( ), 166
enumerating instances in, InstanceOf( ), 153, 156
get instance or class in, 152–153, 154–155
put classes and instances in, Put( ), 164–165
put classes and instances in, PutAsync( ), 164–165
receive instances, InstancesAsync_( ), 166
Rename( ), 222–223
SWbemObject, 161–170
SWbemServices Object in, 151–161
Windows Management Instrumentation (WMI), 126, 128–129
Instances_( ), 166
InstancesAsync_( ), 166
InstancesOfAsync( ), 156
integrated security, 134, 296–297, 303
Intel, WBEM and, 121–122

Internet Information Services (IIS), xv, xvi, 47–69
access type selection in, 52–54
authentication in, 50–51
Data Source selection for, 51–52
Hypertext Markup Language (HTML) and, 47
Hypertext Transport Protocol (HTTP) and, 47
Internet Server API (ISAPI) extension in, 47–48
launching, 48–49
Microsoft Management Console (MMC) and, 47
Object Linking and Embedding Database (OLE DB) in, 48
Secure Sockets Layer (SSL) and, 51
security configuration in, 50–51
Template Files in, 52–53
Uniform Resource Locators (URLs) in, 52–53
virtual directories in, 49–54
XPath and, 52, 54
Internet Server API (ISAPI) extension, 47, 48
Item( ) method
SWbemNamedValueSet object, 179
SWbemPrivilegeSet Object, 175–176
SWbemProperty Object, 174–174

J–L
JScripts, Scripting API in WMI, 182
keys, 236, 240–241, 268–269, 360–363, 391–392
Common Information Model (CIM), 129–130
SWbemObject, 163
Windows Management Instrumentation (WMI), 149–150
language, 296, 303
location paths, XPath, 26–27, 85
location steps, XPath, 27
logical elements, 313–317
logins, 239, 242, 245, 249, 263, 269, 323–324
associate login with SQL server role, 207–208
create new login, 207
get login information, 208–209
scope associations in, 137–138
log shipping in SQL Server 2000, 4

M

Managed Object Format (MOF) in
CIM, 126, 169
management tasks. *See* common
management tasks
management tools, 12, 17–19
mapping, xvi
attribute-centric, 90–91
edge-table, 91–92
element-centric, 88–90
MDAC and, 116–117
memory capacity of SQL Server
2000, 4
metaproperties in, 92
methods, 160–169, 222–223
Common Information Model
(CIM), 128
MSSQL_MethodRtnVal,
399–400
qualifiers for, 129
return values in WMI for,
181–183
Microsoft Data Access
Components (MDACs), xv,
xvi, 108–117
Active Server Pages (ASPs)
and, 114–115
ActiveX Data Objects (ADO) in,
109–112
command dialects for, 108–109
Command object, ADO,
dynamic properties in,
108–110
connecting to database with,
110–112
Connection object in, 110–112
direct queries (T-SQL) with, 113
DOMDocument object for, 112
dynamic properties for XML
data in, 114–115
mapping schema in, 116–117
Microsoft XML Parser for, 112
Named Parameters in, 115–116
parameterized queries in,
115–116
Posting requests with, 113–114
Stream object, ADO, in, 109–112
Windows Script File (.wsf) in,
109–110
XML-to-HTML-to-ASP
translation in, 114–115
XMLHTTP object in, 113–114
XPath queries in, 116–117
Microsoft Desktop Engine
(MSDE), 4, 5
Microsoft Developer Edition of
SQL Server 2000, 4–5
Microsoft Management Console
(MMC) snap-in, 17, 47

Microsoft SQL Server, xv, xvii
Microsoft Windows 2000
DataCenter, 4
Microsoft XML Parser, MDAC
and, 112
Microsoft, WBEM and, 121–122
mixed mode, SQL Server 2000, 14
mode argument, 56, 71–78
modifying data in XML, 87
OpenXML function, 94–95
MSSQL classes
aggregations in, 136–137,
225–230
associations in, 136–141
containment in, 139, 267–269
dependencies in, 138–139,
231–249
extension associations in,
141, 305
identity relationships in, 140
keys in, 150
parent-child relationships
in, 137
permissions in, 141, 251–259
scope associations in, 137–138,
261–266
statistics associations in, 140,
309–311
MSSQL_BackupDevice, 355–357
MSSQL_BackupSetting, 271–275
MSSQL_BaseDatatype, 248
MSSQL_BulkCopySetting,
275–279
MSSQL_CandidateKey, 360
MSSQL_Check, 363–364
MSSQL_Column, 366–368
MSSQL_ColumnDatatype, 248
MSSQL_ColumnDefault, 247
MSSQL_ColumnDRIDefault, 247
MSSQL_ColumnRule, 246
MSSQL_ConfigValue, 299–301
MSSQL_Constraint, 359
MSSQL_Containment, 267
MSSQL_Database, 368–376
MSSQL_DatabaseCandidateKey,
268, 269
MSSQL_DatabaseDatabaseRole,
266
MSSQL_DatabaseDatabase-
Setting, 304
MSSQL_DatabaseDatatype, 266
MSSQL_DatabaseDefault, 265
MSSQL_DatabaseFile, 306–308
MSSQL_DatabaseFileDataFile,
308
MSSQL_DatabaseFileGroup, 246
MSSQL_DatabaseFullText-
Catalog, 245
MSSQL_DatabaseLogin, 269

MSSQL_DatabaseOwnerLogin,
245
MSSQL_DatabaseRoleDatabase-
Permission, 259
MSSQL_DatabaseRoleStored-
ProcedurePermission, 258
MSSQL_DatabaseRoleTable-
Permission, 257, 258
MSSQL_DatabaseRoleUser-
DefinedFunctionPermission,
257
MSSQL_DatabaseRoleView-
Permission, 256
MSSQL_DatabaseRule, 265
MSSQL_DatabaseSetting, 297–298
MSSQL_DatabaseStored-
Procedure, 264
MSSQL_DatabaseTable, 230
MSSQL_DatabaseTransactionLog,
244
MSSQL_DatabaseUser, 263
MSSQL_DatabaseUserDefined-
Function, 264
MSSQL_DatabaseView, 229
MSSQL_Datatype, 365
MSSQL_DBMSObject, 364
MSSQL_DBMSObjectOwner, 244
MSSQL_DBMSUserObject, 321
MSSQL_DRIDefault, 377
MSSQL_ErrorLogDataFile, 243
MSSQL_ErrorLogEntry, 314
MSSQL_ErrorLogErrorLogEntry,
229
MSSQL_Extends, 306
MSSQL_Extension, 305
MSSQL_FileGroup, 314–316
MSSQL_FileGroupDatabaseFile,
228
MSSQL_ForeignKey, 361–362
MSSQL_FullTextCatalogService,
350–352
MSSQL_FullTextWin32Service,
350
MSSQL_Index, 377–380
MSSQL_IndexColumn, 243
MSSQL_IndexFileGroup, 242
MSSQL_IndexStatistics, 310
MSSQL_IndexTableInformation,
311
MSSQL_IntegratedSecurity-
Setting, 296–297
MSSQL_Key, 360–361
MSSQL_KeyColumn, 228
MSSQL_KeyFileGroup, 240
MSSQL_LanguageSetting, 296
MSSQL_Login, 323–324
MSSQL_LoginDefaultDatabase,
249
MSSQL_LoginWin32Group, 249

MSSQL_LoginWin32UserAccount, 239
MSSQL_MemberDatabaseRole, 239
MSSQL_MemberLogin, 242
MSSQL_MemberUser, 241
MSSQL_MethodRtnVal, 399
MSSQL_Permission, 251, 252
MSSQL_PrimaryKey, 362–363
MSSQL_Process, 348–350
MSSQL_ReferencedKey, 241
MSSQL_ReferencedTable, 240
MSSQL_RegistrySetting, 294–295
MSSQL_RestoreSetting, 280–283
MSSQL_Role, 319
MSSQL_Rule, 381
MSSQL_Scope, 261
MSSQL_SQLServerBackup-Device, 238
MSSQL_SQLServerConfigValue, 304
MSSQL_SQLServerConnection-Setting. 134, 283–285
MSSQL_SQLServerDatabase, 227
MSSQL_SQLServerErrorLog, 238
MSSQL_SQLServerIntegrated-SecuritySetting, 303
MSSQL_SQLServerLanguage-Setting, 303
MSSQL_SQLServerLogin, 263
MSSQL_SQLServerRegistry, 302
MSSQL_SQLServerRole, 325
MSSQL_SQLServerServerRole, 262
MSSQL_SQLServerSQLServer-ConnectionSetting, 302
MSSQL_SQLServerUser, 268
MSSQL_StoredProcedure, 382–383
MSSQL_StoredProcedure-Parameter, 398
MSSQL_SystemDatatype, 365–366
MSSQL_Table, 383–389
MSSQL_TableCheck, 237
MSSQL_TableColumn, 227
MSSQL_TableFileGroup, 237
MSSQL_TableIndex, 236
MSSQL_TableKey, 236
MSSQL_TableTextFileGroup, 235
MSSQL_TableTrigger, 235
MSSQL_TransactionLog, 316–317
MSSQL_TransactionLogDataFile, 226
MSSQL_TransferSetting, 286–292
MSSQL_Trigger, 389–390
MSSQL_UniqueKey, 391–392
MSSQL_User, 321–322

MSSQL_UserDatabase-Permission, 253, 254
MSSQL_UserDatatype, 392–393
MSSQL_UserDatatypeDefault, 234–235
MSSQL_UserDatatypeRule, 232–233
MSSQL_UserDefinedFunction, 393–394
MSSQL_UserLogin, 232
MSSQL_UserStoredProcedure-Permission, 253
MSSQL_UserTablePermission, 255
MSSQL_UserUserDefined-FunctionPermission, 255, 256
MSSQL_UserViewPermission, 254
MSSQL_View, 394–395

N

name-value pairs, 55
Named Parameters, MDAC, 115–116
named values
SWbemNamedValue Object in, 180
SWbemNamedValueSet Object in, 178–179
namespaces, 38–40, 126, 133, 148–149
Common Information Model (CIM), 129–130
ConnectServer( ) method and, 151
declaration of, 40
event queries in WQL and, 196–198
security setting, 131–132
xmlns= in, 40, 79
nested elements and attributes, 25, 43–44
NextEvent( ), SWbemEventSource Object, 180
node tests, XPath, 28–31
node-set functions, XPath, 28, 29
non-abstract classes, Common Information Model (CIM), 129–130
notification events
ExecNotificationQuery( ), 160
ExecNotificationQuery-Async( ), 160
SWbemSink Object in, 170–173
Novell, WBEM and, 121–122
NT log, register NT log events, 218–219
numeric functions, XPath, 28, 30

O

object creation in WMI, 141–144
Object Linking and Embedding Database (OLE DB), IIS, 48
objects, XPath, 26
OnCompleted, SWbemSink Object, 171–172
Online Analytical Processing (OLAP), 4
OnObjectPut, SWbemSink Object, 172
OnObjectReady, SWbemSink Object, 172
OnProgress, SWbemSink Object, 172–173
open content models, 41
OpenXML function, 87–88
attribute-centric mapping in, 90–91
DELETE statement in, 95–96
deleting data in, 95–96
edge-table mapping in, 91–92
element-centric mapping in, 88–90
inserting data, 92–94
metaproperties and, 92
modifying data with, 94–95
Query Analyzer and, 89, 92
stored procedures and, 87–88
system stored procedures in, 88
UPDATE statement and, 94–95
XPath and, 89
operating systems support
by SQL Server 2000, 4, 5
by Windows Management Instrumentation (WMI), 122, 123
operations, Common Information Model (CIM), 128
operators
WMI Query Language (WQL), 193
XPath, 32
overriding a class, 129, 222

P

parameterized queries, MDAC, 115–116
parameters, 181–182, 223
Common Information Model (CIM), 128–129
enumerate parameters of stored procedure, 214
MSSQL_StoredProcedure-Parameter, 398
MSSQL_StoredProcedure-StoredProcedure-Parameter, 262

Named Parameters in, 115–116
queries, parameterized queries in, 68–69, 115–116
SWbemObject, 162
updategram, 100–101
parent-child relationships, 27, 41, 137
parsers, 21, 24
MDAC and, 112
Microsoft XML Parser for, 112
passwords, 14, 134
Perl, SWbemSink Object and, 170–173
permissions, 141, 213–214, 251–259
Personal Edition, SQL Server 2000, 4
POST method, MDAC, 113
predicates, XPath, 32–33
primary key attributes, 83, 362–363
processes. See service and process classes
processing-instruction( ) node test in XPath, 28–31
properties, 222, 223
Common Information Model (CIM), 126, 128
dumping properties of table, 209–210
qualifiers for, 129
SWbemObject, 162, 163–164
Properties configuration, Enterprise Manager (EM), 17–18
Providers, WMI, 19
Put( ), 164–165
Put_( ), 203, 206, 212, 223
PutAsync( ), 164–165
Python, SWbemSink Object and, 170–173

Q

qualified names (Qnames), 38
qualifiers, 122, 126, 129, 152, 191–201
queries, 54–65, 85
associator return in, Associator-Async_( ), 167–168
associator return in, AssociatorOfAsync( ), 158–159
asynchronously receive query objects, InstancesOf-Async( ), 156
attribute-based documents and, 57
Auto mode in, 73–75
content types in, 58–59

database objects in, 59–60
element-based documents and, 57–58
ExecQuery( ) execution in, 154
execute asynchronous query in, ExecQueryAsyn( ), 157–158
execute query in, ExeQuery( ), 157
Explicit mode in, 75–78
Extensible Stylesheet Language Transformations (XSLT) in, 60–61
FOR XML clause in, 55–56, 71–78
HTTP embedded parameters for URLs in, 56
Hypertext Markup Language (HTML) and, 59, 61
image display using, 59–60
MDAC and T-SQL, 113
mode argument in, 56, 71–78
notification event execution, ExecNotification-Query( ), 160
notification event execution, ExecNotificationQuery-Async( ), 160
optimization of, in WQL, 199–200
parameterized, 68–69, 115–116
querystring of URL in, 54–55
Raw mode in, 71–73
root parameter in, 57
SELECT statement in, 55
singletons, 57–58
stored procedures and, 65–68
streaming binary data in, 59
template files in, 61–65, 85–86
top-level elements in, 57–61
Uniform Resource Locators (URLs) in, 54–55
views for, 78
XPath and, 85, 116–117
Query Analyzer
OpenXML function and, 89, 92
SQL Server 2000, 3
querystring of URL, 54–55

R

Random Access Memory (RAM), SQL Server 2000, 4
Raw mode, 71–73
references, 223
MSSQL_ReferenceTable, 240
References_( ), 168
ReferencesAsync_( ), 168–169

REFERENCES OF statements in WQL, 195–196
ReferencesTo( ), 159
ReferencesToAsync( ), 168
registry, 294–295, 302
relationships among data, 82–83
aggregations in, 136–137, 225–230
antecedent classes, 138–139
associations in, 136–141, 142–144
containment in, 139, 267–269
dependencies in, 138–139, 231–249
extension associations in, 141, 305
identity relationships in, 140
parent-child relationships in, 137
permissions in, 141, 251–259
scope associations in, 137–138, 261–266
statistics associations in, 140, 309–311
relative locations, XPath, 26–27
Remove( ) method
SWbemNamedValueSet Object, 179
SWbemPrivilegeSet Object, 176
SWbemProperty Object, 174–174
Rename( ), 222–223
restore, 280–283
rights, Windows Management Instrumentation (WMI), 133
root elements, XPath, 26
root parameter, Extensible Markup Language (XML), 57
root-level elements, 25

S

schema in CIM, 126
Common Model for, 127–128
Core Model for, 127–128
schema in XML, xvi, 40–45, 221–223
annotated, 79–86
attributes in, 41–43
building a, 79–83
caching of, 45
configuration of, 83–85
data types in, 80–81
elements in, 41–43
foreign key attributes in, 83
hiding fields in, 82
locating data in, 85–86
nested elements and attributes in, 43–44

open content models in, 41
primary key attributes in, 83
relationships among data in, 82–83
template files in, 85–86
top-level elements in, 80
tree structure in, 82–83
typed elements in, 41
XML Data Reduced for, 41, 79
xmlns= in, 40, 79
schema queries, WMI Query Language (WQL), 191, 199
scope associations/scoped objects, 137–138, 261–266
Scripting API in WMI, 124–125, 147–190
  associator return in, Associator_( ), 167
  associator return in, AssociatorOf( ), 158
  associator return in, AssociatorAsync_( ), 167–168
  associator return in, AssociatorOfAsync( ), 158–159
  asynchronously get class or instance in, GetAsync( ), 155
  asynchronously receive query objects, InstancesOf-Async( ), 156
  asynchronously receive subclasses, Subclasses-OfAsync( ), 157
  class or instance in, DeleteAsync( ), 166
  class or instance in, DeleteAsync( ), 155–156
  compare objects, CompareTo_( ), 170
  ConnectServer( ) method in, 151
  create derived class, Spawn-DerivedClass_( ), 170
  create instance, Spawn-Instance_( ), 170
  delete class or instance, Delete( ), 155, 165
  enumerate instances, Instances_( ), 166
  enumerate instances, InstanceOf( ), 153, 156
  execute asynchronous query in, ExecQueryAsyn( ), 157–158
  execute query in, ExeQuery( ), 157

JScripts and, 182
languages and output parameters in, 181–182
method execution, ExecMethod( ), 160
method execution, ExecMethod_( ), 169
method execution, ExecMethodAsync( ), 161
method execution, ExecMethodAsync_( ), 169
method return values in, 181–183
MOF of current object, GetObjectText_( ), 169
namespaces and, 148–149
notification event execution, ExecNotification-Query( ), 160
notification event execution, ExecNotificationQuery-Async( ), 160
put classes and instances in, Put( ), 164–165
put classes and instances in, PutAsync( ), 164–165
query execution in, 154
receive instances, InstancesAsync_( ), 166
references, References_( ), 168
references, References-Async_( ), 168–169
references, ReferencesTo( ), 159
references, ReferencesTo-Async( ), 168
scripting languages and variants in, 183–184
subclass enumeration in, SubclassesOf( ), 156–157
subclasses, Subclasses_( ), 166–167
subclasses, Subclasses-Async_( ), 167
SWbemEventSource Object in, 180
SWbemLastError Object in, 178
SWbemLocator Object in, 148–151
SWbemMethod Object in, 173–175
SWbemNamedValue Object in, 180
SWbemNamedValueSet Object in, 178–179
SWbemObject in, 161–170
SWbemObjectPath Object in, 177–178

SWbemPrivilegeSet Object in, 175–177
SWbemProperty Object in, 173–175
SWbemPropertySet Collection in, 174–175
SWbemPropertySet Object in, 174–175
SWbemServices Object in, 151–161
SWbemSink Object in, 170–173
VBScripts in, 182–183
scripting languages and variants, Scripting API in WMI, 183–184
Secure Sockets Layer (SSL), Internet Information Services (IIS), 51
security, 130–132, 134, 296–297, 303
  Internet Information Services (IIS) and XML, 50–51
  in SQL Server 2000, 4
  virtual directory management, 106
SELECT statement, 55, 78, 192–193, 211
Server Agent, SQL Server 2000, 13–14
service and process classes, 320–352
Service Manager for SQL Server 2000, 15–17
services account, SQL Server 2000, 13–14
services in SQL Server 2000, 16–17
side-effects of operations, Common Information Model (CIM), 128
Silicon Graphics, WBEM and, 121–122
Simple Object Access Protocol (SOAP), 22
singleton queries, 57–58
slash, backslash character, 25–26
Software Development Kit (SDK) for WMI, 19
sorting, XSLT, 34–36
SpawnDerivedClass_( ), 170
SpawnInstance_( ), 170
special character encoding in XML, 25–26
SQL Server 2000, xv, 3–20, 45–69, 132–144, 262–263, 268, 283–285, 302–303, 325
  ActiveX Data Objects (ADO) and, 10

adding components to, 15
advanced installation options for, 8
Analysis Services in, 4, 15
applications for, 3
associate login with SQL Server role, 207–208
authentication mode for, 14
auto-starting services in, 16–17
backup of data in, 11
books online for, 13
capacity of, 3–4
client connectivity in, 13
Client Tools Only installation in, 9–10
clustering in, 4
code samples for, 13
collation settings for, 14–15
component selection for, 12–13
console for, 19
data mining with, 4
data types in, 80–81
decision trees in, 4
defining installation type for, 9–10
development tools for, 13
domain user accounts in, 13–14
English Query in, 15
Enterprise Edition of, 3–4
Enterprise Evaluation Edition of, 4, 5
Enterprise Manager (EM) for, 3, 17–19
Extensible Stylesheet Language Transformations (XSLT) and, 4
failover support in, 4
firewalls and, 4
HTTP listener for, 4
Hypertext Transport Protocol (HTTP) and, 4, 45–46
indexed views in, 4
installation of, 5–19
instance name for, 10–11
invoking installation for, 6–7
launching, 6
log shipping in, 4
management tools for, 12, 17–19
memory capacity of, 4
Microsoft Data Access Components (MDACs) in, 10
Microsoft Desktop Engine (MSDE) in, 4, 5
Microsoft Developer Edition of, 4–5

Microsoft Management Console (MMC) snap-in for, 17
Microsoft Windows 2000 DataCenter and, 4
mixed mode in, 14
multiple instances in, 10–11
naming computer for, 7
Object Linking and Embedding Databases (OLE DB) in, 10
Open Database Connectivity (ODBC) in, 10
operating systems supported by, 4–5
Personal Edition of, 4
Query Analyzer in, 3
Random Access Memory (RAM) in, 4
remote installation of, 7
security in, 4
selecting installation type for, 8
server components for, 12
Service Manager for, 15–17
services account in, 13–14
services in, starting, stopping, pausing, 16–17
Setup type selection, 12
Standard Edition of, 4
starting and stopping, 209
unattended installation of, 8–9
Uniform Resource Locator (URL) access in, 4
updategrams for, 97–101
user information dialog for, 9
virtual server and, 8
Windows CE Edition of, 4, 5
XPath and, 4
SQLVDir directory object, virtual directory management, 104–106
SQLVDirs collection object, virtual directory management, 104, 105
Standard Edition, SQL Server 2000, 4
Standardized Generalized Markup Language (SGML), 21–22
start/end tags, XML, 24–26, 24
start/stop SQL Server, 209
static classes, 135–136, 271–292, 293–304
CIM, 127
static methods, 223
statistics associations, 140, 309–311
CIM_StatisticalInformation, 310
CIM_Statistics, 309

storage classes, 353–357
stored procedures, 17, 65–68, 78, 87–88, 253, 258, 262–264, 382–383, 398
assign permission to stored procedure, 213–214
create stored procedure, 211–213
enumerate parameters of stored procedure, 214
scope associations in, 137–138
Stream object, ADO, in MDAC, 109–112
streaming binary data, xvi, 59
string functions, XPath, 28, 29
Structured Query Language (SQL), 3
COMPUTE expressions in, 78
FOR XML clause in, 55–56, 71–78
INSERT statement in, 78
SELECT statement in, 55, 78
WMI Query Language (WQL) and, 191–201
style sheets, 23–24, 38
subclasses
asynchronously receive subclasses, SubclassesOf-Async( ), 157
Common Information Model (CIM), 129
subclass enumeration in, SubclassesOf( ), 156–157
Subclasses_( ), 166–167
SubclassesAsync_( ), 167
Subclasses_( ), 166–167
SubclassesAsync_( ), 167
SubclassesOf( ), 156
SubclassesOfAsync( ), 157
superclasses, 129, 222
SWbemEventSource Object in, 180
SWbemLastError Object, 178
SWbemLocator Object, 148–151
SWbemMethod Object, 173–175
SWbemNamedValue Object, 180
SWbemNamedValueSet Object, 178–179
Add( ) method in, 179
Item( ) method in, 179
Remove( ) method in, 179
SWbemObject, 161–170
classes and instances in, 161
compare objects, Compare-To_( ), 170
create derived class, Spawn-DerivedClass_( ), 170

create instance, SpawnInstance_( ), 170
creating managed objects with, 162–163
delete class or instance in, DeleteAsync( ), 166
delete class or instance, Delete( ), 165
enumerate instances, Instances_( ), 166
keys in, 163
methods in, 162, 163–164
MOF of current object, GetObjectText_( ), 169
parameters for, 162
properties in, 162, 163–164
put classes and instances in, Put( ), 164–165
put classes and instances in, PutAsync( ), 164–165
receive instances, InstancesAsync_( ), 166
subclasses, Subclasses_( ), 166–167
subclasses, SubclassesAsync_( ), 167
SWbemObjectSet in, 161–165
SWbemObjectPath object, 177–178
SWbemObjectSet, 161–164
SWbemPrivilegeSet Collection, 175–177
SWbemPrivilegeSet Object, 175–177
  Add( ) method in, 175–176
  AddAsString ( ) method in, 175–177
  Item( ) method in, 175–176
  Remove( ) method in, 176
  SWbemPrivilegeSet Collection Object in, 175–177
SWbemProperty Object, 173–175
  Add( ) method in, 174
  Count( ) method in, 174
  Item( ) method in, 174
  Remove( ) method in, 174
SWbemPropertySet Collection, 174–175
SWbemPropertySet Object, 174–175
SWbemServices Object, 151–161
  associator return in, Associator_( ), 167
  associator return in, AssociatorOf( ), 158
  associator return in, AssociatorAsync_( ), 167–168

associator return in, AssociatorOfAsync( ), 158–159
asynchronously get class or instance in, GetAsync( ), 155
asynchronously receive query objects, InstancesOfAsync( ), 156
asynchronously receive subclasses, SubclassesOfAsync( ), 157
delete class or instance in, DeleteAsync( ), 155–156
delete class or instance in, Delete( ), 155
ExecQuery( )query execution in, 154
execute asynchronous query in, ExecQueryAsyn( ), 157–158
execute query in, ExeQuery( ), 157
Get( ) method in, 152–153, 154–155
InstanceOf( ) enumerating instances in, 153, 156
method execution, ExecMethod( ), 160
method execution, ExecMethod_( ), 169
method execution, ExecMethodAsync( ), 161
method execution, ExecMethodAsync_( ), 169
notification event execution, ExecNotificationQuery( ), 160
notification event execution, ExecNotificationQueryAsync( ), 160
references, References_( ), 168
references, ReferencesAsync_( ), 158–159
references, ReferencesTo( ), 159
references, ReferencesToAsync( ), 168
subclass enumeration in, SubclassesOf( ), 156–157
SWbemSink Object, 170–173
  OnCompleted, 171–172
  OnObjectPut, 172
  OnObjectReady, 172
  OnProgress, 172–173
  Windows Script Host and, 170
syntax, xvi
systems management, WMI, 122, 123
system stored procedures, 88

T
tables, 17, 223, 235–237, 240, 243, 246–248, 255–258, 311, 366–368, 383–389
  add new column, 206
  bulk copy a table, 215–216
  create new table, 205–206
  dumping properties of table, 209–210
tags, 24–26
template files, 61–65, 85–86
  Internet Information Services (IIS) and XML, 52–53
  parameters in, 68–69
  stored procedures and, 67–68
  XSLT, 33, 37
text( ) node test in XPath, 28–31
top-level elements, 25, 57–61, 80
top-level classes, 397–400
Transact SQL, xv
transaction log, MSSQL_TransactionLog, 316–317
transfer setting, MSSQL_TransferSetting, 286–292
Tree pane, Enterprise Manager (EM), 17
tree structure, 73–78, 82–83
  XSLT, 33
triggers, MSSQL_Trigger, 389–390
T-SQL query statement, 113
typed elements, 41

U
unattended installation of SQL Server 2000, 8–9
Uniform Resource Identifier (URI), 38
Uniform Resource Locator (URL)
  access in SQL Server 2000, 4
  Extensible Markup Language (XML), 54–55
  HTTP embedded query parameters for, 56
  Internet Information Services (IIS) and XML, 52–53
  mode argument in queries using, 56, 71–78
  name-value pairs, 55
  parameters in, 69
  querystring in, 54–55
  stored procedures and, 65–68
UPDATE statement, 94–95
updategrams, xvi, 97–101
  before and after elements in, 97–99
  elements and attributes in, 100–101

installation of, 101
updg prefix for, 98
updating data in XML
   UPDATE statement and, 94–95
   updategrams for, 97–101
updg prefix, 98
user-defined functions, 17,
   255–257, 264, 393–394
   scope associations in, 137–138
usernames, 134
users, user account classes,
   319–328

V

VBScripts, Scripting API in WMI,
   182–183
VDirControl management object,
   103–104
View Provider, Windows
   Management Instrumentation
   (WMI), 126, 135
views, 78, 254–256, 394–395
virtual directory management,
   xvi, 83–85, 103–108
   Connect( ) method in,
      103–104
   Disconnect( ) method in, 104
   graphical user interface (GUI)
      of, 103
   Internet Information Services
      (IIS) and XML, 49–54
   security setting for, 106
   setting properties for, 104–106
   SQLVDir directory Object in,
      104–106
   SQLVDirs collection Object in,
      104, 105
   VDirControl management
      Object in, 103–104
   VirtualName Object for, 107–108
   VirtualNames collection for,
      106–107
virtual names, 106–107
virtual servers, 8
VirtualName Object, 107–108
VirtualNames collection, 106–107

W

wbemComparisonFlagEnum, 185
wbemFlagEnum, 185

wbemPrivilegeEnum, 189
wbemQueryFlagEnum, 185
wbemTextFlagEnum, 185
Web-Based Enterprise
   Management (WBEM),
   121–122, 126
WHERE clause, WQL, 200
Win32_Account, 320
Win32_BaseService, 331–340
Win32_Group, 327–328
Win32_GroupUser, 226
Win32_Process, 340–346
Win32_Service, 345–348
Win32_UserAccount, 325–327
Windows 2000, xvii, 122
Windows 2000 Advanced
   Server, 4
Windows 2000 Professional, 4
Windows 2000 Server, 4
Windows 95/98, 4, 122
Windows CE Edition of SQL
   Server 2000, 4, 5
Windows Management Service
   (WinMgmt.exe), 123–125
Windows Millennium Edition,
   xvii, 1, 122
Windows NT, 122
Windows NT Advanced
   Server, 4
Windows NT Server Enterprise
   Edition, 4
Windows NT Workstation, 4
Windows Script File (.wsf),
   MDAC, 109–110
Windows Script Host (WSH), xvi,
   xvii, 170–173
Wizards, Enterprise Manager
   (EM), 18–19
WMI Query Language (WQL),
   xvii, 122, 152, 191–201
   ASSOCIATOR OF statements
      in, 194–195
   BY argument in, 198
   data queries in, 191, 192–195
   event programming and,
      200–201
   event queries in, 191, 196–198
   GROUP clause in, 198
   HAVING clause in, 198
   operators in, 193

query optimization in,
   199–200
query types supported by,
   191–200
REFERENCES OF statements
   in, 195–196
schema queries in, 191, 199
SELECT statements in,
   192–193
Structured Query Language
   (SQL) and, 191
WHERE clause in, 200
World Wide Web Consortium
   (W3C), 22
writing, deleting, modifying data,
   87–96

X

XML Data Reduced, 41, 79
XMLHTTP object, 113–114
xmlns=, 40, 79
XPath, xvi, 26–33, 79, 85
   absolute locations in, 26–27
   attributes in, 27
   axes in, 27, 30
   Boolean functions in, 28, 30
   core functions in, 28
   execution of, 31–32
   expressions in, 27–28
   extensions for, 79
   filtering in, 32–33
   Internet Information Services
      (IIS) and XML, 52, 54
   location paths in, 26–27, 85
   location steps in, 27
   MDAC and, 116–117
   node tests in, 28–31
   node-set functions in, 28, 29
   numeric functions in, 28, 30
   objects in, 26
   OpenXML function and, 89
   operators in, 32
   parent-child relationships
      in, 27
   predicates in, 32–33
   queries in, 116–117
   relative locations in, 26–27
   root elements in, 26
   SQL Server 2000, 4
   string functions in, 28, 29